THE HORSEMAN'S BIBLE

Revised Edition

(SUE MAYNARD)

THE HORSEMAN'S BIBLE

Revised Edition

Jack Coggins

Illustrated by the Author

DOUBLEDAY
NEW YORK LONDON TORONTO SYDNEY AUCKLAND

ACKNOWLEDGMENTS

The author owes thanks to many people for advice and comment. In particular he wishes to thank the following busy men who took time to make suggestions, read text, and answer innumerable questions.

Knute Rondum, all-around horseman, trainer and instructor, of Valhalla Stables, Pottstown, Pa.

John Patt, V.M.D., Boyertown, Pa., for his help in general, and with the veterinary section in particular.

John Ehmer, Chukkar Valley Farms, Gilbertsville, Pa., one of the horsemen through whose efforts polo is now making an amazing comeback as a popular sport.

My father, whose twenty-five years in the cavalry and lifetime interest in horses made his advice invaluable.

PUBLISHED BY DOUBLEDAY

a division of Bantam Doubleday Dell Publishing Group, Inc.

1540 Broadway, New York, New York 10036

DOUBLEDAY and the portrayal of an anchor with a dolphin
are trademarks of Doubleday, a division of Bantam Doubleday
Dell Publishing Group, Inc.

Library of Congress Cataloging in Publication Data
Coggins, Jack.
   The horseman's bible.
   1. Horses.   2. Horsemanship.   I. Title.
SF285.C566   1984   636.1   83-16500
ISBN 0-385-18343-7

CONTENTS

INTRODUCTION

A century ago the most common form of transportation in America was the horse. The highways and byways echoed with the clip-clop of hoofs and every community had its livery stable and its blacksmith's shop. Half a century later, the aroma of hay and horse manure was rapidly giving way to the stink of oil and gasoline—and there were those who predicted that the horse would become all but extinct. Today, thanks to the tremendous rise in popularity of riding as a sport, the horse is not only far from extinction, but increasing in numbers every year. And each year thousands of new riders appear on the bridle paths and in the show ring, or join in the ranks of those who breed horses for fun, or for profit, or both.

There has been a great deal of literature published in the last few years on every phase of riding, showing, horse care and breeding. In addition there are magazines devoted to horses in general, and to certain breeds in particular. Naturally, the proponents of each breed noisily tout the advantages of their choice, but this can be confusing to the newcomer who may easily receive the impression that certain "makes" of horse are designed for specific purposes only. This is far from the truth; almost any animal, providing he is sound and of good disposition, can be trained for range work, for polo, or used as an all-purpose riding horse. Too much has been made of the differences between breeds, and perhaps not enough of the differences between individual animals. One of the first things the new rider will learn is that horses, irrespective of breed, are as different in personality as humans. They can be dull, lively, gentle, mean, mischievous, bold, nervous, hard-working or lazy. Their physical characteristics differ also. Some can run faster than others, some can run longer, some can jump higher. And while a great deal has been written on the subject of breeds and specialization, it should be remembered that a Thoroughbred may make a perfectly good stock horse, while for years one of our best jumpers was an army mule.

Riding for enjoyment covers a vast field—from the Sunday rider who hires a mount for an occasional hour's fun to the dedicated horse lover, who devotes a great deal of time and effort to keeping a horse or horses. Certainly this rider, while not necessarily a more skillful horseman, will gain an insight into the world of the horse which will be forever denied to the casual rider. Stabling, feeding, grooming, exercising may be onerous chores to some, but to the true horseman they are as rewarding a part of his hobby as a brisk trot down the bridle path or a good gallop in the hunting field. In between the two extremes are many who, while they might like to own and care for their own horses, find themselves unable to do so. This group is a large one, and numbers many keen riders in its ranks. Included are the many polo players who hire mounts by the chukkar, and who would otherwise be excluded from what is undoubtedly one of the finest games (and, incidentally, one of the most thrilling spectator sports).

It is impossible to cover all the many facets of horses, horse care and ownership, and horsemanship in a volume of this length. Each has been the subject of many books. What this book attempts to do is to touch on the most important aspects of horses and riding, and to answer some of the questions which may bother the beginner. I should like to make clear that in learning how to ride and handle horses there is no substitute for a competent instructor. Also that, while a little home doctoring can be most useful, there is no substitute for a competent veterinarian.

THE HORSEMAN'S BIBLE

Revised Edition

Chapter 1

THE HORSE

The sports-car owner knows and cares a good deal about the mechanics of his automobile, and for the rider to fully enjoy his moments of relaxation and sport on horseback, it is necessary to have some understanding of the complex and wonderful piece of mechanism which is the horse. No machine made will do everything, and a good mechanic knows the limitations of his equipment. The horse is a very powerful and flexible piece of machinery, but it too has its limitations, beyond which it will function poorly and inefficiently, or not at all.

But the horse has one factor which a machine does not have; it has a brain. Not a very large one, it is true, but large enough to introduce a random element of uncertainty into its operation. For while a machine is wholly predictable, given a certain set of circumstances, a horse is not, and the rider therefore has to cope not only with the mechanics of directing and regulating his mount, but also with the unex-

pected reactions of a very large animal with a very limited intelligence. The results of these reactions are always interesting, sometimes frightening, at least to the novice, and occasionally disastrous.

The riding horse itself is a product of centuries of breeding and refinement. It was evolved with the sole idea of providing a safe, comfortable, and speedy means of transporting a rider over a variety of terrains and under many conditions. There are different kinds of horses, some more suited to the particular needs of an occasion than others. Basically the average horse is a large animal weighing half a ton or over, standing some five and a half feet at the shoulders, and about nine feet in length from nose to tail. It has a deep chest, to accommodate a large heart and lungs, and powerful hindquarters—the hind legs act mainly as the propellers, while the front legs are the supporters. As in all long-legged grazing animals, the neck is long and muscular. The legs, while slender, are exceedingly strong, but are by far the most vulnerable part of a horse's anatomy. Serious damage to the legs often results in complete disability. In most cases a break means the destruction of the animal.

PHYSICAL CHARACTERISTICS

It is a difficult task, calling for the talents of an expert judge, to set up a standard for the perfect horse. All breeds have different characteristics, and animals within the breed classification vary considerably. For the newcomer unfamiliar with the fine points of the breeds, the job of picking good from bad, of recognizing the differences between minor faults and major disqualifications, may seem impossible. Yet there are certain characteristics which even a beginner can soon recognize and which he can correlate with the functions which the type of horse in question is supposed to perform. Form follows function in the make-up of animals, just as it does in architecture, and definite limits are placed upon the usefulness and adaptability of a horse in a specific field by the structural features of the ani-

mal's make-up. With this in mind, one may also remember that a pedigreed animal will have a beauty of proportion and a symmetry all its own, which even an amateur fancier will soon be able to recognize.

The size of the head should be in proportion to the rest of the body—not so big that it appears coarse. In humans, a smaller head than normal, unless ridiculously out of proportion, may give the rest of the body the appearance of being more massive and well developed than it actually is, while a large head has exactly the reverse effect and is noticeably misproportioned and ungainly. The same is true of horses: a head that is too large is far more noticeable and objectionable than one that is a little too small. Stressing the similarity between the human animal and the equine one again, foals and colts, like young people, are likely to have heads large in proportion to their bodies, but here we realize that this is merely an indication of growth to come. A small head on a foal or yearling, on the other hand, usually indicates that the animal will lack size and substance when fully developed.

The shape of the head, while not affecting the animal's performance, is important to breeders and

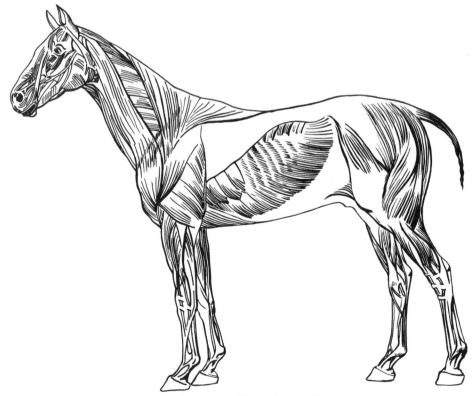

Diagram of horse's muscles

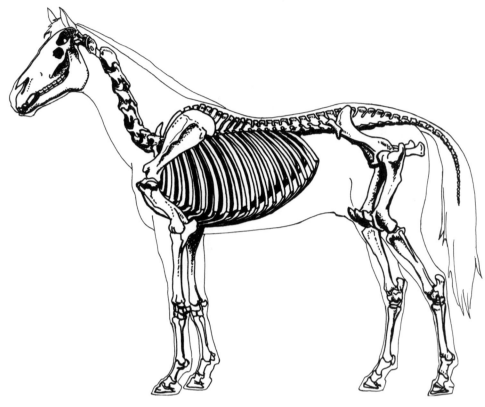

Horse skeleton

those intending to show. The straight head, with good width between the eyes, and width of jaw and muzzle, is preferred. Long thin heads with "dished" faces, and short heavy ones with "Roman" noses, are equally undesirable. Ears should be in proportion—mule ears make a head look coarse. Of the two, a smaller ear is more acceptable than one that is too large. They should be set well upright (ears set out at the side, "lop ears," give a horse a common, mulish look) and not too far back to the poll, nor too low down over the eyes. Movement of the ear is said to be an indication of the horse's temperament. Ears always kept in motion may show a nervous disposition, or even impaired vision. Ears that seldom or never move are thought to show a slow, lazy animal. Horses can do peculiar things with their ears at times, but the most pleasing position, the best "picture" angle, is when the animal is alert and the ears are pricked up at an angle of about forty-five degrees with the axis of the head.

The eyes should be large and prominent, and a dark hazel in color. Too prominent an eye—bovine or "pop" eyes—is objectionable, as are eyes in which the iris is completely white, without pigment—"wall eyes" or "glass eyes," as they are called. Eyes that are small and narrow are referred to as "pig eyes." Eyes with a bluish cast are considered to be weak or unsound.

The nostrils should be large—this indicates good breathing capacity, and usually goes with good depth of chest. The nasal passages are the lungs' only means of air intake, horses being unable to breathe through their mouths. Horses normally discharge at the nostrils, and this discharge should be clear and transparent and odorless. Colored discharge usually indicates an ailment of some sort. The mucous mem-

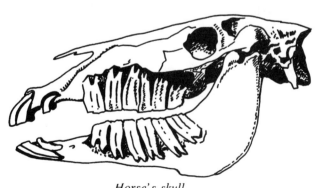

Horse's skull

brane which lines the nostril itself should be a rosy color when the animal is at rest and a deeper red after exercise.

The mouth is made up of the lips, teeth, gums, bars, the lingual canal, tongue and palate. The lips are flexible and help in the intake and mastication of food. The lips should meet evenly, as should the jaws. Lower jaws which protrude or recede—"monkey" mouths or "parrot" mouths—are as unsightly as they are undesirable in any horse.

The teeth are classed as incisors, canines and molars. There are six incisors in each jaw, two canines and twelve molars. In the mare, the canines or tushes are undeveloped. Occasionally a supplementary molar tooth, known as a wolf tooth, appears in either jaw. These serve no useful purpose, may cause trouble and are usually removed.

A horse's age can, up to a point, be judged fairly accurately by the condition of its front teeth or incisors. After six years, the permanent teeth are in place and no further structural change takes place. Thereafter only an approximately correct opinion of the horse's age can be given by the effects of wear, alteration in the shape of the teeth, and by the receding of the gums, as these factors may be influenced by many circumstances. The following gives some general rules to follow in attempting to determine an animal's age.

At birth a foal usually has two, sometimes three temporary molars in each side of each jaw. During the first ten months the temporary incisors also appear. When about a year old, another molar, a permanent one, appears; and before the animal is two, a fifth, also a permanent molar, appears. At about two and a half, the two front temporary molars are replaced by permanent teeth, and between three and four, the third is also replaced. At the same time the sixth permanent molar begins to appear, so that at four years of age the horse has its full set of twenty-four permanent molars.

The temporary incisors are smaller and whiter and smoother externally than the permanent teeth. The necks are more distinct and they have but little attachment to the gums. When a year old the horse has six incisors in each jaw, but the corner teeth are mere shells. All teeth appear close together at this stage. The two-year-old shows center incisors with considerable wear, and they appear to be smaller, because of the growth of the jaw. The inside walls of the corner teeth have, by this time, grown level with the outer walls. At two and a half the horse sheds the two center incisors, and these baby teeth, or milk teeth, are replaced by permanent ones. The jaw of a three-year-old has two permanent center teeth and two temporary ones on each side. At three and a half years or thereabouts the next two milk teeth are shed and replaced by permanent ones, so that at four years the horse has four permanent teeth and one milk tooth on both sides in each jaw.

The remaining milk teeth are shed before the horse is five. The set is complete, but the corner teeth, the two last ones to be replaced, are just shells, having no inner walls. These inner walls grow up level by the time the animal is six years old, and no further structural change in the teeth occurs. Thus these structural changes afford, up to the age of six, an accurate indication of the animal's age. After that time other, and less precise, signs of age must be noted.

There is a hollow or "mark" in the center of each tooth. This hollow speedily becomes the repository for food particles, and shortly after its appearance in the new teeth, becomes black. As the edges of the teeth are gradually ground down, the hollow disappears; but the dentine under the hollow, being somewhat softer than the surrounding enamel, has become stained for some distance below the surface. These marks themselves in time are worn away, but the rate of wear depends upon the natural hardness of the individual horse's teeth, and on the kind of food which it has been fed. The use of such marks as a gauge of age, therefore, can give only a relatively accurate idea of the animal's true age.

Generally speaking, at six the marks are wearing

| Ten months (milk teeth) | Three years (two permanent teeth) | Four years (four permanent teeth) | Five years (complete permanent teeth) | Six years (marks wearing from center pair) |

Incisors showing changes with age

out of the two center teeth. They are plainly to be seen on the next two, and appear fresh on the corner teeth. At seven the marks on the center teeth are no longer visible, the next two are disappearing, and they are only plain on the corner teeth. At eight, the marks are becoming indistinct in the corner teeth and have vanished from the others; at nine years of age, the teeth usually show no marks at all. For this reason dealers will sometimes automatically give "nine" as a horse's age. At this age marks are sometimes burned into the teeth by unscrupulous dealers, to deceive the unwary. However, while it is possible to imitate the marks with caustic or an iron, it is quite impossible to build up the surrounding walls of enamel, so this particular fraud can be easily detected.

After nine, the best indications of age are the gradual alterations in the shape of the teeth. As the teeth wear they show a more triangular top surface. Whereas at six to eight years the teeth are broad laterally, at nine the two center teeth will have become somewhat triangular. At ten the next two begin to show a similar shape, and at eleven the next two, the corner ones, are becoming triangular in shape also. At twelve all teeth show marked triangular characteristics on their upper surfaces, and this increases with age. In a very old horse, the depth of the teeth from front to rear exceeds the lateral width. There is often, in old horses, a considerable space between the teeth, which in younger animals appear close-set.

The bars are that part of the lower jaw which lies between the incisors and the molar teeth in mares, and the canines and the molars in stallions and geldings. It is on the bars, which are covered with mucous membrane, that the pressure of the bit is brought to bear. When this mucous membrane becomes toughened and calloused, the sensitivity of the horse's mouth is deadened and the animal is said to be "hardmouthed."

The tongue is situated in the lingual canal, which occupies the space between the branches of the lower jaw. The tongue performs the functions of prehension, tasting and swallowing, and also aids in mastication. The tongue also supports and receives pressure from the bit, and, with the lower lip, receives signals through the reins.

The hard palate forms the forward part of the roof of the mouth, and is joined to the soft palate at a point just forward of the root of the tongue. The hard palate extends in front as far as the incisors.

The conformation of the neck varies greatly from breed to breed. Generally speaking, the Thoroughbred and breeds developed for speed are long and slender in the neck, the Saddlebred and work types are thicker, and the great draft horses are exceedingly heavy in the neck. Necks also vary in the way they are carried; straight, when the curve from the poll to the withers approaches a straight line; arched (arch and crest of the neck are the same thing), when the line is convex; swan-necked, when the front part is distinctly convex, giving it a resemblance to the neck of a swan. When the top line of the neck shows a distinct hollow just in front of the withers, the animal is said to have a "ewe neck." This is just the opposite of what a good neck should be, so it is often called a neck "set on upside down."

The withers is the region behind the crest of the neck, between the shoulders. It is from the highest point of the withers that the height of a horse is measured, the measurement being given in hands (one hand equals four inches) and inches. Withers should be reasonably prominent. If they are low and thick they affect the horse's motion and prevent a long stride of the forefeet.

The back lies between the withers and the loin. It should be straight and in length should be in good proportion to the rest of the animal. A convex back is called a "roach" back, while one that is concave is known as a "sway-back." Of the two the sway-back is the more objectionable, in extreme cases giving the impression that the animal is about to collapse in the middle. A short straight back with well-sprung ribs is usually the most desirable.

Seven years

Eight years

Nine years
(marks have
disappeared. Center
teeth showing signs of
triangular shape)

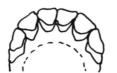

Fifteen years
(all teeth show marked
triangular
characteristics)

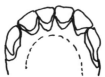

Twenty-one years
(depth of front teeth
greater than width)

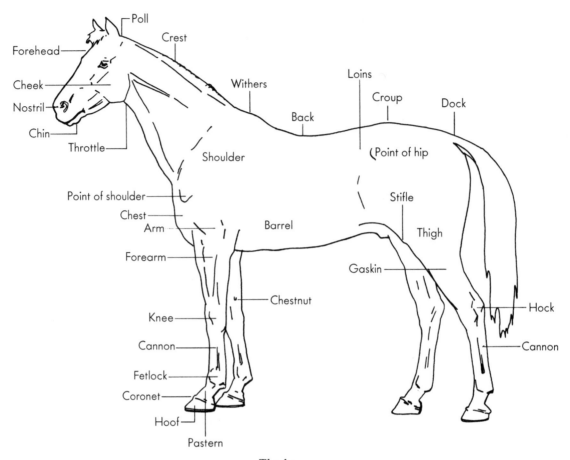

The horse

The muscular region back of the rearmost ribs and extending to the hips is called the loin. The muscling here should be short and heavy. A horse well muscled over the loins is said to be "close-coupled." Behind the loins and reaching back to the tail is the croup. This region should be wide; horses that taper too abruptly from hip to tail are called "goose-rumped." The line of the croup should not slope too steeply, as this conformation tends to place the hind legs too far forward, while if the croup is too straight, that is, parallel with the ground, it has the opposite effect, leaving the horse with a poorly supported back.

The chest contains the lungs and heart, and should have great depth and capacity. To its framework are anchored many of the muscles which are part of the horse's system of locomotion. Depth of chest—that is, the distance from the point of the shoulder to the middle of the last rib—is desirable. Width should be commensurate with the size of the animal. Too narrow a chest does not give sufficient capacity, while with too much chest, a "barrel chest," a horse may be uncomfortable to ride. The breast, that part which lies below the neck and as far back as the arm, should also be well proportioned. Too narrow a breast gives the legs the appearance of being joined together, while too great a width results in the front legs being set too far apart. This gives a rocking, paddling sort of gait and makes for a slow horse.

Unlike man and the members of the monkey tribe—who can move their forelimbs outward from the body, as well as backward and forward—the horse, along with the dog, deer, lion and most other mammals, has forelimbs which have no skeletal attachment to the trunk. The shoulder blade, or scapula, is attached to the body solely by muscles. This shoulder should be long and sloping, thus allowing a longer and more powerful stride and a higher action of the front legs. By reason of the greater angle it forms with the arm, it also affords greater shock-absorbing qualities, thus reducing concussion. In comparison with the shoulder, the arm—the humerus—should be short. This, coupled with a long forearm—the area between the elbow and the knee—gives a maximum amount of stride. The humerus is a single bone; the forearm is composed of two: the radius, and fitting in behind, the ulna, the projecting upper part of which is called the olecranon. The arms should be parallel with the center line of the horse. Too much deviation will result in poor leg conformation. Hinging the forearm to the cannon bone is the knee. This joint should be wide and thick and consequently able to take a lot of wear and punishment. Correct placement of the knee is important. If the knee is set too far forward the horse is "knee-sprung"; if too far back, it is called "calf-kneed." A "knock-kneed" horse has its knees set inward; and if the knees are set outward, it is termed "bow-kneed." From the point of view of looks and of efficiency of the machine, the knee should be properly centered and thus able to function correctly as hinge and support.

The knee, or carpal joint, is made up of seven or eight small bones (in roughly half of all horses one of these bones, about the size of a pea, fails to develop) and is, strictly speaking, not a knee at all but a wrist. The bones below the wrist are actually the bones of the foot. The ancestor of the horse ran on three toes, and the bones below the carpal joint make up the toe, the horse walking on what is a much changed and enlarged toenail. On each side of the cannon bone, or large metacarpal bone, of the forelimb, and of the metatarsus of the hindlimb are attached two splinters of bone, extending part-way down the central bone. These splint bones terminate in small knobs, and are the vestigial remains of the other two toes. To avoid confusion, however, it should be pointed out that when a horseman refers to a horse's foot, he means the part below the fetlock.

Below the cannon, which should be short in comparison with the forearm, is the fetlock or ankle. This joint takes up a great deal of the concussion when the weight of the body is thrown on the pasterns, which are set at an angle of approximately forty-five degrees with the leg as the horse stands.

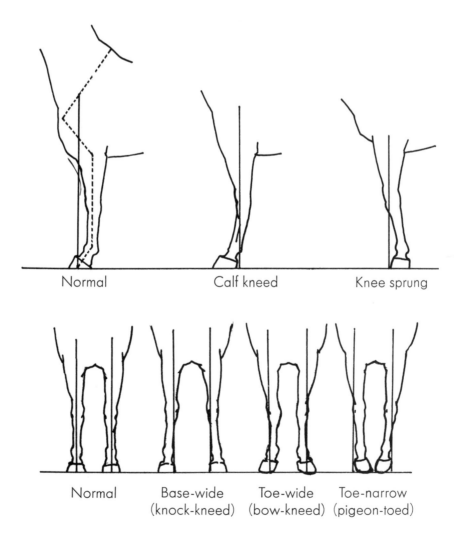

Normal   Calf kneed   Knee sprung

Normal   Base-wide   Toe-wide   Toe-narrow
                (knock-kneed)   (bow-kneed)   (pigeon-toed)

When galloping, as the full weight is thrown momentarily on one leg, the pastern takes almost a full ninety-degree angle, and it is the fetlock joint which absorbs much of this shock. The pasterns—there are two, the long pastern and the short (or first and second phalanx)—should not be too long, or appear too low when the horse is standing. "Coon-footed" is the term used for a horse in which the pasterns are sloped at too great an angle with the rest of the leg. On the other hand, too straight a pastern will not absorb concussion, making for a rough ride, and also not providing the spring and snap which good pasterns add to a horse's stride.

The foot is made up of three articulated bones, the coffin or pedal bone (the third phalanx), shaped like a horse's hoof in miniature; the navicular bone, which is located behind the foot, where the pedal bone and the second phalanx come together; and the second phalanx or short pastern, noted above.

The hoof is described more fully in the chapter on shoeing. The bones of the foot and leg are strapped and laced with the tendons, which are very strong and flexible springs of the leg mechanism's driving and shock-absorbing apparatus.

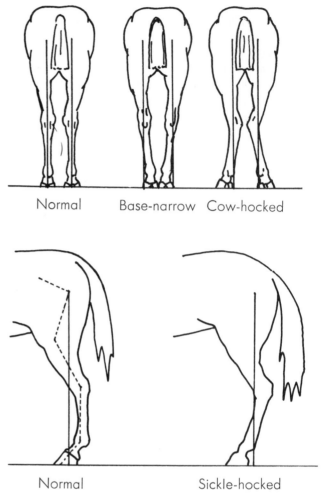

Normal   Base-narrow   Cow-hocked

Normal   Sickle-hocked

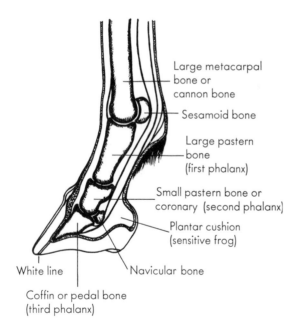

Large metacarpal bone or cannon bone

Sesamoid bone

Large pastern bone (first phalanx)

Small pastern bone or coronary (second phalanx)

Plantar cushion (sensitive frog)

White line   Navicular bone

Coffin or pedal bone (third phalanx)

The foot

The hindquarters are the horse's main propelling machinery. Because of this the framework of the hindquarters is very heavily muscled. The thigh, or femur, which roughly corresponds to the arm, is hinged (also at an angle) to the pelvis at the hip joint. The stifle, or patella, which joins the thigh and

the gaskin, made up of the tibia and fibula, and the hock joint below the gaskin are equivalents of the elbow, forearm and knee. The hock joint, or tarsus, and the muscles and tendons which sheathe it, carry a great deal of the horse's working load. It is important both in propulsion and in absorbing shock (notice the tremendous springing and thrusting action when a horse is jumping) and bears the weight when a horse is rearing. Here again the direction of the set of the hocks has considerable effect on a horse's appearance and way of going. Hocks whose points turn inward are called "cow-hocked." Too much outward set results in a twisting motion—"rotating hocks." Hocks which form too small an angle between gaskin and cannon tend to shorten the stride. Those in which the angle is too great ("sickle hocks") throw the feet too far forward.

The cannon bones of the hind legs, the metatarsals, are longer than those of the forelimbs, although very similar. The hind feet and forefeet are also very much alike.

INTELLIGENCE

The horse is by nature a grazing animal and as such he lacks the claws and fangs of the predators. His safety lies in his heels, literally as well as figuratively, for a horse can lash out with deadly effect on occasion. But if he can, he will run. This age-old tendency of the fleet-footed herbivores—horses, deer, antelope and such—is reflected in the naturally apprehensive, high-strung temperament of most horses. Certainly, not all horses are constantly tense and nervous, but even the quietest is suspicious of anything strange, while a sudden move may momentarily startle the steadiest animal.

This inborn apprehensiveness is at the root of most of the troubles which frequently plague trainer and owner. The great majority of horses are co-operative animals, and when one does "act up," some fear, some danger, fancied or remembered, is usually the cause. Only patient work in finding the cause and overcoming it will effect a cure. Shouts, and punishment with whip or spur will only serve to confuse his small equine brain, and will ultimately drive him to viciousness or reduce him to a nervous wreck. Horses are seldom or never born vicious, and any tendency in this direction is usually the fault of handler or trainer.

Horses have little reasoning ability, but a long memory. They are also creatures of habit. Their memory stands them in good stead when being trained, although it must be realized that they will remember bad habits—or the source of a scare or an injury—just as easily. Unfortunately, horses, like people, seem to acquire bad habits more easily than they lose them.

Much has been written (a lot of it nonsense) about the horse's intelligence, and almost human traits of love, courage, and devotion have been attributed to him. Actually the horse comes out rather low on most animal I.Q. charts, a fact which may surprise people who have read about horses, but not those who have spent much time around them. What horses do, they usually do from habit, or the memory of simple, often repeated, signals. Much "love" is of the cupboard variety—the knowledge that some tidbit may be forthcoming—for any creature will soon learn to associate humans, and one human in particular, with food and water.

This is not written with the idea of downgrading the horse, but rather to warn the uninitiated not to expect too much. New owners, who have been raised on the oversentimentalized type of horse story, may be disappointed when their mounts do not turn out to be the paragons of virtue and intelligence that they have been led to expect. However, if not overly bright, the majority of horses are willing and anxious to please and will give a great deal in exchange for a little praise and kind treatment.

GAITS

A horse's gait is his way of going, either natural or taught. The natural gaits are the walk, trot, pace and gallop. These gaits have been modified and additions made by selective breeding and by training.

The walk is a slow, flat-footed gait. Because each foot strikes the ground separately it is called a four-beat gait. There are always at least two feet on the ground. The feet fall in the sequence: (1) right fore, (2) left hind, (3) left fore, (4) right hind.

Notice that the horse nods his head up and down for balance as he walks—the faster the walk, the more pronounced the up and down motion—and because of this Tennessee Walkers were sometimes called "nodders." The body of the horse is not "lifted" during the walk. The legs are used only to push the feet backward, bearing the weight evenly on both front and hind legs.

Stride is measured by noting the difference between two tracks of the same foot. At a normal walk the hind foot will touch the ground at about the same place as the front foot of the same side, the hoofprints sometimes overlapping.

The trot is a more rapid, two-beat, diagonal gait, in which the front foot and opposite hind foot strike simultaneously. The rate of speed varies, as does the leg action, some breeds using a more high-stepping action than others. The legs impart an upward spring to the body at this gait, as well as forward motion. It was formerly believed that the horse always had two feet on the ground while trotting, but photographic experiments in 1872 showed that for a brief period all four feet are clear of the ground.

The trot is an uncomfortable gait, and "trotters" were not held in high favor as riding horses in older days. Amblers and pacers were a more comfortable ride, and it was not until "posting" came into style that the gait became acceptable. The term "posting," by the way, is said to derive from the postilions who rode the near horses of a coach team. To save their rear ends from the eternal jarring, the postboys "invented" the idea of rising in the stirrups on each alternate diagonal.

The gallop is a fast three-beat gait. Two diagonal legs are paired, falling between the beats of the other two legs. The hind foot, say in this case the left, makes the first beat, the other hind foot, the right, and the diagonally opposite forefoot, the left, makes the second beat simultaneously, and then the right fore. The horse then has all four feet clear of the ground, when the left hind comes down and the cycle starts over.

In the cycle above, the left hind foot and the right forefoot bear more weight than the two which are paired. A horse "leads" with one leg or the other and can be taught to change leads on command.

The hind legs are gathered under the body and when extended propel the animal forward in leaps with a pushing motion. The forelegs are mainly used for support and balance, the hind legs doing most of the work.

The canter is really a restrained gallop. The beat and sequence are the same. In the gallop the horse is stretched out; in the canter the horse is collected, his weight is more on his haunches and the movement is slow, with much of the energy expended in vertical rather than horizontal motion. The left or right shoulder leads, the foot on the lead side touching the ground a little in front of the other. The leads can be changed at command. The canter is not necessarily a fast gait, although it is sometimes an intermediate gait between the trot and a gallop. A fast trot can be quicker than a slow canter.

The pace is a fast two-beat gait in which the two legs on the same side move at the same time. There is a moment when all four feet are off the ground. The pace is faster than the trot, but as a riding gait may be uncomfortable because of the rolling motion (pacers are sometimes referred to as "side-wheelers").

The running walk, the gait of the Tennessee Walking Horses, is a slow four-beat gait. The hind foot oversteps the front, sometimes as much as thirty-four inches. The gait is characterized by a smooth gliding motion. It is the working gait of the South and Southwest, where long distances are covered with great ease and comfort to both horse and rider, at rates of six to eight miles per hour.

The fox trot is a rather peculiar gait, perhaps best described as a cross between a walk and a trot. It has four beats but they are spaced differently from the walk; left hind, right fore, pause, right hind, left fore. Instead of the even one-two-three-four of the walk, there is a one-two——three-four cadence.

The stepping pace or slow gait is the flashy four-beat gait required in the show ring by the five-gaited saddler. The feet fall in this order: right rear, right fore, left rear, left fore. The gait should be executed with rhythm and precision, slowly but with a great deal of action.

The rack is an evenly spaced four-beat gait. Sequence: left hind foot, right forefoot, right hind foot, left forefoot. It is fast and showy, and performed with high knee action. It is comfortable for the rider but tiring to the horse and can only be endured for short periods. It is also a required gait of the five-gaiter.

Somewhat similar is the single-foot of the West. This is also a four-beat gait, but characterized by a shuffling movement, which is much slower than the rack. As it is to be expected, it is not only very comfortable for the rider, but exceedingly easy on the horse as well.

COLORS AND MARKINGS

A black horse is one that is true black, with no light areas. A brown animal is one that is black with the exception of light areas around the muzzle, the eyes, and the inside of the legs. Both can have white markings on face and legs.

Bays run from light shades (bright bay or cherry bay) to dark mahogany. They all have a reddish cast, and all have black manes and tails and usually black lower legs.

Chestnuts vary from golden yellow to dark reddish brown. Their coats are often similar to the bays and their manes and tails are the same color as their bodies or a bit lighter. The dark shades are called liver chestnuts while the lighter red or golden ones are sometimes called sorrels. Chestnuts often have white markings on face and legs.

Palominos vary from creamy yellow to golden. Tails and manes are silver or flaxen. They often have a white blaze or star and white legs.

Grays (there are no pure white horses except albinos) are born almost black, and grow gradually lighter with age, this lightening varying with the breed. There are several markings: dappled, flea-bitten, iron, etc.

Dun horses are a grayish-yellow with a black mane and tail. There are various slight differences in color: mouse dun, claybank and buckskin.

Horses with solid colors with the overall admixture of white hairs, giving a gray effect, are called roans. Those black or near-black with white hairs are called blue roans; bays with white are called red roans; and roan chestnuts are called strawberry roans.

Spotted horses, if they are white and black, are piebalds, while those white with any other color are skewbalds. Odd markings and combinations sometimes occur; the peculiarly marked Appaloosa is an example.

These diagrams show the more common facial markings, and the markings of the legs.

| Blaze | Bald | Star | Spot | Race | Stripe |

Facial markings

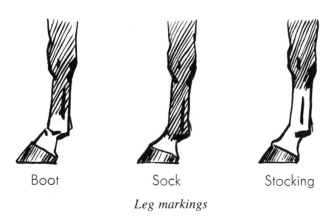

| Boot | Sock | Stocking |

Leg markings

Chapter 2

THE BREEDS

A breed may be defined as a strain or species having characteristics peculiar to the group and not common to others of the same genus. These characteristics are capable of being uniformly transmitted.

While the various breeds—and there are many—are man-made creations, the product of centuries of careful and selective breeding, the pre-history of the horse is a matter of speculation. Because the earliest remains of the dawn horse discovered to date have been unearthed in the trans-Mississippi region of North America, some contend that the horse originated in this country and migrated, via the now vanished Alaska-Siberia land bridge, to the Asiatic mainland. Others reverse the procedure, making the early horse a visitor to this country. Stranger or native, the ancient horse eventually vanished from this continent, leaving the Americas horseless until the coming of the Spaniards.

It is generally held that the common ancestors of

the horse as we know it lived in Asia, probably in the north central section. From there it spread through Asia, Europe and North Africa. The migration seems to have been divided into three main channels. One stream flowed westward, and from these were descended the herds of primeval horses which roamed the forests and plains of Europe. From the quantity of their remains found around the dwelling sites of prehistoric man, the wild horse must have been found in abundance, furnishing an important part of the Stone Age peoples' food supply. Later the wild horse became domesticated, but it is doubtful if attempts at improvement were made by the savage clans who hunted and fought over the northern portion of the continent. From the appearance of the bones, and from rough but lifelike carvings on bones and antlers, this descendant of the equine migrants from the steppes of Central Asia was small and heavy, with a shaggy coat and a long

Modern European descendants of the wild horse (PHOTO RESEARCHERS, INC.)

mane and tail. The head was relatively large and lacked any depression or ''stop'' in the skull in front of the eye. With the possible exceptions of such types as the dun ponies of Norway and the Celtic ponies of Iceland, the original wild horse of northern Europe has been so altered by admixture of ''hot-blooded'' strains, associated with Libya and North Africa—the Barbs—as to become unrecognizable. The wild pony of Mongolia, Przewalski's horse, discovered in 1879, was the last true wild horse remaining in the twentieth century.

The eastward flow resulted in the Chinese and Mongolian types. These, separated from the rest of the world by the Asiatic land mass, remained apart and had no influence on the development of the breeds from which the modern American horse is descended. The most important migration flowed southwest into Asia Minor, Persia, India and Arabia, and finally through Egypt into North Africa. These were the lands where flourished the early civilizations from which our Western culture springs.

Here the breeding of horses for specific purposes became a science. Strains developed in widely distant localities were crossed to further improve existing stock, and with the rise of the great Mediterranean civilizations we may find the beginnings of the

species from which the present-day horse is descended.

The foundation stock of all improved types of the light riding horse as we know it today is the ''Oriental'' as represented by the Arab and the Barb. The characteristics of these closely related strains were fixed many hundreds of years ago. By exerting the utmost care and rigid control over breeding, and by great attention to bloodlines, the species was kept pure over the centuries. The fame of these magnificent desert-bred animals spread throughout the Old World. Over the years, many strains have been improved by the addition of Arab and Barb blood, while the pure-bred Arabian, long the jealously guarded possession of the fierce inhabitants of the Arabian peninsula, is today one of the most popular and sought-after breeds in America.

THE ARABIAN

There is some difference of opinion as to when the horse was introduced into Arabia. This is of little moment. The important thing is the great care which the warlike inhabitants of that arid land lavished on the breeding and raising of an animal which was more a comrade and household pet than a mere means of locomotion. To this love and devotion with which the Bedouin treated his mount may be traced the wonderful disposition of the Arabian horse. Centuries of such treatment (which included the freedom of the family living quarters, which Westerners customarily reserved for their favorite dogs) coupled with careful breeding for temperament has produced an animal which, while possessed of magnificent spirit, is extremely docile, and which makes an admirable pet.

The harsh conditions under which even the most pampered denizens of Arabia exist aided in the development of an animal which is exceedingly hardy and one of the soundest of horses. Hoof and leg trouble is rare, and respiratory diseases are almost unknown. The strong back—the Arab has one fewer lumbar vertebra than other breeds—enables the breed to carry great weight for their size. The Arab has also the ability to travel long and far and yet to make a rapid recovery from exertion. For this reason the Arab has been used with success as a polo pony

and as a roping horse. The Arabian horse is noted for its genetic prepotency and an Arab sire will improve any half-bred.

When the Arabs conquered most of Spain, they took with them their Arabians and Barbs, breeding them to the noted horses of Andalusia. At various times other Arabian stallions found their way into the Christian lands, often as presents from some sultan to royalty. The Crusades, too, did much to infuse the blood of the Arab and Barb into the horses of the West. During the fifteenth and sixteenth centuries the demand in Western Europe was for sizable horses. Henry VIII laid down laws governing the size of horses, stipulating, among other things, that in certain counties no stallions of less than fifteen "handfulls" should be grazed on common or waste land. Later, the increased use of firearms and the consequent abandoning of heavy armor enabled the cavalryman to use a lighter and faster mount. Coupled with this fact was the increasing interest in horse racing, fostered in great part by the sports-minded Stuarts. James I, who ascended the throne in

Arabian stallion Sea Captain, owned by Mrs. Garvin Tankersley of Al-Marah Arabians (LOUISE L. SERPA)

1603, imported what is believed to be the first Arab stallion brought into England. The succeeding monarchs further encouraged the introduction of Eastern blood, and in the reign of William III the famous Byerly Turk and Darley Arabian appeared, followed some twenty-five years later by the Godolphin Arabian or Barb. To one or the other of these three Eastern horses all modern Thoroughbred race horses trace their lineage in the direct male line. Today almost all the world's finest horses boast at least some Arab blood.

The Arab is comparatively small, seldom weighing more than a thousand pounds and averaging about 14.2 hands. The back is short and straight and the tail is set high. The neck is long, slim and finely arched. The legs, though strong, are long and slender. The distinctive head is short from muzzle to poll, broad between the eyes, and very definitely "dished" due to a rather bulging forehead. The nostrils are able to distend, or flare, considerably. The eyes are large, and set low in the head. The ears are short, the nose is small, and the jaw deep and wide. The skin of an Arab is dark but the coat may vary, bay, gray or chestnut being the most prevalent colors, with occasionally blacks, browns or whites.

The Arab has a very easy flat-footed walk and the canter and hand gallop are smooth, although the trot is inclined to be short and choppy. Lack of size handicaps the breed for hunting and jumping.

THE THOROUGHBRED

Because the name has come to stand for the epitome of breeding and elegance, the term "Thoroughbred," besides being bestowed on such diverse objects as beautiful women and expensive automobiles, is often mistakenly applied to purebreds of other breeds. Technically, of course, the word is properly applied only to running horses whose ancestry may be traced in the direct male line (in tail-male) to the three Eastern horses mentioned above: the Byerly Turk, the Darley Arabian and the Godolphin Barb. In the female line their pedigrees may trace to other sources, but there is such an intermingling of the blood of the famous trio in the present-day mares

Thoroughbred racehorse Conquistador Cielo, with Laffit Pincay up, reaching the finish line to win the 1982 Belmont Stakes (N.Y.R.A.)

Thoroughbred hunter White Gloves (SUE MAYNARD)

that most Thoroughbreds combine the blood of all three.

Many of the mares to which the Eastern stallions were bred had themselves a considerable infusion of Eastern blood. Proof that this importation of Oriental stock and subsequent breeding of light horses did not meet with universal approval is shown by a memorial presented to Charles I, asking that some action be taken to prevent the type of horse "fit for the defense of the country" from disappearing altogether.

The infusion of Arab and Barb blood in the already excellent English animals produced a breed characterized by a fine, lean head, with broad, flat forehead; eyes full; nostrils large· and dilating; fine muzzle; and small pricked ears. The neck is wide and muscular, allowing for a spacious windpipe; withers moderately high and thin; chest well developed, but rather narrow and not too deep. The shoulders are oblique and well muscled to reduce concussion when at the gallop. The upper arms are long and muscular, with broad, flat sinewy cannons, with good bone. The knees are broad and strong, and the fetlock joints large. The pasterns, which act as shock absorbers, are springy and sloped at forty-five degrees. When at a gallop, the flexibility of the Thoroughbred's pasterns is such as to allow the fetlock of the foot bearing the weight to touch the ground. The back and hindquarters are powerful, for weight-carrying and propelling power. The croup should not fall away but should be continued in a straight line to the tail, which is set high.

The general appearance is of a long, lean animal, standing some fifteen to sixteen hands high and weighing from one thousand to fourteen hundred pounds. The colors are mainly bay, brown and chestnut, with occasional grays, roans or blacks.

While known mainly as a race horse, the Thoroughbred is also used for jumping, hunting or polo. His spirit, strength and conformation make him ideal for the former, while his speed and stamina come into play in the hunting field or on the polo ground. In addition, the Thoroughbred is much used for plain everyday hacking (riding).

As might be expected with a highly bred animal, Thoroughbreds are frequently high-strung and temperamental. In some cases animals have been bred for great speed at the expense of other qualities. On the other hand, breeding has produced in others great fighting spirit and will to win. Such a horse, while a delight to the experienced rider, may be wasted on a beginner.

THE AMERICAN SADDLEBRED

Today most people ride short distances for pleasure, and gait does not greatly matter. But when the horse was the sole means of transportation and long hours each day had to be spent in the saddle, gait meant a great deal. As compared to the mother country, the old English colonies in America were vast places. The colonials, especially those living in the South, where everything—farms, plantations and pasture lands—was on a lavish scale, naturally favored a mount whose gait was as easy and comfortable as possible, and which could carry them at fair speed but with a minimum of jouncing and thumping.

For this gait the colonists turned to the amblers and pacers, horses who naturally moved by lifting the two feet on one side together, alternately with the two feet of the other. This gait, while a good traveling pace, was also a great deal more comfortable than the trot, especially as the Southerner customarily rode with long stirrups and did not rise to the trot, or "post." Horses showing signs of possessing this easy ambling lateral gait were selected for breeding. There were soon many gaited stallions and mares transmitting their characteristics, and the breeding and use of these easy-riding horses became general in the South. These comfortably gaited saddlers had been in favor for many years before much thought had been given to anything but performance. However, there gradually evolved a definite type. A Thoroughbred stallion named Denmark, foaled in Kentucky in 1839, helped stamp his own characteristics on the breed. He was designated foundation sire of the recognized breed by the American Saddle Horse Breeders Association, founded in 1891 as the National Saddle Horse Breeders Association. (The present breed organization is The American Saddlebred Horse Association Inc., 929 S. Fourth Street, Louisville, KY 40203.) Denmark was recog-

Three-gaited American Saddlebred (AMERICAN SADDLE HORSE BREEDERS ASSOCI-ATION)

Five-gaited American Saddlebred (AMERICAN SADDLE HORSE BREEDERS ASSOCIATION)

nized because, of close to three thousand entries in the first volume of the saddle horse register, over half traced directly to him.

The American Saddlebred is characterized by a slim and elegant build, a small head and a long, graceful neck. The ears are pointed and set well forward. The eyes are large. The back is short, and the tail set high. The whole effect should be one of beauty, style and animation. At the same time, horses of this breed are noted for intelligence, docility and tractability. Weights usually run from nine hundred to twelve hundred pounds and most Saddlebreds stand from fifteen to sixteen hands in height. Usual colors are brown, chestnut, bay, black or gray.

A list of qualifications agreed upon in the past by the breeders' association put sure-footedness first, surely an excellent endowment for a good riding horse. A good disposition and a good mouth came next, while gaits and manners trailed at the end of the list. This sensible emphasis on the working char-

acteristics of the breed is especially noteworthy in view of the growing tendency to subordinate these qualities to showiness and looks. This unfortunate trend is true of many breeds, and the very qualities which gave them pre-eminence in the first place are in danger of being passed over in favor of mere size and appearance.

Today's Saddlebred falls into two classifications, the show horse and the working animal. The former exhibits several artificial modifications which are strictly for the show ring. The hoofs are allowed to grow to excessive lengths, thus altering the natural placing of the feet. This is suitable for the tanbark of the show ring but is impractical for anything but the smoothest going. The action is still further modified by the addition of weighted shoes.

The high movement of the legs, so characteristic of the breed, is developed still further by training and exercise. Tails are "set" to make them stand straight and high. This is done by cutting the tendons under the tail so that when they heal they are longer than they were originally. The tail is then "set" to heal in a contrivance called a crupper. While this can be removed when the tendons are healed, it is usually worn throughout the show season. Sometimes, to further ensure a peppy, prancing, "tail-up" performance, a rectal massage with a preparation containing ginger is administered. Under those questionable circumstances, who wouldn't prance?

The schooling of the show horse, which is nothing more or less than a performing animal, is a long and complicated business compared with the training of the working saddle horse. The working saddler comes close to being the ideal pleasure horse. For looks and ease of gait it is hard to beat, and the breed is characterized by good manners and good disposition. Besides the walk, trot and canter, the Saddlebred horse, by breeding and training, can acquire two other gaits, the slow gait and the rack (see p. 20). In the show ring the three-gaited saddlers, also known as plain-gaited, are shown with roached manes, that is, clipped short so that the mane stands upright. Five-gaited Saddlebred horses, also called gaited saddlers, are shown with full manes and tails.

THE TENNESSEE WALKING HORSE

The Tennessee Walking Horse is a composite, the foundation sires and dams having pedigrees tracing to Thoroughbred, Standardbred, American Saddlebred horse and Morgan blood. However, for over a century breeders have practiced careful selective breeding with such success that the best qualities of the parent stocks have been mingled, and a truly separate breed, with breed characteristics uniformly transmitted, has been developed.

The Tennessee Walking Horse originated over one hundred years ago in Tennessee. The horse was bred for utility and was used in the old days for riding, driving in harness, and light plowing and cultivating—a true all-purpose farm work horse. Today the Tennessee Walker is a riding horse, and his distinc-

Tennessee Walking Horse (TENNESSEE WALKING HORSE BREEDERS' AND EXHIBITORS' ASSOCIATION OF AMERICA)

tive and comfortable gait, nice manners and good disposition have in recent years made the breed many friends in the riding fraternity, both on the bridle trail and in the show ring.

Although long a favorite in his native Tennessee, the breed has only comparatively recently achieved nationwide popularity. The Tennessee Walking Horse Breeders Association was not organized until 1935. Since then the number of registrations has grown by leaps and bounds.

Standing, on the average, just over fifteen hands and weighing between one thousand and twelve hundred pounds, the breed is noted for balance and conformity. They are, as a rule, short-backed, with strong legs, muscular hindquarters and rather large knees and hocks. The shoulders are long and sloping. Tennessee Walkers are seen in a variety of colors: bay, brown, chestnut, sorrel or roan, occasionally a palomino gold, black or white and gray. Head and leg markings are of all kinds. For show purposes the mane and tails are left long, and the tails "set" like those of the Saddlebred horse.

Perhaps the chief claim to fame of the Tennessee Walking Horse is the swift (up to seven or eight miles an hour) and very comfortable running walk which is so characteristic of the breed. This stride, in which the front foot strikes the ground a moment before the diagonal hind foot, gives a gliding motion very much more comfortable than the jar of the trot, which necessitates posting on the part of the rider. Undoubtedly this stems from the blood of the amblers and pacers of old. In this connection it is interesting to note that some believe that the massive war horse of medieval times was also a pacer. Granted that the knight's charger was led as close to the scene of action as possible, while the ironclad warrior himself rode a lesser steed; even so, the act of trotting for only the shortest distance must have been a wearing and painful procedure (not to speak of the noise) for both horse and rider.

This running walk gait is inherited, and while it cannot be taught to a horse which does not naturally possess it, it can be improved and developed by proper schooling in one that does. Besides the fast walk, the breed has a flat-footed walk and is noted for a comfortable "rocking chair" canter.

Like any other breed, the Tennessee Walker has its limitations. It was not bred for sustained speed and is not recommended as a jumper or a hunter. On the other hand, for quiet, safe, relaxed hacking it has no equal, and is particularly suitable for elderly people who take up riding late in life.

THE MORGAN

If there is some mystery as to the ancestry of the Tennessee Walking Horse, there is none at all about the Morgan. The foundation sire of this justly popular breed was a remarkable stallion called Justin Morgan, named after the man who bred him. This "big little horse" as he was called, was foaled in Vermont in 1789. Rich in Thoroughbred and Arabian blood, the stallion was prepotent enough to stamp his characteristics on his descendants regardless of the quality of the mare. When he died in 1821 he had established a definite type, one which has had considerable influence on a number of American breeds, particularly the American Saddlebred and the Standardbred.

Justin Morgan was small, a little over fourteen hands, and weighed about a thousand pounds. He was exceedingly muscular and won fame in the log-pulling contests in Vermont in those days, defeating horses of sixteen hands which outweighed him by hundreds of pounds. He was a good runner, and often beat the best of the local horses in the quarter-mile straightaway courses typical of the period. He was noted for his endurance, another of the qualities which he has passed on to the breed bearing his name (and incidentally he was the *only* horse to have a breed named for him).

In appearance he was a stylish little horse, dark bay with black legs, mane and tail. His head was clean-cut with full and prominent dark eyes and small, pointed, widely set ears. His body was deep and short-backed, with exceedingly powerful shoulders, short legs and sloping pasterns. Besides being a champion all-rounder, he had great style and substance, and was all in all a most remarkable little horse.

Besides contributing greatly to the foundation stock of the American Saddlebred and to the Tennessee Walking Horse, the Morgan horse also profoundly influenced the Standardbred. Justin Morgan was himself a trotter of note and his descendants won distinction on many tracks.

The modern Morgans are of several types but they all retain the general characteristics of their famous progenitor. They are mostly on the small side—15.2 hands is a tall one—and usually weigh from one thousand to twelve hundred pounds. They are marked by delicate heads showing Arabian features, very heavy shoulders and width of chest, short backs (another Arabian characteristic) and well-muscled hindquarters.

Morgan Horse (THE MORGAN HORSE CLUB, INC.)

No longer pre-eminent in the harness racing field, the Morgan is now primarily a saddle horse. Years ago the breed was introduced into the West, where it met with great approval. Today there are many Morgans raised both as saddle horses and as cow horses, where the breed's power, endurance and good disposition have made it popular on the range.

THE AMERICAN QUARTER HORSE

In colonial Virginia, before the days of Thoroughbreds and regular race courses, the pioneer "improvers of the breed" used to race over paths that were usually merely trails hacked out of the brush. These primitive race tracks were generally a quarter of a mile long; and a type of horse evolved which performed best at such a distance, one which could get off to a flying start and sustain a burst of speed for a few hundred yards. In 1752 Janus, a grandson of the Godolphin Barb, was imported from England to Virginia, where his contribution to the breed was such that all but two of the earliest Quarter Horse families trace back to him.

As the more refined and expensive long-distance racing became established in the East, the quarter-mile course and the kind of horses who ran it moved with the pioneers to the West and Southwest, where it is still popular today. During the 1840s, two other famous sires, Steel Dust and Shilo, were progenitors of the two principal families in Texas. The mixture of Quarter Horse blood with that of Spanish mares, which had already won fame as range horses unequaled for cow-sense and endurance, produced a compact, heavily muscled animal of greater weight and speed, without diminishing the good qualities of the dams.

More recently, Thoroughbred crosses have tended to refine the Quarter Horse without altering its distinctive characteristics: a compact body with a deep, broad chest, wide-set forelegs, very short cannons, a short, close-coupled back, full and powerful across the kidneys, broad hindquarters with hindlegs muscled inside and out; a short, broad head with little fox ears, wide-set eyes and a short muzzle; and, last but not least, unusual cow-sense, steadiness, endurance, sure-footedness, level-headedness, and incredible sprinting speed.

A better description of the ideal ranch horse would be hard to find, as the number of Quarter Horses working on Western ranches testifies. With the rise in popularity in the East of Western-style riding and activities such as barrel-racing and cattle-cutting, the Quarter Horse population has increased nationwide. Even in New York State there are now more Quarter Horses than Thoroughbreds. Another reason for this increase is the discovery that Quarter Horses can perform honorably in many activities aside from their traditional racing and ranch work, and so more and more of them are seen in the hunting field, on the polo grounds, in competitive long-distance rides, in the show-jumping arena, and in combined training events.

THE APPALOOSA

The red-skinned population of the Southwest in all likelihood viewed the first horses to penetrate their region with some awe. However, once it was demonstrated that man and beast were not one creature, and that the four-legged monster would carry a naked red man as well (in fact, better) than it would a steel-clad Spaniard, the local inhabitants took enthusiastically to horseback. As more horses strayed, were bartered for, or were stolen, the foundations were laid for the great horse herds which roamed the West in the old days. The impact of the horse on the way of life of the Indian was as great as that of the automobile on American civilization in the opening decades of the twentieth century. Yet, dependent as the red man of the West became on the horse, with one exception there seems to have been no attempt to improve their herds by selective breeding. The exception was the Nez Percé tribe, who at one time ranged over what is now parts of Washington, Oregon and much of Idaho, while their buffalo hunters often pushed eastward into the great hunting grounds

American Quarter Horse stallion Hank Will, owned by Robert Kieckhefer (LOUISE L. SERPA)

of Montana. By careful breeding, and gelding of inferior stallions, they produced a type which was a combination war horse, buffalo hunter, long-distance traveler and race horse. Any horse which would serve all these purposes in that rugged, often mountainous country must of necessity have stamina, speed and toughness even in excess of that usually found in the hardiest of Western horses.

These were the characteristics which appealed to the white men who penetrated and finally settled those regions. They are still prized by stockmen, and the Appaloosas have made a name for themselves as rugged work horses on some of the great Western ranches. In 1938 admirers of the breed founded the Appaloosa Horse Club, which has its headquarters in Moscow, Idaho (P.O. Box 83843).

The breed's name is taken from a small river, which flows into the Snake, named the Pelouse or Palouse by French-Canadian fur trappers. The riverbank was evidently the grazing grounds of a herd of the distinctly marked horses and to the white settler they became known as Pelouseys. How or why this changed to the presently accepted spelling of Appaloosa is anybody's guess. As odd as the name are the breed's characteristic markings. These are of several patterns, no one being given preference as far as judging goes. The Appaloosa may be white with dark spots over the whole body, the spots sometimes running together on the head and neck to give the appearance of a solid color, but also common are those with solid color foreparts and dark or white spots on loins and hips. Another variation is a dark coat with white spots over the body, while some are mottled dark and light all over.

In physical appearance the Appaloosa closely resembles the Quarter Horse. In recent years their fine conformation and unusual appearance have interested many Westerners in the breed, and the increasing number of Western-style riding clubs in the East will undoubtedly spread the spotted horses' popularity.

THE PALOMINO

The Palomino, strictly speaking, is not a breed at all, but a color. Any type of light horse is acceptable as long as the color standard is maintained. There are Palominos in harness, on the cattle ranges, in the

Appaloosa stallion owned by Al Levin (LOUISE L. SERPA)

Palomino B' Jazz Bar owned by Cathy Coyner (LOUISE L. SERPA)

show ring in both three-gaited and five-gaited classes and on the bridle path. However, no horse can be registered with The Palomino Horse Breeders Association unless it or its sire or dam is registered as an American Saddlebred, Quarter Horse, Morgan, Tennessee Walker, or with the Arabian Horse Club, The Jockey Club or The United States Trotting Association.

The golden horse, typically enough, was found in California when that territory was "liberated" from Mexico over a century ago. The horse-loving people of that sunny land had developed the strain for pure beauty of color, and the Palomino was strictly a high-class saddle horse, ridden by the owners of the great *estancias* both as a beautiful show and parade horse and also as a racer. Like most horses of Spanish descent, the Palomino shows its Arabian and Barb ancestry, although the infusion of blood of heavier stock has resulted in an animal of increased size and weight. Today it is impossible to classify the Palomino as to height and weight, as Thoroughbreds as well as Arabians figure in the pedigrees of many present-day horses. The distinctive golden coat should have the color of a new gold coin, although cream and very light chestnut are also seen. The skin

should be basically dark, and is considered to be so if the skin around the nose and eyes is dark or black. The eyes should be dark hazel color. Mane and tail are a flaxen color, almost white. White stockings, blazes and white stripes on the face are permissible, but there should be no white spots on the body. Nor should the Palomino have dark markings on the body; spots, dorsal stripes on the back or zebra stripes on the shoulders and legs, etc. The mating of two Palominos will often result in too light a color—almost an albino—and the breeders usually use a chestnut cross to obtain the desired golden color. The association forbids the use of draft horse blood, also that of Shetlands. The use of piebalds, pintos and other off-colors is also forbidden. There are two associations for the registration of Palominos. One, The Palomino Horse Breeders Association of America, has its headquarters at Mineral Wells, TX 76067 (P.O. Box 249); the other, The Palomino Horse Association, is at Jefferson City, MO 65101 (P.O. Box 324).

Horses are sometimes registered both with the association for their breed, with The Morgan Horse Club, for instance, and with either of the Palomino associations for color.

THE STANDARDBRED

The term "standardbred" includes the trotters and pacers. The history of these goes back into colonial days, when roads first became good enough so that a light carriage could not only be used, but driven at some speed. Harness racing, the sport which has grown out of this early means of transportation, has become firmly established as a major American sporting event.

The earliest racing was between ordinary citizens, who were naturally curious as to whose roadster could go fastest. As such a rig was a necessary part of most households, and as the horses were work horses, raised for pulling a load, the local churches in the puritanical Northeast, who frowned on horse racing as the sport of kings and of the ungodly, could hardly object if two farmers both wished to be first to market or to church! So the sport spread, and soon, men being what they are, horses began to be bred more with an eye for speed than for honest labor. The descendants of the English stallion Messenger, who was a runner and the sire of runners, also sired offspring on cold-blooded mares, who, it was noted, could outtrot any competitors. The progeny of this stallion, who was imported in 1788 and died twenty years later, were among the most famous trotters of their day. Other fine animals were descended from Ethan Allen, himself a descendant of the famous Justin Morgan. However, in 1849 a great-grandson of Messenger, Hambletonian, proved to be the greatest sire in trotting history. This bay stallion, with his black points, small star and two white socks on the hind feet, has so influenced the trotting field that it is estimated that out of all horses racing in the 1950s about 99 per cent traced directly to him. He was tremendously muscled, and his long powerful hind legs were placed well back, giving plenty of drive. Like many fast trotters, his croup was higher than his withers, 16 hands to 15.2—the so-called "trotting pitch." Although never seriously raced, his get proved such consistent winners, some forty doing the mile in 2:30 or better, that his stud fee rose to the then huge sum of five hundred dollars, with a demand larger than he could fill.

Prior to 1823, all harness racing was still done on

Standardbred trotter, the legendary Greyhound, driven by Sep Palin (U.S. TROTTING ASSOCIATION)

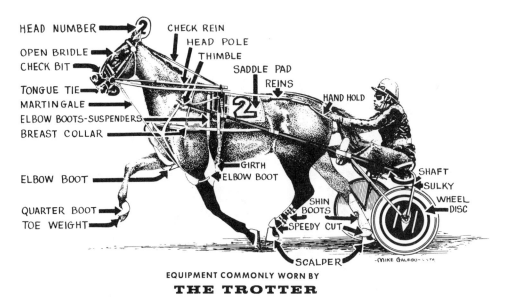

EQUIPMENT COMMONLY WORN BY
THE TROTTER

Equipment commonly worn by the trotter (U.S. TROTTING ASSOCIATION)

the roads, the Bowery in New York being a favorite "track." Complaints from pedestrians, long-suffering then as now, finally drove the speedsters further afield, but it was not until some years had passed that regular race tracks came into use. It was due to this lack of harness tracks, and also to the comparatively clumsy vehicles then in use, that before 1830 most races for big stakes, or for records, were run under saddle. Rules and regulations were not standardized and many races were between paired teams, and a variety of vehicles was used. It was not until the invention of the pneumatic tire and the ball bearing, both of which developed as part of the growing bicycle industry, that the light sulky came into being in 1892 and the old high-wheeler gradually disappeared. The modern rig weighs about twenty-five or thirty pounds.

Meanwhile harness racing has passed along many trails. The gentleman-driver has all but vanished, and harness racing might have followed but for the formation in 1870 of an association, the forerunner of the present United States Trotting Association (750 Michigan Ave., Columbus, OH 43215). This association regularized trotting racing and cleaned up the tracks (temporarily, at least, although the phrase has an all too familiar ring).

Pacers differ in gait from trotters, the "side-wheelers" moving both legs on one side at once. This gait, while fast, is not a comfortable one for a rider; and perhaps because many of the carriage horses in early times also doubled as riding horses, the pacers were not as popular as those animals with an easier gait.

Even when harness racing became a recognized sport the pacer suffered a disadvantage. If a pacer once broke stride he could not resume his gait, while a trotter who momentarily broke into a gallop could be checked and would resume the trot. Against this drawback was the fact that pacers were fast, a fraction faster than the trotters. The first harness horse to break the two-minute mark for the mile was a pacer, Star Pointer, who did the distance in 1:59¼ in 1897.

In 1885 the exasperated owner of a pacer who frequently "broke" invented a leg harness, the "hopple," that prevented the animal from using any gait *but* the pace. There were many objections to the use of this contraption, and also much ridicule, but it worked, and eventually the hopple, or hobble, was accepted, although the free-legged, or clean-gaited pacer (one that does not use hopples) is considered the better animal. Many horses use both gaits; one in particular, Calumet Evelyn, won many events in each division (best time, 1:59½ trotting, 1:59¼ pacing). In 1938 the legendary trotter Greyhound set a record for the mile in 1:55¼, which stood unbroken until 1966, when Nevele Pride did it in 1:54⅘. The present pacing mile record holder is Niatross, with a time of 1:49⅕, set in 1980.

Handicapping, which in flat racing is done with weights (this does not work when applied to vehicles), was for a long time a major problem. Harness horses are now handicapped on the basis of their money earnings and their current performance (timed with great exactitude) over the mile course. The greater speed of the modern trotters and pacers has led to a shortening of the courses; many events are now under one mile. This has in turn placed greater emphasis on the fast horse as opposed to the stayer.

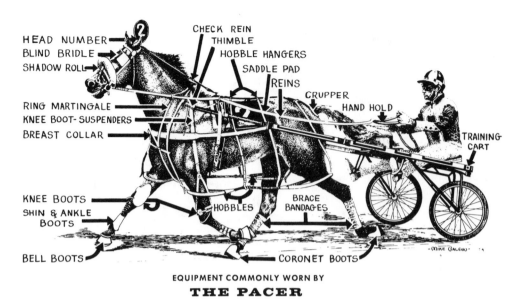

EQUIPMENT COMMONLY WORN BY
THE PACER

Equipment commonly worn by the pacer (U.S. TROTTING ASSOCIATION)

Standardbred pacer Niatross, driven by C. Galbraith (U.S. TROTTING ASSOCIATION)

By long years of selective breeding, the modern Standardbred has acquired great quality and finish. On the average, heights run from 15.2 to 16 hands, with weights of from 850 to 1000 pounds. The old idea that the harness racer should have an exceptionally long body (sometimes a hand longer than in height) seems to have disappeared. All Standardbred horses in the United States are registered with The United States Trotting Association.

Standardbreds, regardless of gait, can be registered "Standard" if purebred or "Non-Standard" if crossbred. The former classification covers all progeny of established bloodlines, and also all horses registered through their bona fide accomplishments on the track. Speed at either gait renders them eligible to Standard registration, if they have sufficient basis of Standard breeding.

A Non-Standard horse is the trotter or pacer whose bloodlines are not clear or whose proof of ancestry has been lost.

In each and every case of requested registration, both for the Standard and Non-Standard, all applicants must provide a true statement of breeding, which is checked in detail by the U.S.T.A. registration department for accuracy and authenticity.

PONIES

There is some difference of opinion among instructors as to the value of the pony as a means of teaching children to ride. Some contend that the pony is too stubborn, as well as sometimes ill-tempered, and that the youngster is better off being started on a regular mount. The opposite school contends that a child will feel more at home on a mount in proportion to his size, that the young rider will have difficulty posting to the trot of a large horse. The horse's large barrel, all out of proportion to the child's short legs, prevents him from proper placement of legs and thighs and does not permit him to contact the horse behind the girth with his legs in order to give the proper signals. Finally, the ground looks very far away indeed to the young beginner on a tall horse, and an actual fall from that height could be serious.

A child's pony (SUE MAYNARD)

As a general rule ponies are considerably more intelligent than horses, are less easily frightened and seldom panic. Their more phlegmatic disposition also enables them to tolerate the rough-housing and the excess of petting and attention which the kids enjoy so much. Also, their small size and the corresponding light weight of their tack enables even the very young rider to saddle and care for his mount by himself. This, added to the fact that he can mount unaided (which is impossible with a large animal), gives him considerably more feeling of independence and self-reliance. Eleven hands is plenty tall enough a pony for youngsters under eight. Children up to ten can usually handle a pony up to twelve or thirteen hands, while for older children ponies in the fourteen-hand class are ideal.

Ponies are economical to house and care for, as they do best all year round in a paddock, with an open shed for shelter. Ponies are naturally hardy and this meager accommodation suffices in even the worst winter weather. Grain feeding is unnecessary unless the pony is being worked especially hard, or is in very poor condition.

Proper training of the pony is essential. It is a mistake to assume that just because a pony is small that a child will automatically be able to manage it.

THE SHETLAND PONY

Perhaps the best-known of all the small breeds is the tiny Shetland. Its native home is far to the north of Scotland in the bleak and rugged Shetland Isles, barely four hundred miles south of the Arctic Circle. The breed is supposed to have been located there at least as early as the sixth century A.D. If this is so, it would make it one of the oldest in existence. Undoubtedly it is an offshoot of the ancient Icelandic- or Celtic-type pony, dwarfed by the harsh climate and scanty vegetation.

The average height of the true Shetland is only about ten hands, and weights vary from three hundred to four hundred pounds. But they are exceedingly sturdy, their chief occupation in their native land being the carrying of 140-pound loads of peat. In the old days many were used in Britain to haul coal carts in the underground mine galleries. In the Shetland Isles, the Shetland pony grew up in and about the primitive cottages, along with the children and the dogs, from which close association it derives its gentle and pleasant disposition.

Chiefly because of its small, almost "toy" size,

the Shetland has always had great appeal to children. They make good pets, and, like most intelligent animals, are easily spoiled. They are noted for hardiness and longevity. Their coats, particularly in winter, are long and shaggy.

The Shetland pony today falls into two distinct types. The "English" type, as still found in the Shetlands, is really a miniature draft horse, chunky and very strong, "cute" but not particularly stylish and with a tremendous barrel, which is too pronounced for him to make an ideal saddle animal. The "American" type, as developed in the United States, is a more graceful, slender animal; a real miniature horse, retaining the older breed's good disposition and hardiness but less clumsy in movement and more active. A pony of this type, standing some forty-two inches at the shoulder, can sometimes clear a three-foot-high obstacle.

The registration of Shetland ponies in this country is in the hands of the American Shetland Pony Club (P.O. Box 435, Fowler, IN 47944). Both the foregoing types of ponies, if of registered stock, may be registered with the association. In America the maximum permissible height is 11.2 hands. In England it is 10.2 hands. In addition, the association is promoting a third type—a half-breed cross between registered Shetland on Hackney or Shetland on Welsh. This breeding produces a good-looking, active pony from eleven to thirteen hands suitable for children from eight to twelve.

THE WELSH PONY

The Welsh pony is another ancient breed, having been established in England as long ago as Saxon times. It gradually became localized in Wales where for hundreds of years these ponies have ranged the mountainous country in semiwild bands, living off the sparse vegetation. Under conditions such as this the weaker specimens do not survive for long, and only the more rugged and active animals pull through.

Attempts were made from time to time to improve the wild stock. Long ago (some say the early eighteenth century, others the early nineteenth) a small race horse, retired after a successful career, was turned out to run with the Welsh mares. A great improvement in the herd headed by this stallion was noted. Years later, small Hackney stallions were crossed with the native ponies, resulting in some fast trotting, harness and saddle horses. However, these endeavors and their results were only local, and be-

Welsh pony owned by Mrs. Jean Austin Dupont (FREUDY)

cause of the way the herds were allowed to mingle and run wild, only temporary.

In any case, the hardiness and agility of these native ponies made them much in demand for children who had outgrown the Shetland. They were also used for driving and for light farm work.

The Welsh pony averages about 12.2 hands and weighs in the neighborhood of five hundred pounds. In appearance they have been likened to a miniature coach horse. Heads are small and clean-cut, with small prick ears, set on a longish graceful neck. The face is slightly "dished." Shoulders are deep and the back is short and strong. The animals are well muscled, with good bone. They possess both speed and endurance. They make excellent jumpers, and one, Little Squire, was for many years one of the leading open jumpers in the United States. In competition the little champion, standing just over thirteen hands, could clear jumps from five to six feet high.

The Welsh ponies are generally more spirited than the Shetlands, without the latter's tendency toward stubbornness. At the same time they are docile and intelligent. They are becoming increasingly popular in America, where their worth as a mount for the more advanced youngster is much appreciated.

Besides riding, Welsh ponies are seen in driving classes, pulling light two- and four-wheeled vehicles. Welsh pony classes are divided into two sections. The "A" section must not exceed 12.2 hands, while the "B" section includes ponies from 12.2 hands to 14.2 hands, which is the height limit.

Besides his desirability as a children's mount, the Welsh pony was used to improve the quality of the polo pony in the early years of the game. The need for a better grade of pony for the increasingly popular game was recognized and the Polo Pony Society was formed in England in 1893. Thoroughbreds and Arabians were crossed with several types of native British ponies. The most successful of these were the Welsh, and their good conformation, speed and hardiness did much to upgrade the British polo pony.

The Shetland and the Welsh are the most popular and most numerous of the recognized pony breeds. However, there are the Chincoteagues from the Virginia coast, Connemaras from the Emerald Isle, hardy Icelandic ponies from just below the Arctic Circle and Galicenos from Mexico. As any animal below 14.2 hands is classed as a pony, there are Arab ponies, Tennessee Walker ponies and Thoroughbred ponies, too.

Pony breeding has become a popular hobby and

small farm business in recent years. With more people moving to the suburbs and country where they have room for a pony for their children, the demand has grown tremendously.

In addition to those listed above there are many crossbreeds. Also new "breeds" are being created by crossing existing breeds. Among them are the "Pony of the Americas," a cross between the Shetland and the Appaloosa, and the Americana—a cross between the Shetland and the Hackney (the Hackney pony—bred from the Hackney horses of coaching fame—is seldom ridden).

The best sources of detailed information about these and other breeds and their breeders are the breed associations. These are listed, along with many other useful addresses for horsemen, in the *Horse Industry Directory,* which is published annually by The American Horse Council (1700 K Street NW, Washington, DC 20006. Tel. 202–296–4031).

Mary Ann Tauskey and her pony Marcus Aurelius, an outstanding team in three-day eventing (SUE MAYNARD)

Chapter 3

BUYING A HORSE

By far the majority of American horsemen and horsewomen ride rented mounts. This is the easiest, cheapest and, for many, the only way in which they can engage in this sport. Sometimes a rented horse may give a satisfactory ride. In many cases, if the riding stable nag is not much good, neither is the rider—they deserve each other. But there may come a time when a rider who has progressed to a point where he feels that a rented mount can no longer give him satisfaction, feels the urge to own a horse of his own. In many (probably most) cases this urge should be firmly suppressed. Ruling out the question of acreage and location few people realize the amount of time and work involved. We in America are a fairly well-mechanized society. We are more used to pushing buttons than shoveling manure. The machines which carry us hither and yon are always on tap. A touch of the starter and we are off. Given an occasional checkup and oil change and regular

feeding of gasoline, our motorized mounts are always at our service.

But unless one belongs to the very small and very fortunate class which can order their favorite horse saddled up and brought to the front door when a little exercise is contemplated, preparation for even a short ride entails considerable work. Few horse owners today can afford the luxury, upon returning from an hour or two in the saddle, of throwing the reins to a waiting groom or stable boy and relaxing with a julep. Nor can an animal be run into a stable and conveniently forgotten during the long winter months. The daily chores must go on, whether you ride or not. Unless you can cultivate a dependable horse-sitter, forget about those weekends on the ski slopes or on Southern beaches.

The prospective owner should ask himself first of all if he really likes horses or merely enjoys riding—there is a difference, and there are many competent

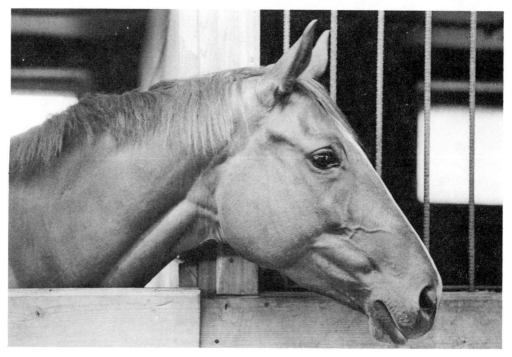

(SUE MAYNARD)

horsemen who crave the exercise, the challenge, the thrill of riding without caring particularly about their mounts. Then there is the question of the amount of work involved. Will the daily routine, plus the little odd jobs that crop up from time to time, be fun or sheer drudgery? Is the owner-to-be a "Mr. Fixit" capable of making minor repairs (both to stable and animal) or is he the helpless type always on the phone to carpenter, plumber or veterinarian? So think twice before joining the ranks of the stableboy owners.

On the credit side, the horseman who realizes that he may spend more time with bucket, broom and pitchfork than in the saddle is in for a rewarding experience. For one thing there is pride of ownership. Most people prefer to own the things they like and the thought that the sleek and graceful creature eating his head off in the stall is one's very own makes up for a lot of hard work, expense, petty annoyances, veterinarian's bills and the like. Horses do not make the best pets in the world but they—or the majority of them—respond to good treatment and affection, and the true animal lover will get a good deal of pleasure in their care, training and company.

Then, too, the handyman type will get satisfaction from the efficient, well-designed and well-run stable, stout fences and a handsome layout and well-kept tack.

If there are children involved in the operation,

then there is a chance for some willing, if unskillful, co-operation at times. And, of course, there is no finer way to interest youngsters in horses and horsemanship than for them to grow up in an environment where horses are part of their everyday life.

Once the decision has been taken, there remains only the problem of finding a suitable horse at a suitable price. First there is the question of the use to which the horse is to be put. Is he to be a hunter, for the show ring or just ordinary hacking around the countryside? Involved also are the buyer's own size, age and experience. It is a mistake, usually brought on by pride, to buy an animal that is too much to handle.

Few people, men especially, care to admit that they are not capable of tackling anything on four legs; and indeed, some riders actually seem to enjoy an animal which they constantly have to battle. There are plenty of riders who care more for dash and spirit than for comfortable going, while on the other hand the more elderly might prefer something a little less fiery, perhaps on the order of an easy-gaited Tennessee Walker.

For the same reason given above—pride—or perhaps through a mistaken idea that bulk in horseflesh gives a greater prestige, people often purchase a mount which is too big. Size is no criterion, however, and at best a horse is a poor choice as a status symbol. Fellow horsemen will be only too happy to pick your prized possession to pieces point by point, and non-horselovers will think you are nuts anyway.

Remember that a small rider perched on an outsize mount looks, and probably is, as uncomfortable and out-of-place as a large man on a pony.

After deciding on the breed which will best suit the buyer's needs, there comes the question of sex. Generally speaking, unless the buyer is an experienced rider, it would be well to rule out a stallion. There are exceptions, but most are too much horse for the beginner. Mares, on the other hand, have many of the characteristics of the fair sex, both good and bad. They may be gentle but also may be a bit skittish at times. Unless the buyer has a breeding program in mind, a gelding makes the best mount. They are quiet and dependable and comparatively easily trained, lacking the rambunctiousness of the stallion and the flightiness of the mare.

Now as to age. Don't buy too young. A horse is ready to go to work when he is three or four years old. If the buyer wishes to do his own training this can start at two or three. The beginner will probably want a well-broken horse, something from four years up to, say, eight or nine. A horse which has not been handled before it is five or six may be difficult to break. A horse reaches its prime at about the age of five and with care should be perfectly sound at fifteen. Horses have been known to live more than forty years—but in general a horse of more than twenty-two or three has just about had it as far as any work is concerned.

Anyone who is new in any endeavor needs advice, and no one can use it better than the novice buying his first horse. Unfortunately the word "horse trader" has come to mean something a bit risky—as far as the customer is concerned—and conjures up visions of tricky deals involving shifty-eyed gypsies, dyed horses and suchlike hokum, all ending with the saddling of the victim with a spavined worn-out animal, possibly stolen into the bargain.

Actually a reputable dealer in horses is one of the best bets for anyone in the market for a suitable piece of horseflesh. Like any businessman, he has his reputation to maintain and, as much of his adver-

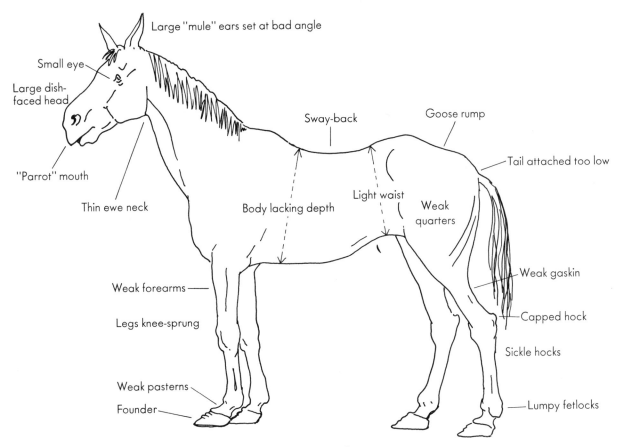

A horse not to buy

tising is by word-of-mouth, he has to be particularly careful in the matter of satisfied customers. Such a dealer is infinitely to be preferred to the friend who knows "all about horses."

Especially to be avoided by the uninitiated are auctions. Here good bargains are occasionally to be found, but more often than not the animals to be found at auctions are there because other attempts to sell them had failed. Such sales are fine for knowledgeable horsemen with lots of experience and an eye for a bargain, but unless you can find one to help you, you will do well to leave auctions alone.

By and large, one gets what one pays for, with horses as with everything else. While it is sometimes possible to pick up a good horse which for some minor reason has been disqualified for show or hunting, this usually involves knowing or meeting the right party at exactly the right time.

Trainers are sometimes able to furnish useful tips as to likely horses for sale, as are horseshoers. Many, if not most, of these latter today cover considerable territory and are in touch with many of the owners in their locality.

Probably the best procedure is to contact the nearest breeders of the particular breed you are interested in. They—like the dealers—are interested in a satisfied clientele, and, while sometimes higher in price, usually have a wider selection to choose from than a dealer who handles anything and everything that comes along. A letter to the breeders' club or association will procure advice as to the breeders in your locality.

Before the horse is finally purchased, the buyer should insist on riding it, preferably for a good ride across country, rather than a few turns around a ring or paddock. If it is possible to arrange for a two- or three-week trial, so much the better. The personality and temperament of the horse can be judged much better if the buyer has actually worked with it for a few days.

It is also a good idea to have a veterinarian look the animal over and report on its soundness. While a veterinarian is not necessarily a good judge of a horse, as far as points are concerned, he is able to remark on its general fitness.

Last, but certainly not least, is the matter of price. This varies considerably according to breed and location. It also depends on the age and condition of the animal, its immediate ancestry and the amount of training, if any. In the East it is usually possible to pick up a good sound animal, one that has been broken, and saddled and ridden a few times, for around twelve or fifteen hundred dollars. The same horse, however, after being trained to the aids (to respond to pressures of leg and reins), and to take correct leads on signal, and after having been hunted a couple of times, would be a bargain at three or four thousand dollars and, depending on conformation, breeding, etc., would be more likely to fetch twice that amount. The same holds true of ponies. The initial cost will be about the same, and so will the training—which is what you are paying for.

For hacking around a lot of people are perfectly happy on the twelve hundred dollar animal. Like many drivers, the fine points of a superb machine are wasted on them.

Some set out to train their own animals, and by dint of painstaking work are sometimes successful in producing a well-schooled animal. Certainly an amateur has the advantage over the professional in that he has much closer contact and personal relationship with his horse than can a person responsible for the care and training of many animals.

On the other hand, the schooling of a mount requires knowledge and experience, as well as patience, and the well-meaning but amateurish efforts of a novice may only succeed in ruining a horse completely. The money paid to a professional trainer is money well spent if it results in greatly increased riding pleasure.

When purchasing a horse you should receive a bill of sale. There is no set form for this. A description of the horse should, of course, be included. If the animal is registered with one of the breeders' associations, then the registration papers are transferred to you at the time of the sale.

Chapter 4

THE STABLE

The novice who is about to purchase or has recently purchased a horse or horses would be well advised to keep his mounts at the nearest professional boarding stable. If, after the first burst of enthusiasm has worn off, he really knows that riding is for him, and if he has time and space to house and care for his animals, he may prefer to keep his horses at home. He is then faced with the problem of providing adequate accommodations.

Naturally the location and design of the stable depends on many factors: the number of horses to be kept, the amount of money available (most important of all, for most of us), the lay of the land and the location of the house and roads. There are some rules for stabling which are musts; there are others which are preferable but not vital and which can be omitted or changed in the interest of economy.

Some compromises made with money-saving in mind turn out to be false economies in the long run

and the owner ends up by spending more on alteration and repair than the initial cost of a better but more expensive job.

In the following suggestions for the ideal small stable, I am presupposing that the owner has sufficient acreage for at least a small paddock (even one as small as thirty feet by forty feet is better than nothing), has access to riding territory without having to traverse heavily-built-up areas and, if within town limits, has thoroughly checked the zoning laws. While neighbors in the ''ranch house estate'' community may think your neat split-rail paddock, cute barn and pretty horses add tone to the area, they will probably not approve of the inevitable by-products and may object to the aroma of manure mingling with that of their barbecued spareribs.

Granted then that the prospective stablebuilder has enough land in or adjacent to good ''horse country,'' the next problem is locating the stable in relation to the house and grounds. Let me say here that any idea of combining stable with garage is out. Fire hazards and exhaust fumes make it entirely too dangerous, not to speak of the disturbance to the horses by car engines, garage doors, etc. Besides this, it will be found to be as impossible to keep dirt and dust out of the garage as it is to keep the exhaust fumes out of the stable.

Existing sheds and outbuildings may sometimes be modified to accommodate horses, but the expense of remodeling often comes close to the cost of a new building, while the results will never be as satisfactory.

If the property was once a farm it may include a cow barn or a stable for work horses, or both, in good enough repair to warrant renovating. The location in relation to the house is already determined. Also, all working barns had easy access to the storage sections so the road problem is eliminated, too. A former cow barn is not the ideal stable, however, as the ceilings are usually too low, and also light and ventilation in many old barns leave much to be desired. However, if the structure is solid it may be possible to work out a plan incorporating most of the desirable features wanted in a stable for riding horses.

If the barn is set into the side of the hill, as are many barns in some parts of the country, the stable floor can usually be excavated sufficiently to give sufficient headroom (a minimum of nine feet is desirable, otherwise a rearing horse may injure his head). Such barns have masonry side and back walls to the lower section (sometimes the whole barn is of stone or brick). These walls are often wet, with water from the hill backing up against them. Outside drainage and interior application of waterproof masonry paints, capable of sealing off water under considerable pressure, can usually take care of this problem. Condensation from moisture, due to inadequate ventilation, can be controlled by putting in new windows or enlarging old ones (this may be cheaper and simpler than attempting to cut through masonry walls, which are often thirty-six inches thick). If the installation of more windows is not feasible, one or more exhaust fans, operated for a short time when necessary, will draw sufficient fresh air into the interior to keep it dry.

The upper section of old barns were often floored with wide boards (a friend of mine discovered his to be of walnut). These, none too carefully fitted in the first place, shrink and warp with age, allowing a rain of debris to drift down between the cracks. Unless the original floor is overlaid with plywood or tongue-and-groove sheathing, it is impossible to prevent horses, blankets, water containers and everything else from accumulating a constantly renewed coating of dust, bits of straw and the like.

On the credit side, an old barn is usually large, with more square footage than most people would build into a new structure, and the upstairs offers ample storage room for hay, bedding and grain, if the latter is to be stored in quantity.

The ideal stable, one built after much planning and forethought, is, of course, tailored exactly to meet the owner's requirements: not too big, which is wasteful both of time and money; and not so small that horses are crowded, or that even a possible addition of a horse or pony would be impracticable.

It should be located close enough to the house so that an undue disturbance may be heard, and the business of getting to and from the stable not too difficult in bad weather.

Flies are always a problem when livestock is present, so there should be at least a hundred feet (more in the South) between stable and the nearest living space—house, patio, pool, etc.

While on the subject of flies, there is no way of eliminating them entirely. Removing the animals and spraying the inside of the stable will give only temporary relief, as does spraying the animals themselves. Spraying will help while grooming an animal, but as soon as the horse begins to sweat, the spray is no longer effective. Good cross ventilation (and a clean stable) is a great help.

If the stable can be sheltered on the south side of a hill, so much the better. It should have a road leading to the storage section, so that feed trucks can deliver in wet and wintry weather.

Whatever the construction, it should have a good deep concrete foundation to discourage rats, and if a tack room and grain storage room are to be included in the ground floor plan, these should have poured concrete floors. The floors of the stalls themselves usually used to be of clay with a couple of feet of rock or crushed stone underneath for drainage. This is the traditional flooring, but it has its disadvantages. No matter how good the subsurface drainage, clay is inclined to be damp. It is impossible to thoroughly clean a clay floor. The best that can be done is to rake and sweep and then lime. Rats will dig and tunnel in clay, and it is not unusual to see an old horse barn literally honeycombed with rat holes.

I recall with a great deal of pleasure rat hunts in one such stable during my youth. After turning out the work horses and closing the doors a water hose would be applied down one of the many openings.

An attractive two-horse backyard stable in Connecticut (SUE MAYNARD)

This would speedily result in the eruption of numbers of indignant rats, which were instantly and enthusiastically assailed by small dogs of the terrier variety. Those survivors who swarmed up walls, stairs and ladders were met, with equal enthusiasm, but less accuracy, by a fusillade from .410 shot guns, .22 rifles and revolvers. The row was terrific and the slaughter, at least by the dogs, impressive. But age brings caution, and few adults, myself included, care for such a noisy, not to say dangerous, way of keeping down the rat population.

Horses, at least some of them, are great diggers too, and are given to pawing large holes in earth floors at night, which excavations have to be filled in and tamped down again the next day.

The advantage of clay is that while often damp, it does not long stay wet on the surface and furthermore is fairly soft and easy on the horse's feet.

Another school of thought believes in concrete floors throughout. Concrete (a dirty word to the clay-floor clan) is undoubtedly hard and cold, and thicker bedding is necessary. On the other hand, if evenly sloped to a drain or gutter it drains quickly, preventing the accumulation of urine in pockets and hollows. It is rat- and hoof-proof and can be thoroughly hosed down, scrubbed and disinfected with a minimum of effort. It would be my preference if building a new stable. However, if adapting an old barn with a good clay floor, I should be tempted to leave the clay.

Wood floors are sometimes used but they soak up moisture, retain odors, are slippery when wet and are subject to rot. Also they afford wonderful protection to rats and mice. The wood floors are warmer than clay or concrete, but in many people's opinion this is outweighed by the numerous disadvantages.

Cobblestones, brick and asphalt are also used for flooring. They have no apparent advantages over concrete, while the brick and cobblestones are harder to clean.

For the walls, wood, covered with siding, clapboards or shingles is probably the best and cheapest building material. Fire- and weatherproof asbestos shingles over plywood or building board are good and have the advantage of never needing paint. Some people claim that in cold climates, barns should be insulated. If they are, care should be taken that the insulating material is rodentproof. While on the subject of rodents, there is nothing like a good, hard-working barn cat or two to help solve the rat and mouse problem. My old Pennsylvania stone barn used to be jumping with rodents but our three Siamese house cats cleared it and kept it cleared.

There is no point in insulating the top part of the stable if yours is to be a two-storied affair; the hay and bedding help insulate the ceiling of the stalls below. Under natural conditions, horses are able to withstand very low temperatures, and given quarters that are airy, draft-free and dry, and plenty of bedding, a properly fed horse will do well in even the coldest stable. Naturally, if the animals have been clipped and nature's winter underwear removed, adequate blanketing is necessary.

Most animals suffer more from heat than from cold, and horses are no exception. One of the great advantages of the two-story barn is the insulating effect of the upper story. If a stable is to be built on one level, then some form of insulation, in the form of an air space, bats of insulating material, or both, should definitely be provided between the ceiling of the stalls and actual roofing.

The top section (and if you plan to keep more than two horses it will probably pay you to build up rather than out) should have a good-sized loading door on the side where your road runs. A pulley arrangement is not necessary in the average stable. The top layers of bales on the delivery truck will be about floor level of the storage loft. The rest can be heaved up without much trouble, especially if the smaller bales are used.

Bales usually can be had in two sizes. The large three-wire bales are quite heavy, often well over a hundred pounds, and manhandling them around is no joke. The smaller, two-wire bales weighing around forty-five pounds are much handier. Figuring roughly 250 cubic feet of hay to the ton and 3½ tons per horse per year, plus 250 bales of bedding per stall, the hay and bedding for one horse will take up approximately 2300 cubic feet. This storage space must be allowed for when you are designing your barn, multiplied by the number of horses you expect to keep. This is assuming that no pasture is available, and that hay and bedding is bought once a year.

The simplest design for a stable is one in which there is a single row of stalls. These should have double-Dutch doors, and should face south or as close to south as the lay of the land permits. This ensures a maximum of warmth and consequent drying and airing of the stalls. Also the back—the north side—can be left doorless, thus cutting down on the drafts. A projecting roof or porch should extend out at least ten feet. This will keep out all but driving rain, provide shade in hot weather and a sheltered working space. If the stable is to have a second story, building the top story out with an overhang will serve this purpose as well as increasing loft space.

If two rows of facing stalls are to be built with doors on both ends of the stable, then the central passageway should run east and west. If only one entrance is planned then the stable door should be on the south side. A small building, two or three stalls on a side, might well be of the latter type. A long stable, on the other hand, might well do with the extra ventilation given by a door at either end of the central passage.

In any event, this passage should not be less than ten feet wide, allowing plenty of room for horses to be led out of their stalls, saddled, groomed, etc. The stable doors at either end of the passageway should be of the sliding type. These are less trouble to open in windy or snowy weather and are out of the way when not in use. If swinging doors are used, be sure they open outward. Stall doors should be at least four feet wide. Those opening on the central passage should also be of the sliding type. A good door is of wood, some four and a half feet wide with vertical iron bars above spaced close enough so that there is no danger of the horse getting his head between them. Heavy galvanized mesh of the "anchor post" fence variety may also be used. Wooden bars are not recommended because a horse will chew anything he can get his teeth into. For this reason all wooden edges of partitions, etc., which a horse can reach should be covered with sheet metal. The iron bars or heavy mesh over wood makes an excellent partition between stalls, although some owners prefer a stall built solid up to or within a few inches of the ceiling.

If adapting an existing barn, poor ventilation may necessitate using open-type construction of stall partitions and doors. Be sure the boards are no more than two inches apart. There will be less chance of damage from kicking and biting if the boards run vertically instead of horizontally. However, in climates where cold weather can be expected, solid partitions cut down on drafts.

Stall doors which open to the outside are always double, and made to swing out. Horses like to look out of the top door, and in doing so, often put considerable weight on the lower door. A heavy wooden bar, made to slide across the inside of the top of the lower door and an inch or two back from it, will save strained latches and hinges.

All wood in stalls and doors should be two inches thick, preferably oak. Anything smaller will not stand the heavy wear and tear. A "kicker" will reduce lighter lumber to splinters in short order.

Stalls are of two types: box stalls, or loose boxes as they are sometimes called and straight stalls. The box stall should be at least eleven feet by eleven feet. A pony needs only eight by eight. Straight stalls take up much less room but are not as comfortable for the horse—six by ten for a hunter down to four by eight for a pony. Some horses become

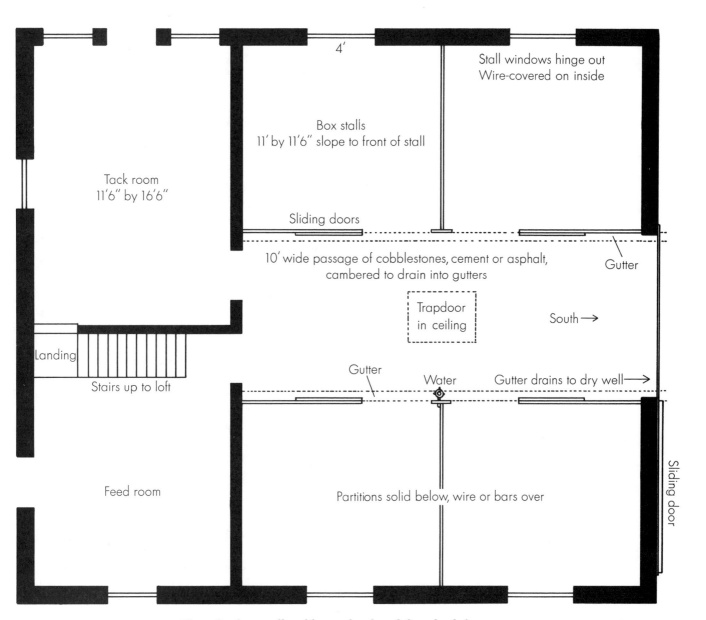

Plan of a four-stall stable, 34 feet by 38 feet, hayloft over

restless and excited in box stalls and do better in a straight stall, but for the majority of animals the box stall is best.

The more light and ventilation in a stable the better. Besides having an open top, each stall should have at least one window. These should be placed high—above the horse's line of sight. Horses are skittish and the sudden appearance of a head or some other moving object may startle them. All windows should be barred or wired with heavy-gauge wire.

Stall floors, whether of clay or concrete, should slope slightly (one inch in eighteen is sufficient) to the point where the drainage gutters are located. With proper bedding, which soaks up most of the moisture, very little actually runs out, but a slight slope is advisable.

Stalls opening on an inside-passageway type of barn should slope toward the passage, which should be of concrete with a shallow gutter on each side. These gutters may either drain outside the barn or through metal grid covers into drain tile in under the gutters and leading to dry wells on the outside. A dry well, for those who have never seen or built one, is a hole into which waste water can flow and drain away into the soil. It can be as large as necessary—four feet in diameter by six deep is a good-sized one—and can be loosely filled with large stones to keep the earth sides from filling in, or it can be built with drainage blocks such as are used in lining cesspools. They are also often used to dispose of rain water from roofs.

If a small feed room is to be built on the lower level, then it should have a concrete floor, and should be as completely rat tight as you can make it. Grain is best kept in metal containers. Fifty-gallon steel drums with latch-on tops are best. This is particularly important if grain is kept anywhere where a horse breaking out of its stall can get at it.

The tack room contains racks and pegs for saddles and bridles and storage space for all other loose gear. It is also a good place for your medical supplies. A rack or frame to hold a saddle while cleaning it will be a big help. There should be a sink with running water. The tack room is a work area as well as a storage space, so allow enough space to comfortably house your gear, while still leaving ample room to move around. It should be completely enclosed from the stall section of the barn. If there is no space for a separate tack room, tack may be hung from pegs beside the stall doors. However, besides being in the way, tack hung in this manner soon gets covered with dust and chaff. If at all possible, a tack room is recommended.

Mangers for feed are best placed in a corner of the stall, about breast high. They should be metal, or wood lined with sheet metal. A rack for hay may be built under the manger. Many old hayracks were put up high, but because of dust from hay affecting horses' eyes, this practice has been abandoned. Some owners who keep their animals in box stalls just pile the hay ration on the floor in one corner on the theory that in any case many animals pull their hay out of the racks onto the floor anyway. However, this is asking for trouble from worms and is not recommended. Hayracks should be made of iron; wooden slats will rapidly be chewed to splinters.

A long flap door on the front of the stall, opening directly over the hayrack, feedbox and water bucket, may be a great convenience for owners who want to be able to hay, feed and water without going into the stall (handy for those last-minute chores before leaving for a party or the office).

If the hay and bedding is kept in a loft above the stable a trap must be provided to allow for dropping bales into the alley. As hay will probably be kept up at one end of the loft and bedding at the other, the trap should be located between the two. If space in the loft allows, traps may be installed above each rack. This permits haying without the necessity of dumping hay in the alley and distributing it from there, with the attendant mess.

In some stables, where the grain is also kept in the loft, pipe chutes lead down to the mangers permitting the feeding of the grain ration without entering each stall separately. With most people today, time is an important factor, and any such labor-saving devices as these more than pay for the initial effort.

Horses should have access to water at all times. A bucket, set in a corner of the stall so that it cannot be kicked over, is the cheapest way of watering. Water pipes should be laid in the stable below frost level. Carrying water is a chore, so arrange your spigots with an eye to saving as much bucket-toting as possible. Automatic fountains are popular, and horses soon learn to use them, but in very cold climates they are subject to freezing. For barn spigots the antifreeze type, in which the valve is below frost level, is the best.

Good lighting is important. When planning this arrange to have at least one outside stable light which will operate from the house. This does away with a great deal of stumbling around on dark paths between house and stable.

All wiring should be in conduit. Rats may chew through ordinary insulation and horses will pull on any loose wiring which is in their reach. Bulbs should be protected against breakage with wire guards.

THE PADDOCK

Along with stabling comes the question of proper exercise space. Besides good quarters it is necessary to provide for some sort of stable yard or paddock, or both. A stable yard can be quite small, and is usually an enclosure large enough to turn the horses into while their stalls are being cleaned, or where on fine days work may be done on the horses; where they may be saddled up—in fact, where any of the outdoor functions of the stable can be carried on without the animals being able to wander outside the enclosure. The stable yard is sometimes, as in the case of a large stable built on the U plan, merely made up of the area enclosed by the wings of the buildings, with a stout fence and gate across the open end. The yard itself should adjoin a larger exercise field or paddock. The paddock should enclose an acre or two, although anything, even a thousand square feet or so, is better than nothing. An area as small as this will provide a little exercise and fresh air and will greatly reduce the amount of time needed for cleaning the stalls.

A small paddock (SUE MAYNARD)

An acre of ground (approximately seventy yards by seventy yards) is better and is probably sufficient for the small stable. Anything smaller gets cut up badly. Grass never has a chance to get started and the area soon becomes soiled. If more space is considered desirable it might well be divided into two one-acre paddocks instead of one large one, as it is sometimes handy to be able to separate certain animals.

If larger areas are under consideration it should be decided just what is a paddock and what is a field. To the writer, a paddock should be large enough to permit adequate exercise, and to permit a little green cover to grow, so that a rain will not turn the area into a sea of mud. It should also be small enough so that a horse turned into it can be caught easily when needed. It should not necessarily be considered as a grazing area—that is the function of the pasture, and the larger that is, the better.

Whatever the area that necessity or fancy dictates, be sure that it is strongly fenced. Here it is well to remember that animals, like children, get bored in confinement; a horse penned in a very small area and not worked more than a few hours a week is likely to spend a good part of his time trying to get out. Any attempt to economize on fencing is a mistake, and may result in strayed or injured animals. And it might be well to remind the horse owner that he is liable for damage to crops, gardens, shrubbery, lawns, etc., caused by his animals straying on other people's property. Furthermore, in the unfortunate event of a motorist striking a stray horse on the road, the owner not only loses a valuable animal but will be on the receiving end of a lawsuit. The damage caused to an automobile, and often to the car's occupants, by hitting a half ton of horse can be very serious indeed.

FENCES

The best fences, both for strength and for looks, are of wood. They are also expensive. The two kinds most used are the post-and-rail variety in which the wood is left natural, or the board fence, which has to be painted. If the latter is used, seven-foot locust posts (cedar can also be used, but any other wood soon rots, even if chemically treated) are dug in at ten-foot intervals, and sunk to a depth of two and a half feet. Boards—oak is generally used—are then nailed (use galvanized nails) on the inside of the posts. If you do use oak, drill a pilot hole for your nails. Three rails will do; four is better. The lumber should be an inch and a half by six inches, or two inches by six inches, and may be had rough from a local sawmill. It will need painting, and a nontoxic fence or barn paint should be used. A liberal splash of paint should be put on the post and on ends of the boards before they are nailed in. If a piece one and a half inches by four inches, or one and a half inches by six inches, is nailed along the top of the upper board and over the posts as a cap rail, a much stronger and neater-appearing job will result.

Wire may be used; a heavy stock fencing (never use barbed) wire strung tight between locust posts. The addition of an extra-heavy-gauge wire along the top or a board will help prevent breakage when horses lean over the top, as they inevitably will. In place of the heavy-duty wire or board, an electrified wire may be used along the top of the wire fence. A "hot" wire by itself, though, is not to be recommended. Unlike cattle, which are usually inclined to be placid and slow-moving, a horse is more likely to run into an electric fence and, snapping the wire, break the current.

Rosa multiflora, the living hedge, so much advertised, may be used to advantage where space is not at a premium, and where there is time (about three years) for it to attain sufficient growth. When fully grown it attains a width of some ten to fifteen feet and stands about eight to ten feet high (it can, of course be trimmed, if desired). It forms an effective barrier and an excellent cover for small game. One disadvantage is the spreading of the seed by birds.

Two or more horses may be run in the same paddock if they are reasonably gentle and get along together. There is always some risk of horses kicking each other. And if, as sometimes happens, two horses definitely do not get along together they must be run in at different times, or put in a separate enclosure. If the two paddocks are separated by a strip a few feet wide (one on either side of a lane or driveway is ideal), it will prevent any fighting and biting over the fences.

Gates should be sturdy, and fitted with latches which cannot be jarred loose, or worked open by a horse's teeth (some of them get quite clever at this).

Chapter 5

FEED AND BEDDING

In the wild state, a horse lives on grass. Unless frightened or escaping from natural enemies he will take little exercise. He will feed almost constantly, wandering from one good grazing spot to another. When not feeding he is resting. For this normally quiet existence on pasture a grass ration is sufficient. However, a domestic horse is called upon to do work, and occasionally very strenuous work. To provide the required energy the natural grass feeding, which, in most cases, the domestic horse receives in the form of hay, must be supplemented by the addition of a grain ration.

This grain ration is concentrated food, unlike the grass, which is taken in slowly and digested as the horse eats. Not only is grain not as readily digested as grass, but the horse is likely to eat it too quickly, with the result that, instead of the natural little-and-often feeding of the pasture, his entire meal is taken into his stomach at once. The horse's stomach is

small as compared to his size, and his digestive juices relatively weak. His stomach is not provided with muscles which permit him to vomit anything that disagrees with him. It will be seen, therefore, that great care must be taken that the grain ration be given often, in small amounts, rather than all at once. Then, too, grain has a tendency to swell when wet. A horse watered *after* a grain feeding will be likely to suffer a bad case of colic. A horse should therefore always be watered before feeding.

To lessen the chance of the animal bolting his grain it is advisable to feed hay first, to take the edge off his appetite. The sequence then is: water, hay and grain, and the smaller and oftener the feedings the better for the horse. Most horse owners of the do-it-yourself type work out a schedule which fits in comfortably with their way of life.

A medium hay feeding and a light grain ration is sufficient in the morning, followed by a medium grain feeding at noon (if this midday feeding is not feasible the morning grain ration may be increased to compensate). A late afternoon medium feeding of hay (if the animals are to be ridden, the hay should be given after the ride) and should be followed in an hour or two by a grain ration. Later in the evening a large hay feeding should be given which will carry the animals through the night.

If there is sufficient water, an occasional variation in the feeding timetable will do no harm. Most domestic animals, and this includes household pets, are more likely to suffer from overfeeding than from undernourishment.

It has been estimated that the owner who does his own work will spend about three-quarters of the amount of money needed for his horse's upkeep on hay, grain and bedding. It is difficult, if not impossible, to price these essential articles, as costs vary greatly in different parts of the country, from season to season, and from year to year. Poor crops may send prices skyrocketing, or overproduction bring them down to bargain levels. Then, too, if good pasture is available a fair amount may be deducted from the hay expenditure. One thing is certain: No attempt should be made to economize at the expense of quality (this applies mainly to hay), while skimping on bedding will prove to be not only unsatisfactory but actually wasteful.

While supplying some food value, hay provides mostly bulk. As a general average, one and a half pounds of hay per hundred pounds of horse per day will prove sufficient. More will often be wasted. Feed a horse what he will readily clean up and you will not go far wrong. Allowing 1200 pounds for the average horse, this will amount to some 550 pounds a month, or about three and a half tons per year.

Hay varies in food value and should be chosen with care. They are often classed as grass hays, grain hays and legume hays. Grass hays include brome, millet, Johnson grass, Sudan grass, prairie grass, and the best and most widely known, timothy.

The grain hays, wheat or oat, are cut when just about to ripen and should include the kernels. Although making good hay, a storage problem is involved, as the kernels attract rats and mice.

The legume hays, of which clover and alfalfa are the most common, are high in protein, vitamins and calcium. By themselves, they are too rich, and if fed exclusively will cause upset stomachs. A mixture (20 per cent to 30 per cent) of the legumes with timothy or other grass hays is most satisfactory. Actually few hay crops yield pure cuttings of any one variety and in many cases mixtures are grown, clover and timothy being a common crop.

Some horse owners recommend timothy half the time, a mixture of clover and timothy one-third of the time and alfalfa the rest of the time. In any feeding program, local conditions play a large part, as some crops do better in certain parts of the country than in others.

Crops also vary with local conditions; some hays, grown on depleted soil, have far less calcium and trace minerals than those grown in better soil. In the old days upland hay was preferred in many parts of the country, but in many cases such hay, being grown on badly washed soil, was of inferior quality. The main thing is to see that the hay diet is balanced, with sufficient proteins and calcium.

Condition of the hay is most important. It should be a good green; clean and bright, not dirty or dusty, easy to pull apart when unbaled, and most important of all, should not be moldy. Moldy hay is poisonous and can kill a horse.

Hay should smell sweet, and any musty-smelling bales are suspect. A great deal of the success of a hay crop depends on the care with which it is cured and baled. Hay left too long to dry loses some of its goodness and appears brown and lifeless, while if it is baled while damp it is likely to become moldy. Hay baled early in the morning while covered in dew, after a shower, or that laying in shady portions of a field may all produce moldy hay.

Hay, especially alfalfa, which has a woody stem, is best if it is crushed after cutting. This splits open the stems and promotes quick drying.

Many farmers tend to adjust their baling machines to make too tight a bale. This is inclined to produce moldy hay, as there is insufficient circulation of air inside the bale. Surprisingly enough, many farmers do not know, or care, a great deal about curing and baling.

Because the successful curing of a hay crop is dependent on a spell of dry weather, more and more farmers are artificially drying hay as soon as it is cut. Hay dried in this manner is higher in protein and there is no danger of it being moldy.

The owner who does not raise his own hay or buy from local farmers must rely on the integrity of his feed merchant. A reputable dealer will replace a batch of moldy hay (a farmer might be reluctant to do this). Some hays, while perfectly wholesome, are more palatable than others. It may be well to buy a sample bale and try it on your animals before ordering a large amount. If storage permits (see stabling),

Grazing (SUE MAYNARD)

it is more economical to buy hay in quantity. A truckload, three to four tons, a year's supply for one horse, can be purchased in summer or early fall when hay is cheapest.

If buying direct from the hay field, occasionally check the temperature of the bales. Hay baled too damp and too tight cannot only mold, it can heat to the point of combustion. This condition is aggravated if the bales are stacked without sufficient air space between them. Work your fingers as far into a bale as you can. It will normally feel slightly warm, but if it feels really hot, to the point where you can't leave your finger there, then you have a problem. If you have space in your loft, break the bales open and spread them to dry; if not, get them outside and open them, making as neat a stack as you can, and cover the top with a tarpaulin. This sounds like a lot of trouble and mess, and it is—but if you don't you will certainly lose your hay (if it is that hot it will mold anyway) and you may lose your stable. Starting a day or two after the hay is baled, check several bales each day for at least three or four more days.

The horse's grain ration varies with his weight, his condition and the amount of work he is being called upon to perform. One pound of grain per hundred pounds of horse may be sufficient if he is

worked hard, otherwise it may be too much. Yearlings and pregnant and nursing mares can usually stand a heavier ration. An eye should be kept on the horse's condition and the balance of grain and hay regulated accordingly.

D. J. Kays in his book *The Horse* recommends that a thousand-pound horse being ridden five or six hours a day, four days a week, be given a morning ration of five pounds of crushed oats, one-half pound of bran and six pounds of mixed timothy and clover. At noon, when the horses are being worked, they get two or three ears of corn; and in the evening, five pounds of crushed oats, four pounds of steamed barley, one-half pound of bran and another six pounds of timothy-clover mixture.

On the other hand, it is very inexpensive to provide food for a pony, and many authorities do not advise feeding grain at all, or at the most, just enough to keep the animal in good condition. Hay is figured as for the horse, but if pasture is available no hay may be needed.

Oats are the standard grain feed. Although they can be fed whole they are best rolled, being more easily digested. Even with a good set of teeth, many horses pass whole kernels. If whole oats are fed they should not make up more than 10 per cent of the oat ration.

Barley is not used a great deal in the United States, although it is usually cheaper than oats and has more food value. It is high in carbohydrates, being similar to corn in this respect. As part of a ration it is a good feed. Barley kernels are very hard and the grain must be rolled.

Corn is fattening and should be given sparingly to horses not accustomed to it. It is more often used for riding horses in the West and South than in the East, although it is used in the Middle West for work horses. It may be fed shelled, cracked, or whole, on the ear, in which form it is good for teeth and gums. It is high in carbohydrates and caloric value, but low in protein.

Bran is the outer layer of the wheat grain. It is a laxative and is used in small amounts as a dietary supplement. A double handful to each grain feeding is usually enough. Sometimes it is fed as a mash once a week. Bran mash is made by mixing bran with enough boiling water to make a thick porridge, covering and allowing to steam until cool. Salt should be added to make it tasty.

Horses need salt. They lose a considerable amount through sweating, especially in the summer months. This must be replaced, and salt should be mixed in with grain feed or kept in the stall in brick or lump form. Bricks or lumps of salt should be kept in a container which enables the horse to lick it but not to bite off big chunks. Normally a horse will eat one or two ounces per day.

Linseed oil meal is good for the bowels and promotes a glossy coat. About three times a week, add a handful to the grain ration.

A little molasses can be added to grain rations for flavor and to increase appetite. It is hard to mix by hand, although nearly always included in ready-mixed feeds.

Ready-mixed feeds, while more expensive than

A hay net (LOUISE L. SERPA)

standard grain feed, are combinations of grains, assorted trace minerals, salt, fish meal and linseed. Properly made up, they ensure a well-rounded diet, and some such feeds are very good. For the one-horse owner, who does not want to get involved in keeping quantities of grain and supplements around, such feeds may prove economical in the long run, as well as time-saving.

For those who buy their grain from local farmers, or who own land which is farmed on a share-crop basis, receiving bagged grain as their share, a small grinding mill driven by a ⅓ or ½ h.p. electric motor may prove to be a practical investment.

Grass is the horse's natural food, and if suitable pasture is available the hay ration can be drastically cut (halved or even eliminated during the months when the grazing is good). Horses that have been kept off grass for a considerable length of time, such as those having been stabled all winter, on being let out to pasture in the spring should be allowed to get used to grass gradually or an upset stomach may result. Too much grass may cause gas. Grass may be fed to a horse if freshly cut. Grass cut and allowed to lie, without proper curing, may ferment in the horse's stomach and cause colic.

Also, in this age when sprays are used so extensively, be sure the horse does not graze where there is any danger of a lethal spray (and most of them are) having drifted from orchard to pasture. For the same reason it is a good idea when riding not to allow the horse to nibble leaves or grass along the roadside.

Good grass is a fine food, and certainly the cheapest. If sufficient acreage is available, feed bills can be cut in half and stable work reduced to a minimum. Like other crops, pasture needs taking care of, and the soil will need to be fertilized. Soil tests should be taken periodically and any mineral deficiencies made up. Lime is often lacking, especially in hill pastures.

Most pastures include some legumes, which take nitrogen from the air and make it available in the soil. Perennial grasses can use up to eighty pounds of nitrogen per acre every season. With a mixture of legumes this can be cut in half.

Commercial nitrogen is immediately available as nourishment to the pasture roots. Put on in early spring, it will greatly benefit pastures in March and April.

Pasture seeding will depend a great deal on your location. Department of Agriculture or state or county agents will provide such information. Usually good mixtures include a few good grasses and a couple of legumes.

Good pasture grasses, depending again on location, include: Kentucky bluegrass, Bermuda grass, timothy, meadow fescue, carpet grass, redtop, Canada bluegrass, orchard grass, brome grass and Johnson grass. Legumes include the clovers—white, red, ladino and alsike—and alfalfa, lespedeza and trefoil.

A seed mixture tested in California for both palatability and nutrition consisted of: perennial rye, 5 pounds; annual rye, 1 pound; orchard grass, 3 pounds; tall fescue, 7 pounds; alfalfa, 2½ pounds; clover, 2½ pounds; total, 21 pounds per acre.

Besides being rich in nutrition, pasture grass should be vigorous, hardy and resistant to drought. It should also renew itself through reseeding.

A one- or two-acre pasture will provide grazing for a horse for three to six months, depending on the climate. Pastures should be mowed at least twice a year to keep unpalatable weeds under control.

Overgrazing can do great damage to pasture land. Horses should be moved when grass is grazed to about four inches. A stream running through the pasture makes an ideal setup.

Horses need a great deal of water—anywhere from five to fifteen gallons per day depending on the weather and the amount of work. Horses should either be watered three or four times a day, or water should be in front of them all the time. Although horses should not normally be watered after feeding, a horse which has water in front of him at all times is never thirsty, and will only take a mouthful or two at any one time. He may therefore safely have grain and have access to his water at the same time.

Automatic water bowls are a great timesaver, and while the initial expense is relatively high, they probably pay for themselves in time. If these are not available, either a trough, or buckets, fastened so that they cannot be knocked over, and kept filled at all times, is provided.

A horse coming in hot after exercise should not be allowed to drink his fill and then stand. This may cause founder or laminitis, resulting in severe lameness. A hot horse can be watered if he is kept moving afterward.

Horses confined in a stable require bedding. The daily cleaning of the stall and bedding and its periodic removal and disposal is one of the least attractive and most time-consuming of the stable chores.

The primary requisite of a good bedding is that it should be absorbent; if it keeps down odors too, so much the better. A horse does much of his resting

An outdoor manger in a Western corral (LOUISE L. SERPA)

on his feet, but they do lie down on occasion, and a wet, cold bed is not conducive to good health. For this reason bedding should not only be absorbent but should be spread thick enough to do the job properly. If a thick layer of bedding—about six inches—is put down originally, wet spots and droppings can be removed and bedding replaced without the necessity for renewing the bedding every day, which would have to be done if put down in insufficient quantity.

The traditional bedding is straw. Almost any straw will do. Some owners prefer rye, others wheat or oat. As horses are prone to eat their bedding, usually more out of perversity than from hunger, it should be clean and not moldy. Hay suspected of being moldy should not be bought for bedding. Figure about five small bales (forty-five pounds) a week per large stall.

Besides straw, wood shavings are often used; they make an excellent bedding material and are not so ex-pensive. If a sawmill is located in the vicinity, shavings can often be had for the price of the hauling. Three or four grain bags full of shavings should service the average stall for a week. Sawdust is not so satisfactory, being harder to clean and to handle generally. Shredded sugar cane also makes a good bed. Peat moss is good but very expensive. However, it has great absorbent qualities and keeps down odors.

When choosing a bedding material, bear in mind that ultimately it has to be disposed of. Straw is bulky and it doesn't take long for a considerable pile to accumulate. However, if the owner does not have any use for it as fertilizer, an advertisement in the local paper, or a call to a feed mill, will contact some nearby farmer or truck gardener who will be only too glad to remove it, and may even pay for the privilege. Shavings may not be so easy to dispose of, as they do not decompose as rapidly as other types of bedding. Peat moss is ideal in this respect and is a welcome addition to any garden.

Chapter 6

GROOMING

Under ideal circumstances a horse should be groomed once a day. If he has been ridden he should be groomed again after he has cooled off. This is one of the chores sometimes omitted by the owner who has to combine the duties of stableboy and wage earner. However, proper grooming is essential to a horse's health, as well as to his looks. By regular cleaning of the animal's skin with vigorous massage and brushing, oil and sweat glands are opened up, which otherwise become clogged with dried sweat, scurf and dirt. Grooming not only removes this material, but stimulates the oil glands and promotes increased secretion. The glossy coat is in a sense only a by-product—and a very pleasing one, too.

Before working on the animal, secure him by cross-tieing him, that is, fixing a line from each side of the halter to a convenient hook or ring set level with the horse's head. These lines can be left permanently in place, and clipped to the halter with spring clips.

Begin the grooming operation by picking out the feet. Go over the horse's feet thoroughly with a hoof pick to remove packed manure, any small stones, etc. Work from the back of the foot toward the front. Horses are prone to hoof rot or thrush. If this is present, you can usually detect it by a foul odor. Keep an eye open for this and other complaints—swellings, cuts, bruises, etc., when grooming. If discovered promptly, thrush is readily cured, but in severe cases, where the infection has been allowed to go unchecked, the animal may have to be destroyed.

When examining a horse's feet—whether fore or hind—always face toward the horse's rear. If a horse has become accustomed to having its feet lifted from early colthood, it will be a great deal easier to work on its hoofs in later life. Before preparing to lift a horse's foot, be sure that he is in a position to easily bear his weight on three legs. If he is not, move him gently until his feet are well placed under the body. The foot should never be grabbed suddenly.

If it is the right forefoot which is to be examined,

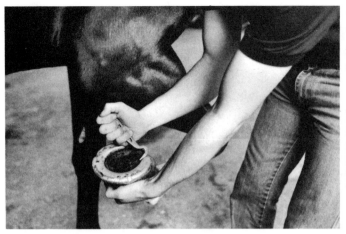

Picking out the feet

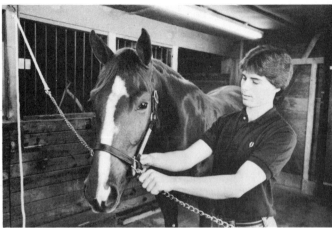

Putting the horse in crossties

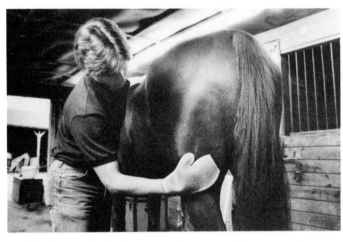

Putting a final sheen on the coat with a grooming mitt

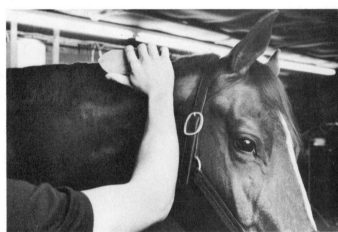

Brushing the mane

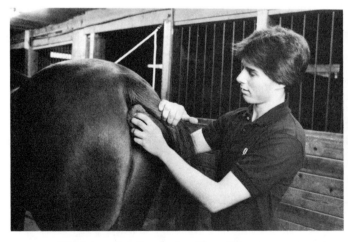

Wiping under the dock with a damp sponge

Brushing the tail

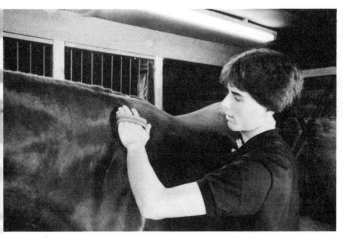

Using a rubber curry comb

Using a dandy brush

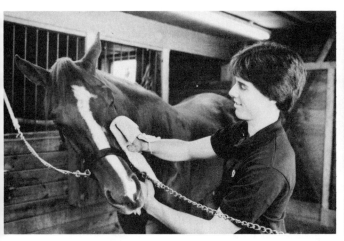

Wiping the face with a clean towel

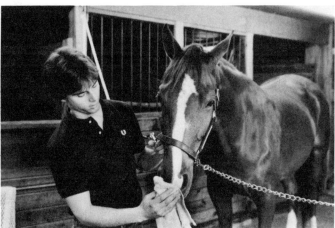

Wiping the nostrils

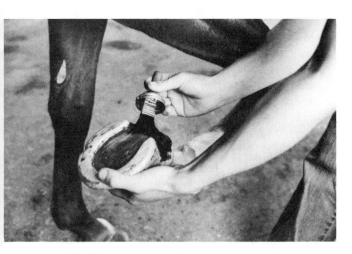

A final grooming touch: painting the hooves

(PHOTOS BY SUE MAYNARD)

stand on the horse's right side. Speak quietly to the animal, place the left hand on the horse's shoulder and run the right hand gently down the front of the leg to the cannon. Grasp the cannon from the front and at the same time press the left hand against the shoulder. The horse will shift his weight from the right leg, and as he does, lift it, and at the same time grasp the pastern with the left, turn slightly, and support the horse's leg on your right leg. If both hands are needed to work on the foot, bring the horse's leg between your own, and clamp it with your legs just above the knees, tightly holding the pastern. Don't raise the forefoot higher than the horse's knee, nor the hind foot higher than the hock. Neither foot should be pulled too far backward.

If the animal is unusually nervous, or is unused to having his feet attended to, it may be necessary to have an assistant steady his head.

Next go over the coat with a rag or towel. This removes surface dust. Place left hand on horse's shoulder (this tends to steady and reassure him) and go over the horse with a currycomb, starting at the withers and working toward the head. Use a circular motion, standing close to the horse as you work. Do not use the currycomb around the eyes or legs, where the skin is thin. In these places a rubber currycomb should be used. Work from the withers back to the rear, using the same circular motion.

The dandy brush is used to clean the dirt and scurf which has been loosened by the currycomb. Start at the back of the neck and work down around the eyes. Use a downstroke with the hair, cleaning cheeks and nose. Using the same with-the-hair stroke, briskly brush the whole body, paying particular attention to the crevices between the legs and the body, and back of the pasterns. Dust and grit can collect in these places, causing irritations. When doing the legs steady them with the hand. Clean well around the dock, holding tail to one side.

Next do the mane. Manes may be worn on either side. Some grow more naturally to the left or to the right. Instead of attempting to brush the whole thickness of the mane at once, stand on the side opposite which the mane will hang and throw the section of the mane you are working on away from you. Brush toward you, picking up a small amount of the mane at a time, until it is all on your side; repeat for the whole length of the mane. Then repeat the brushing operation, brushing toward the side on which the mane will naturally hang. When brushing a long-maned horse, use a softer brush than when working on an animal with a shorter or roached mane.

Now go over the whole animal with the body brush. Brush with the hair. Keep the currycomb in the left hand, and every three or four strokes, scrape the loose hair, etc., from the brush with the currycomb. Occasionally tap the currycomb to shake out hair and the other matter.

Finish off with a clean towel or cloth. This puts a final sheen on the coat, but only if you have done a thorough job with the currycomb, dandy brush and body brush.

After the grooming of the coat is complete, clean out the animal's eyes and nostrils, with a damp sponge, and wipe under the tail.

Be vigorous in your grooming; the harder you brush and rub, the better your animal's skin and coat will be, and the better he will like it.

The excess hair should be trimmed from inside the ear, and the long hair should also be trimmed from the fetlock joints and over the coronary band. Hairy legs look fine on a Clydesdale but a bit out of place on a hunter.

Many stables use vacuum cleaners to clean away loose hair, scales and dirt after currying. These cleaners range from large models on wheels, which with regular attachments can be used for cleaning stables, blankets, etc., to small portable models weighing only a few pounds, which can be taken right into the stall.

The minimum time for grooming is half an hour. To do a thorough job you should spend at least an hour. If, some day, you are unable to give your animal a thorough grooming, spend the time in picking out the feet and cleaning out the crevices and the parts under the saddle.

When you return from your ride, even if your horse has been ridden quietly for the last mile or two, he will in all probability be hot. Cool him off slowly, by walking him quietly, with the saddle on but with a loosened girth. A horse heated from exercise should never be allowed to stand for any length of time without attention. Never take the saddle off a hot horse as soon as you dismount, unless you blanket him immediately. When he has walked enough to stop sweating, dry him off.

Hand-rubbing is the best way of drying a horse. Use a linen cloth or piece of burlap for this. If circumstances do not permit this, he should be blanketed with a woolen cooler. In very cold weather the animal should be blanketed right away, and the blanket turned back to allow rubbing one area at a time. Do not brush the animal while he is wet. Rub down and cool him off first. Before the cloth rubdown, excess sweat may be removed by going over the animal with a sweat scraper. When the animal has been thoroughly dried by rubbing, then go over him with a dandy brush to smooth out the coat.

Washing a horse is seldom necessary, nor do many authorities recommend it. Washing, especially with soap, removes the oil, and the coat will be dull and lusterless for some time.

The mane and tail should be combed with a metal comb and brushed with the dandy brush. Some horse owners advise never combing the manes and tails of breeds such as Tennessee Walkers, Five-gaited Saddlebreds, Morgans, etc., which are worn as long and heavy as they will grow, sometimes sweeping the ground, as they claim that combing will break and pull out the hair. They prefer to untangle the hair by hand, following up with the brush. The mane of the Thoroughbred is usually trimmed by plucking. This will not hurt the horse though it may sound a bit brutal. Just don't try to pull more than half a dozen hairs at one yank. Start on the underside of the mane and pull out the longer hairs until the mane is of uniform length (about four or five inches) and thickness. The Thoroughbred's tail should be fine and thin. Like the mane it is trimmed by plucking. This is done by pulling the long hairs along the dock until it is well thinned and the length you want. When preparing a Thoroughbred for the show ring, the mane is usually done up in tiny pigtails, braided with thread or wool. These pigtails are then turned under, a ribbon passed around the end of the loop and tied with a rosette on top.

Hunters which are not Thoroughbreds usually have their manes roached—that is, cut short, or hogged. This is done with the clippers, and care should be taken to keep the hairline even.

Five-gaited Saddlebred horses and Tennessee Walkers are shown with the manes flowing, but the forelock is braided with three long pigtails and so is the mane immediately back of the poll. These pigtails are not turned under, but the colored braiding material is left hanging.

Three-gaited saddlers are shown with the mane hogged, and the tails plucked short along the dock and plumed out at the end. The tail in both three- and five-gaited horses is set. This tail setting, which is supposed to add beauty and style to the horse, is unnatural and, to many, rather ridiculous.

Horses grow a heavy undercoat in the winter. Brisk and thorough grooming will do much to get rid of the old coats. The dead hair, which deadens the appearance of the coat, will come out, leaving the animal sleek and glossy. If the horse is going to be working hard during the winter, worked, that is, so as to make him sweat profusely, then most owners prefer to clip their animals. This is because of the difficulty of properly drying a heavy coat—an operation doubly necessary in cold weather.

Some horses take readily to clipping; others object violently, and it may be necessary to have help at hand to steady the animal. Clippers tend to heat up, so keep them well oiled. They also clog if not cleaned frequently. The best way to do this is to dip the head of the machine, while running, into a container of kerosene. Horses, like children, are apt to get fidgety after a while, so start with the head, which is the part he will like least. Clip against the hair and try to keep the same pressure on the instrument; otherwise you will end up with bumps and ridges. When clipping the legs, as with all work on a horse's legs, stand well clear as possible. A sudden jerk of the knee or stamp of the foot may prove painful, if not downright dangerous.

Places like the brisket and neck where the skin is loose are tricky. Here the skin must be stretched taut and you may need a helper. When clipping the inside of the legs it may be easier to work from the opposite side by reaching under the horse.

Horses which are hunted or ridden in rough country are often given a "hunting clip." There the hair is left on the legs, which protects them to some extent from brambles and briars, and the hair is also left under the saddle as an additional pad.

Clipping is usually done in October and the horse re-clipped in January. A clipped coat must be replaced by an artificial one, and so a blanket is always used. In extra cold weather (sub-zero) two blankets should be used.

Horses which are not ridden, or ridden very seldom and not hard enough to work up a real sweat, are usually left unclipped, in which case they need no blanket. A horse in his natural winter coat can stand a great deal of cold, and can be left out in all weathers, providing he has a covered place to shelter from drenching rain and sleet. An open shed with plenty of straw is protection enough.

Blankets come in a variety of weights and colors. More important, perhaps, are the arrangements for keeping them in place. Some horses take kindly to blankets, and can spend a day in the paddock or a night in the stall without disarranging their "clothing." Others, like some people, are "messy sleepers." Still others seem to spend much of their time trying to relieve themselves of their blankets. For this reason, breast straps and surcingles are sometimes supplemented by leg straps which fasten round the hind legs and help keep the blanket from shifting.

Chapter 7

TACK

The harness is as old as civilization itself. From the earliest times, the horse has played a vital part in man's everyday life, and, of necessity, working gear was developed before the dawn of history. Horse gear—or tack—is mostly a logical solution to the problem of control and seating. Improvements have been made from time to time, and adaptations made to meet special requirements, but, with one notable exception, horse gear has remained basically the same for hundreds of years.

Presumably the hero who first clambered aboard a horse gripped with his heels, grabbed a handful of mane, and hoped for the best. The seat was not much of a problem. Steering could be done to some extent with pressures of the leg, but some means of holding and braking had to be devised.

A loop of rope or hide solved the holding problem, but this earliest of halters contributed little to the rider's control while mounted. Some means of exerting a restraining pressure on a sensitive part of the horse's anatomy had to be found. The obvious method was to pull back the animal's head, but a horse's neck muscles are very strong and a straight pull on a loop around the muzzle is not sufficient to check the horse in full career. But by putting a loop around the lower jaw (as did the Plains Indians of North America), pressure could be exerted on the jaw muscles, and the jaw pulled back and down. To relieve this pressure the animal slowed and stopped—and the first crude bit was born. As civilization developed, the simple loop was replaced by more elaborate gear.

The various bits which have evolved from the simple loop around the jaw are basically of two types: the snaffle, a jointed bit with two large rings (to keep the mouthpiece from being pulled through the horse's mouth); and the curb, used with a curb chain. The snaffle exerts very little pressure on the

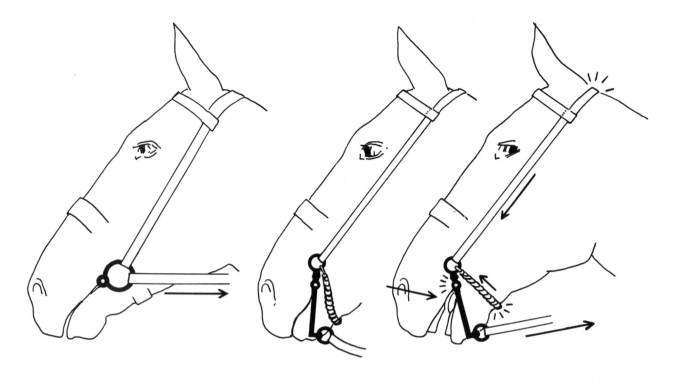

Snaffle bit (direct pull, little pressure). Curb bit (considerable leverage, severe pressure)

horse's mouth, mostly on the corners. The curb, however, anchored by the curb chain, exerts considerable leverage on the horse's jaw. The mouthpiece, or crossbar, of the curb has a half-moon bend in the middle, called the port. The drawing shows different bits and also the way in which the curb exerts its leverage. As you can see, the pressure from this type of bit can be very severe. Bronze Age bits have been found, and the Greeks and Romans used both the snaffle and the curb.

The Greeks rode bareback or on a saddlecloth, as did the early Romans. The saddle proper probably developed by adding rolls to the saddlecloth. High peaked saddles are first seen in late Roman times.

The medieval saddle was a chair-like affair, somewhat like the Oriental saddle, the war saddle being particularly high in front and back. This gave great support when using the long lance, but at the same time, a solid thrust from an opponent's weapon might well result in a broken back. For this reason the jousting saddles of later medieval times—when the knightly tournament had become a gentler sport—were made with high protective cantles but with no back support, so that a direct blow pushed the jouster backward over his horse's crupper.

The deep Spanish saddles brought to the Americas by the Conquistadores were the ancestors of today's Western saddle. The high front, often extended and

Snaffle bit

Port curb bit

Pelham bit

Hackamore

but ensured the rider a far firmer seat—of particular importance to the cavalryman. In fact, before the advent of the stirrup, the lance was used more as a missile weapon or for stabbing, than for thrusting.

In general, stirrups have changed but little, being usually in the form of an inverted metal U, with a crossbar at the bottom for the foot, and a slot at the top for an adjustable strap, or leather, which is attached to the saddle. For variation, the old Japanese stirrup was a large spoon-shaped affair, while the Ethiopian prefers to ride with his big toe thrust through an iron ring.

Spanish spade bit

Old Japanese lacquered stirrup

armored to protect the rider's legs, evolved into a horn around which the lasso or lariat, used for roping cattle, could be secured.

The ladies' sidesaddle is said to date from the twelfth century. Ladies also rode astride, or on a pillion (a pad attached to the back part of the saddle) behind a male rider. Such rigs were also used in medieval times to carry an archer behind a man-at-arms.

The greatest step forward in the history of saddlery was the development of the stirrup. This would seem to have been a fairly elementary idea, but not until after the fall of the Roman Empire did the stirrup appear in the West. Its origin is obscure, but it is believed to have been adopted from some of the nations of nomad horsemen who were then on the move in Central Asia.

This simple device not only made mounting easy,

Brass Moorish stirrup

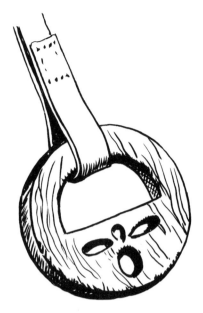

Argentine wooden stirrup

Portuguese stirrup

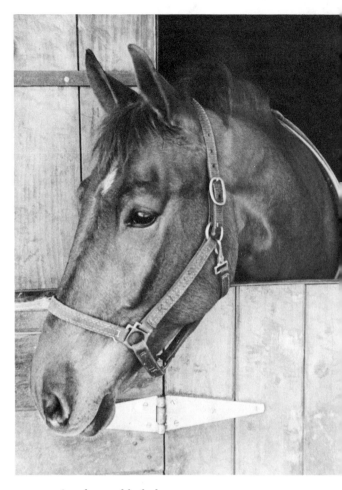

A nylon stable halter (SUE MAYNARD)

PRESENT-DAY TACK

Halters, or head collars, are used for leading or tying up. They are made in various shapes and sizes and of different materials: leather, webbing or rope. Some of the working types of halters are heavily made, while others, for showing in the ring, are lighter and more finished in appearance.

The term ''bridle'' includes the reins, bits, curb chain, head straps and throatlatch. There are various forms of bridles, the simplest being the snaffle bridle which consists of a snaffle bit, crownpiece and browband, cheek straps, a throatlatch and reins. Snaffle reins are usually made with a buckle in the center so that they can be passed through the rings of the running martingale (which is described on p. 74–75). When the snaffle is used as part of the full bridle it is called a bridoon.

The double bridle, or full bridle, consists of a snaffle bit (bridoon), reins, with cheek straps and crownpiece, and over this another crownpiece and cheek straps, curb bit, curb chain, lip strap, browband, throatlatch and reins.

The Pelham bit is a combination of snaffle and curb. It is shaped like a curb bit but has a pair of rings at the ends of the crossbar as well as the lower rings and is used with two pairs of reins. The Pelham bridle is the same as the snaffle bridle, with the

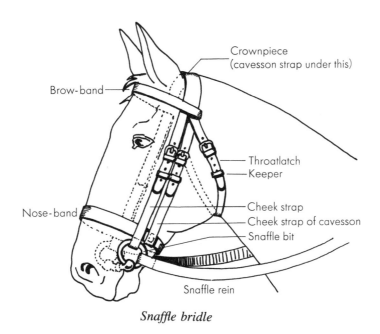

Crownpiece
(cavesson strap under this)

Brow-band

Throatlatch
Keeper

Nose-band

Cheek strap
Cheek strap of cavesson
Snaffle bit

Snaffle rein

Snaffle bridle

Two full-cheek snaffle bridles. Left, with leather keepers to prevent the bit from turning in the horse's mouth. Right, with stylish rounded leather and braided reins (SUE MAYNARD)

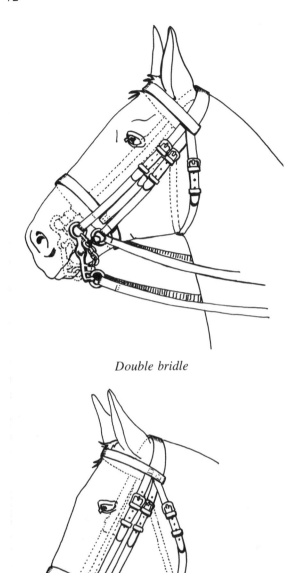

Double bridle

Pelham bridle

Snaffle rein

Curb rein

Curb chain

can be ridden with a simple snaffle bridle. The Pelham bridle has the advantages of the snaffle plus the restraining effects of the curb. It is much used for general hacking and for polo. The double or full bridle, because it has a curb bit as well as a snaffle bit, gives more delicate and precise control, and is preferred by many experienced riders. A regulation snaffle, Pelham or full bridle, all with cavesson nose-bands, are required in the horse show hunter and hunter seat equitation divisions; a full bridle in saddle seat equitation.

As both the Pelham and the double bridle call for two sets of reins, they may be both confusing for the novice (whose main interest at first is staying in the saddle) and painful for the horse. I recommend a snaffle bit only for beginners.

Western tack, which is of Spanish ancestry, calls for a curb bit. The Western bridle usually consists of curb strap, noseband, cheek straps, crownpiece, browband and throatlatch. As noted before, the curb bit can exert great pressure on the horse's mouth, and the beginner, riding Western-style, should remember this. The pony, as originally used in the West, was a work horse, and one whose duties called for sudden stops and lightning turns. A competent rider on a trained mount is capable of handling the curb bit with a light touch, but undoubtedly the average "cowpoke," riding a half-broken mount out of the ranch herd, or "string," cared little for the niceties of gentle handling. So today many riding-stable mounts ridden Western-style have mouths "hard" as iron, due to rough treatment by ham-fisted novices.

The hackamore has no bit. A pull on the reins exerts pressure on the nose and cuts off his air. The animal is checked, but there is no chance of hurting a sensitive mouth. For this reason, the hackamore is used a great deal in training.

Horses have a tendency to relieve the pressure of the bit by opening their mouths. To prevent this, a noseband or cavesson is used with all the above-mentioned bridles. The noseband is a broad strap with slots through which the cheekpieces run.

The cavesson is a similar band with a head-stall which passes behind the horse's ears, through the ends of the browband under the crownpiece of the bridle. Both the noseband and cavesson are adjusted by a buckle under the jaw.

The throatlatch is a thin strap which passes under the horse's throat back of the jaw and prevents the bridle from slipping off. It is opened to allow the bridle to be put on or removed and fastened with a buckle on the near side.

addition of curb chain, lip strap and another pair of reins.

The selection of a bridle is partly a matter of personal choice and partly a matter of the horse's training, temperament and sensitivity of mouth. A well-trained horse with a sensitive mouth (one which reacts to the slightest pressure on the bit, as opposed to an animal with a "hard," or insensitive mouth)

Double (or ''full'') bridles with long shanks are worn in Saddle Seat Equitation classes such as this one (SUE MAYNARD)

A hackamore worn by Wow, ridden by Barney Ward (SUE MAYNARD)

The curb chain's function is to provide purchase for the action of the bit upon the jaws. It should lie flat in the groove of the chin. In the center of the chain is a pendant ring through which runs the lip strap. The lip strap helps position the curb chain. It runs through the ring in the curb chain and fastens in eyelet holes in the lower cheekpiece of the bit.

The crownpiece, which goes behind the horse's ears, is held in position by the browband. The cheek straps hold the bit in place. The straps of the snaffle bridle are fastened to the snaffle rings, and with the curb bit, the cheek straps attach to the upper rings. They adjust with buckles on both sides of the head.

Reins are attached to the bit by either buckling, stitching, hooks or a slide. Stitched reins are stronger, and a good deal easier to clean.

Snaffle reins are usually wider than curb reins. They are usually made to buckle in the center. Curb reins are sometimes buckled, too. The reins of hunting bridles are often braided to give a better grip and prevent the hands slipping in wet weather.

Reins on Western bridles are not fastened together. A properly trained Western horse will stand still when the reins are dropped. Were the reins fastened together there would be a chance of the horse getting tangled up in them.

To prevent a horse tossing his head, or habitually carrying it too high, a martingale is used. There are two types, the standing and the running. Both attach at the lower end to the girth, the strap that holds the saddle in place, and pass between the forelegs and up the chest. They pass through a loop in a narrow strap which is buckled loosely around the lower part of the horse's neck. This neck strap serves to keep the martingale strap or straps in place.

The standing martingale is a single strap which fastens at the upper end to the bottom of the noseband or cavesson. It should be carefully adjusted so as to permit the animal carrying its head normally without being able to toss it back. This type of martingale is sometimes used in the West where it is usually called a tie-down.

Standing martingales are often used on polo ponies and occasionally in the field on hunters. If a horse tends to put frequent strain on a standing martingale, it should be padded with sheepskin where it passes under the breast. The noseband should also be padded.

The strap of the running martingale divides after passing through the neck strap and the ends terminate in rings, through which the snaffle reins run. By altering the direction of "pull" more control is

A standing martingale worn by Emerald Boy, ridden by Gigi Gaston (SUE MAYNARD)

A running martingale worn by Sandsablaze, ridden by Buddy Brown (SUE MAY-NARD)

achieved over the snaffle bridle. It also exerts down-ward pressure on the bars of the horse's mouth when the animal raises its head above normal. The length should be adjusted so that there is no pressure on the bit when the head is carried at the correct level. If a martingale is used with a double bridle the rings are sometimes used on the curb reins, but usually on the snaffle reins. The Irish martingale consists of two rings, joined by a five- or six-inch strap. A pair of reins is passed through the rings. The purpose is to prevent the reins being thrown over the same side of the neck when the head is tossed about.

A breast strap or breastplate is often used with a hunting saddle or where there is much rough cross-country going. This helps prevent the saddle sliding backward, and is particularly useful on a horse with flat ribs where the girth may have a tendency to slip. It consists of two leather straps, the lower ends of which join into a single strap at a point on the horse's chest below the neck. This strap passes be-tween the forelegs and ends in a loop through which the girth runs. The upper ends pass on either side of the neck and are fastened to two rings in the front of the saddle; a short connecting strap joins these two straps across the horse's withers.

In another form, the plate passes around the breast and back across the shoulders, fastening to the sad-dle about level with the rider's knee. It is supported by a light strap fastened to it on both sides and pass-ing up over the horse's withers. Where a martingale is needed a combination martingale-breastplate is used.

SADDLES

Saddles vary with the work for which they are in-tended. They fall into two main classes: the Western saddle, with high pommel and cantle, and the En-glish or "flat" saddle. While there are variations of both types, as we shall see, all saddles are built on the same principle and consist of a frame or tree of wood, steel, or a combination of both, suitably shaped for maximum comfort of horse and rider. This frame is padded and covered with leather and to it is attached the girth or girths which, passing under the horse's belly, hold it in place. From it are also suspended the stirrups. It may have further an-choring in the way of breast and crupper straps, which help prevent any forward or backward move-ment.

The frame is made up of side bars, usually of ash, connected with front and rear arches. Trees were once hand-shaped out of wood, but more recently

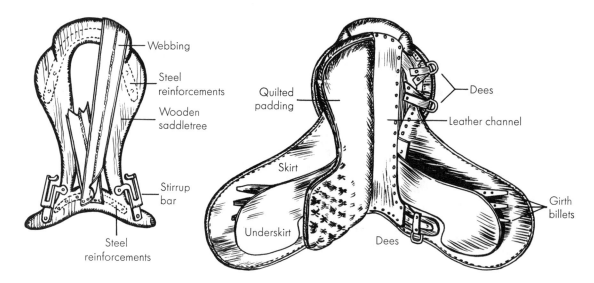

Labels: Webbing, Steel reinforcements, Wooden saddletree, Stirrup bar, Steel reinforcements, Quilted padding, Skirt, Underskirt, Dees, Leather channel, Dees, Girth billets

Underside of flat saddle, showing construction

are of steel or wooden sides with steel arches. These arches have to be strong enough to prevent the tree from spreading and allowing the weight of the rider to come down directly on the horse's withers and spine.

Flat saddles are well padded, and it is not necessary to use a saddle pad or blanket beneath them, although that is the current practice, except with Saddlebreds. Western saddles, and the very similar McClellan, are always used with pad or blanket.

The Western saddle, although often excessively heavy, is ideal for the conditions for which it was developed. It is a comfortable seat for long hours in the saddle, securely "anchored" on the horse to withstand the strain of roping, and has a stout horn around which the lariat is snubbed. To secure a firm support many Western saddles are double-cinched.

Although all Western saddles are basically the same, there have been some changes and variations of the original Mexican type. Some of these were local Texas or California styles, or were merely reflections of individual tastes. The swelled heavily undercut saddle fork which came into fashion about the turn of the century was one such variation. Positions of the cinch vary too. The original Mexican type had the cinch hanging directly under the fork. This allowed some play to the saddle. The Texans added another cinch further back—the double rig. The Californians moved the cinch ring back to the center of the saddle, hence the name "centerfire" or "Californian." Variations on this moved the ring forward a little. These variations in positions are measured in fractions—⅝, ¾ or ⅞—from the halfway placing in the center, to the fork. Cinches are fairly wide—five or six inches for single rigs—while those for double rigs are narrower. They are made

Mexican saddle

of various materials, including cotton, fish cord, canvas, leather, horsehair, or mohair, the last being the most common. Sometimes the hair cinches are woven but when made up of separate corded strands the strands are usually held in place by a bar or bars, of the same material. Often the center bar, or diamond, holds a large hair tassel. Cinch rings are usually leather-covered.

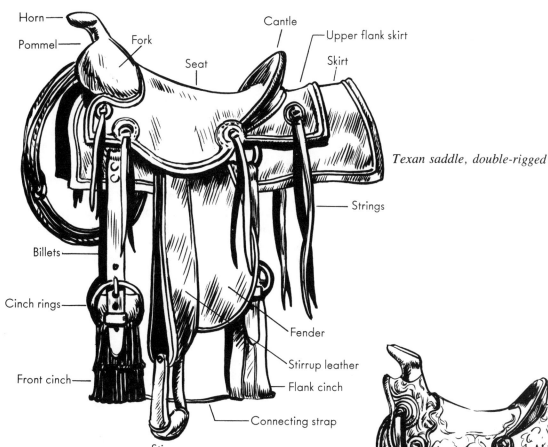

Horn

Pommel — Fork

Cantle

Upper flank skirt

Seat

Skirt

Texan saddle, double-rigged

Strings

Billets

Cinch rings

Front cinch

Fender

Stirrup leather

Flank cinch

Connecting strap

Stirrup

The cow pony's usual gait is a lope, running walk or fox trot, very comfortable for man and beast, and gaits which are capable of being maintained for long periods. There being no need to post, as with a trot, the Westerner rides with legs almost straight, and so the stirrups are usually set closer to the center of the saddle than in the so-called Spanish rig. The long leather flaps are called sudaderos, rosaderos or fenders. Often these and the stirrup leathers are made in one piece.

The skirts are usually lined with sheepskin. The saddle is put on over a blanket or sometimes a pad. Saddle strings are fastened to the skirt back of the cantle for attaching blanket roll, poncho or what-have-you. There is also a strap and buckle on the fork for attaching the lariat.

Western stirrups are usually of wood or steel, leather-covered. In the old days they were often entirely of leather. They came in various shapes—box-like wooden affairs, oxbows, and some consisted of plain iron rings. These last are somewhat reminiscent of the old Californian stirrup of Spanish days, which were often made of a disklike piece of oak, with a slot in the top for the leather and a toehold in the center (the Spanish stockman did not push his

California saddle

foot all the way into the stirrup). These were often protected in front by leather flaps or hoods.

These flaps, or tapaderos, as they are called, are used on many Western stirrups today and are of many shapes and sizes. They protect the feet when riding through thorny brush, and for winter use are made with fleece lining, keeping the feet warm and dry. Almost all fancy rigs include "taps," and some of them are very handsome.

Leather-covered stirrup

Carved leather tapadero

Speaking of fancy rigs, there are few types of saddles in the world which can compare in workmanship and ornament with a really high grade Western or Mexican parade outfit. These, with their carved leather- and silverwork, are magnificent creations and sometimes run as high as ten thousand dollars, depending on the amount and artistry of the adornment. Even the old-time cowpoke was not averse to a little decoration, and frequently his saddle was by far his most valued possession. There are plenty of good, plain working saddles on the market, but today by far the majority of Western-style riders ride for fun, and the fancy saddle is more often the rule than the exception. In parade outfits, the whole harness is designed and decorated to match: saddle, bridle and breast collar, and sometimes the rider's boots and belt besides.

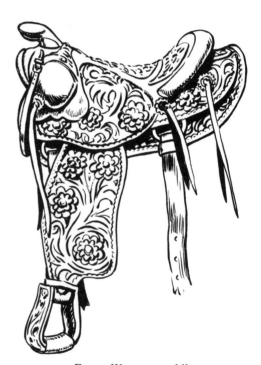

Fancy Western saddle

The breast strap was seldom, if ever, used on working rigs. It is, or was, often a part of cavalry harness. Although it was nonregulation for the U.S. Army it was used by many volunteer regiments and is seen in many Civil War photographs. In rough going it did take some strain off the girth. The breast straps, collars and plates which are part of most Western parade outfits serve no useful purpose, and are just for "pretty," just another place for a little polished metal and decorated leatherwork.

If a saddle pad is used, it is usually cut to fit under the skirts without showing. A corona blanket also fits under the skirt, but has a colorful roll which shows around the edge of the skirt.

The blanket is often a gay Navaho affair, used single or double. Whatever the type, the blanket should be stiff enough to avoid wrinkling, which would chafe the horse's back, and absorbent enough to soak up most of the sweat.

An adaptation of the Western rig is the ever-popular McClellan. This saddle was designed by "Little Mac" just prior to the Civil War and, with minor improvements, was the standard U.S. Army saddle right down to the time that the cavalry was mechanized. It is sometimes called a cross between the Western and English types, but the latter influence, if any, is very slight and the saddle is more a modified version of the former. For many years quantities of these fine saddles were on the market as surplus and could be bought at a bargain price. Many Americans learned to ride on them, and their popularity is such that today they are being copied.

The seat of the McClellan is flatter than in the true Western saddle and the pommel and cantle are lower. There is, of course, no horn. The saddletree is divided in the center, the advantage of this split tree being that the tree does not come in contact with the horse's spine. Stirrups were of wood, leather-covered and with leather hoods.

The English or flat saddle is pretty well what the latter name implies. Compared to the Western saddle it *is* flat. Pommel and cantle are practically nonexistent. The seat and panels are well padded and a properly fitted saddle needs no pad. Fit is important in a saddle, and while it is seldom practical to have a saddle tailor-made to each horse, it is necessary to see that the general fit is a good one. The use of a saddle pad may permit the same saddle to be worn by different horses. But some horses vary considerably in the conformation of their backs, and a horse with high withers, for instance, might be exceedingly uncomfortable with a saddle patterned with a low, wide front arch.

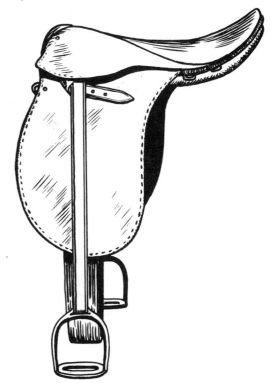

English saddle

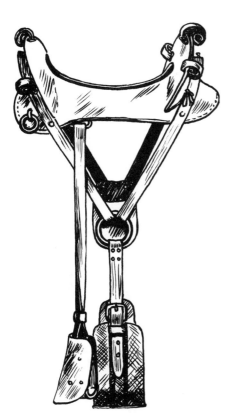

McClellan saddle

The English saddle is ridden with shorter stirrups than the Western, and the rider's weight is forward, over the horse's center of gravity. To ensure this the stirrup leathers are set further forward than in the Western rig. The hunting saddle usually has a deeper seat, set well forward, with flaps set to the front, as it is ridden with a shorter stirrup than the regular saddle. Padded knee rolls are often used under the flaps of the hunting saddle, giving a brace for the knee against the shock of landing after a jump.

The forward seat jumping saddle was developed in Italy in response to the demand created by the riding style invented by Federico Caprilli, an Italian cavalry officer, and promoted by his pupil, Major Piero Santini. This calls for an extreme forward seat, and the padded knee rolls are more pronounced. It is interesting to trace the development of the forward seat from the old-time "tongs across a wall" seat of some 125 years ago. Old prints show our ancestors sitting far back with their weight on the horse's loins, just where we now know it shouldn't be. Even the crouching jockey seat, where the rider perches up on the withers like a monkey, is comparatively recent. This jockey seat—as opposed to the old method of standing in the stirrups of a saddle set well in the middle of the horse—was developed in America and brought to England in the late nineteenth century. American jockeys riding far forward with short stirrups and with hands holding the reins a few inches from the horse's mouth, made such consistent wins that the conservative British finally followed suit. At first, much of the visitors' success was put down to lessened wind resistance, but it was finally found that the horse carries weight better and can stride more freely when the weight is placed well forward on the shoulders.

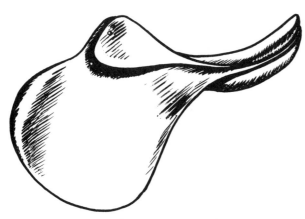

Forward seat jumping saddle

The racing saddle is chiefly noted for its very light weight—one to one and a half pounds without stirrups. The average flat saddle weighs about eighteen pounds with stirrups. Contrast this with the usual thirty pounds of the Western stock saddle.

Stirrups for the flat saddle are of metal, and varied little in design for generations until the development of the offset iron, in which the slot for the leather is off-center (to the right on a right-hand iron). This throws the knee in while treads sloping down toward the rear help keep the heel down.

Stirrup leathers fasten to the saddle by passing through the stirrup bar. This is open at the back, or has a safety catch on it. In case the rider is thrown without being able to disengage his foot from the stirrup and is in danger of being dragged, the leather pulls free from the saddle.

Some "safety" stirrups have movable sides, or are made so that the outer side is composed of a heavy rubber band, hooked top and bottom. Pressure of the foot after a fall wrenches this free, releasing the boot. Under normal circumstances there is little danger of a rider being dragged. Either he frees his foot as he feels himself going, or the act of falling itself does it for him. A good many tumbles involve horse as well as rider, and in that event the rider usually rolls well clear. Most instances of dragging are confined to "horse opera" where the act of being shot while in the saddle might well result in a foot being caught. The best advice is for the reader to stay away from badmen, posses and hostile Indians. However, it is poor practice to use a stirrup iron so narrow that the boot completely fills the width of the tread, or even worse, actually has to be wedged into the stirrup.

Tapaderos are not worn with flat saddle tack although there are small sheepskin-lined hoods on the market, which fit over the front and sides of the stirrup and may save a toe or two on a nippy morning.

As to the price of tack: in harness, as in everything else, you get what you pay for. Most large harness makers offer equipment in three price ranges: cheap, medium-priced and expensive. The cheapest gear, while involving little initial outlay, will usually prove false economy in the long run. Materials and workmanship are inferior, and will last for a comparatively short time. The most expensive, on the other hand, is for those who can afford to indulge themselves with the very finest leather and workmanship. They are paying a premium for "finish" (and sometimes the snob appeal of famous foreign makers' names). Medium-priced tack from a reliable firm will usually give just as much service, even if it does not have quite the elegance of the most costly saddlery.

CARE OF TACK

Tack is expensive, and it will pay to take some pains to keep it in good shape. Given proper care a good piece of saddlery will last the average person, who rides for pleasure, a lifetime. As is pointed out in the section on stabling, a handy and well-appointed tack room is a great incentive to keeping tack in good shape. Good light, space to work and places for stowing cleaning gear all add to the pleasure—and if you like fine saddlery and leatherwork it can be a pleasure—of keeping your tack in tiptop shape. A sturdy movable saddle stand makes taking care of saddles a lot easier, as will a hook or two to hang a bridle on while it is being cleaned. Besides these two useful items, equipment should include a stiff brush for removing mud, washing and polishing cloths, a sponge or two, neatsfoot oil, saddle soap, Dubbin and metal polish.

The best time to clean saddlery is right after it has been used. Wipe clean with a damp sponge and brush off the caked mud, if any. Apply saddle soap as directed on the container, paying particular attention to places where the leather is exposed to much sweating. Saddle soap not only cleans, but softens and preserves leather as well. Soap will not give you a high finish, but if you want more of a polish there are several harness dressings available which are easy to apply and quick-drying.

When cleaning, all buckles, studs, stirrup bars, etc., should be undone, as there is always a great deal of wear around these parts, and this is also where leather, if it is not kept cleaned and supple with oil, begins to show signs of cracking.

New leather usually needs oiling. It should be gone over with a neatsfoot oil preparation, putting plenty on the under surfaces of skirts and flaps. After a few days give it a good going over with saddle soap to remove any excess oil that may still be on the surface. Afterward, work a heavy dry lather of soap well into the leather and then rub up with a dry soft cloth.

Leather loses oil through getting wet with rain or sweat, and by cleaning. This oil should be renewed two or three times a year. For the under surfaces neatsfoot oil is good. For the exterior surfaces and for the reins, girths, bridles, etc., use Dubbin or some similar preparation which replaces oil and yet gives a better-looking finish than straight neatsfoot. Also, neatsfoot can be messy unless great care is taken to remove all excess oil after applying. Metalwork should be kept bright.

How to carry a saddle (SUE MAYNARD)

SADDLING UP

Before saddling up, become familiar with your tack. Be sure you know where each piece goes and what it does. With this in mind, the process of saddling and bridling a horse will—with a little practice—become a simple matter, one accomplished in less time than it takes to read this description.

A quiet horse may be bridled anywhere, but a skittish or head-shy animal will be more easily bridled in the stable, preferably in a straight stall. As in most cases you will be saddling up as soon as the grooming operation is finished; leave the crossties on until the saddle is in place.

The tack should be arranged on the peg in the tack room as shown in the photograph. The stirrups are run up on the leathers, and the girth (buckled to the billets on the off side) is thrown across the saddle. Some prefer to hang the bridle from a hook under the saddle peg. Take the bridle off the peg and slide it over your left arm. Lift up the saddle and carry it

SADDLING UP

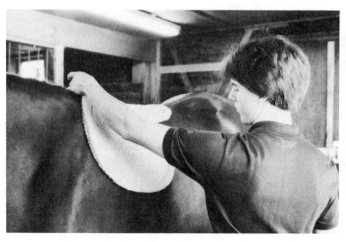

Lay the saddle pad from front to rear so that the coat lies flat

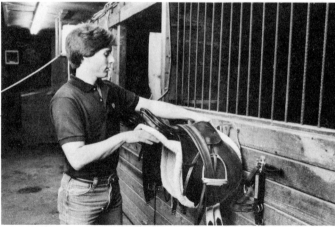

Fetch the saddle

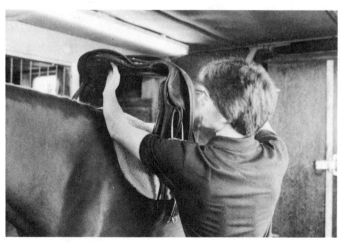

Place the saddle over the pad and slide it back into position

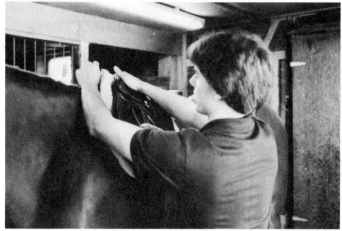

Pull the pad up into the arch of the saddle

Fasten the billet straps

(PHOTOS BY SUE MAYNARD)

over the right arm, thus leaving one hand free for opening doors, etc.

Approach the horse quietly on the near side, take the pommel in the left hand and the cantle in the right and place the saddle over the horse's back, well up on the withers. Slide it back into place until the raised portion under the pommel is just over and a little behind the withers. The saddle should be far enough forward so that the shape of the withers helps keep it from slipping from side to side, but not so far up as to restrict the movements of the shoulders. The saddle is put on far forward and slid back into place so as to ensure that the hair underneath is smooth. Pushing it forward will rub the hair the wrong way and cause irritation. If a pad is used, place it a little to the front of where it is to rest and slide it back into place.

Flip the girth off the saddle, reach under the horse and bring the girth straps up to the billets. The girth should be close behind the horse's elbows. If put too far back it will slide forward and loosen. Lift the flap and buckle the girth straps, snugly but not tight.

If the horse is crosstied, unsnap the ties. Hold the halter with the left hand, and with the right slide the reins from the left arm over the horse's head. Let them rest on the poll just back of the ears, so that if, when the halter is removed, the horse tries to pull away, the reins can be grabbed under the throat, giving an effective grip on the animal.

Remove the halter and take the crownpiece of the bridle in the right hand, the bit in the left. Slip the bridle over the horse's nose. Slide the right arm up and over the horse's poll (still holding the crownpiece in the right hand). Pull up on the bridle with the right hand (the right arm over the horse's neck will help to keep his head steady). Hold the horse's chin in the left hand with the bar of the bit in the palm of the hand up against the teeth (some horses will accept the bit readily, but most will keep their mouths closed). Press the fingers of the left hand in between the horse's lips at the bars (he has no teeth there) on the off side and the thumb on the near side. Not liking the contact, the horse will open his mouth, at which moment pull up on the crownpiece, guiding the bit into place with the left hand, and slip the crownpiece in place over the ears, one at a time, which automatically brings the bit into place.

Step in front and straighten noseband and browband.

Buckle the throatlatch, leaving space for three fingers between the leather and the horse's throat.

Straighten the curb chain and hook it in place, being sure that it is lying flat and not twisted. Care should be taken in adjusting the curb chain. Too loose a curb chain is as bad as too tight. The photo shows the correct angle of the bit when the chain is properly adjusted. Some horsemen recommend that it be adjusted so that three fingers can be slipped under the chain without disturbing the bit.

Walk the horse for a few yards. This allows the saddle and girth to work into their proper places. Then tighten up girth. The girth should be tight enough to prevent the saddle from moving. Some horses will swell their bellies while being saddled, and consequently the girth will later be too loose. Sometimes it is necessary to exert a little pressure with knee or shoulder on the horse's barrel when tightening up, although unnecessary tightening will only prove uncomfortable for the animal. The stirrups are not slid down the leathers until the rider is about to mount.

Final adjustments to the stirrups are made in the saddle. However, a rough adjustment may be made before mounting in the following manner.

Slip your left arm through the left reins, which are looped over the horse's neck. (Never let go of the horse's reins. If you do, and he is startled, he may clatter off, leaving you with no horse, and a red face.) Stand by the left stirrup, keeping the reins around the left arm, pick up the stirrup iron in the right hand and hold it under the left arm, the bottom of the iron touching the armpit. When you step away from the saddle, stretching the leathers, your finger tips should just reach the near side of the pommel at the seam. If the leather needs shortening or lengthening, adjust the strap with the buckle. Move around the horse's head (never the tail) to the other side. (This business of never going too close to a horse's rear end is important. Horses do not have horns; and while they have teeth, and sometimes use them, their main weapon in the wild state is a pair of flying hoofs. Even the quietest horse may lash out behind if startled.) As you move, drop the left rein and slip your right arm through the right rein and adjust the right stirrup in the same manner.

If the horse is not to be mounted immediately, slide the stirrup irons up the leathers, where they are out of the way.

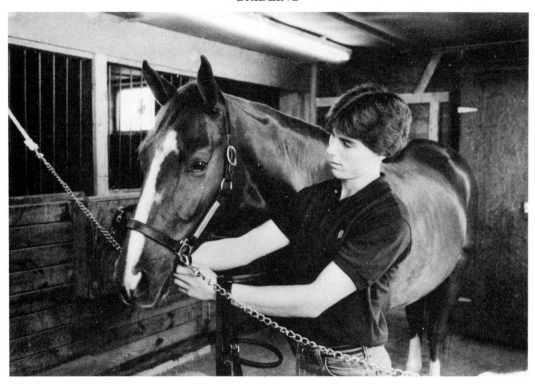

Remove the crossties

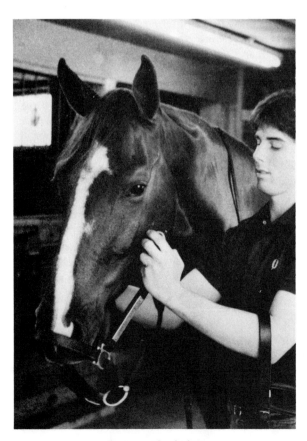

Remove the halter

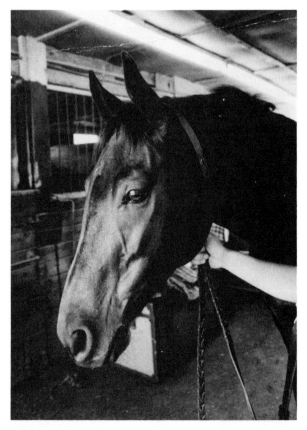

With halter removed, the horse may be held under the neck with the reins if necessary

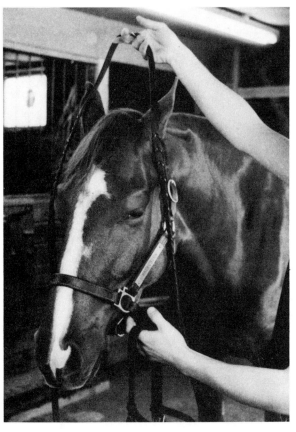

Lay the reins on the horse's neck

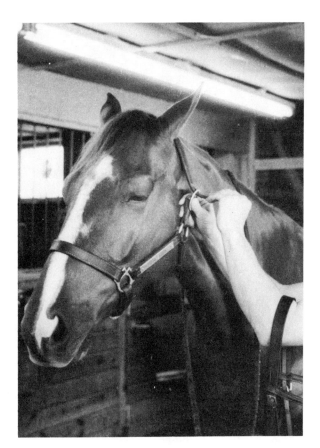

Unbuckle the halter

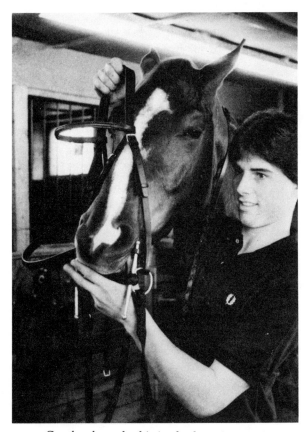

Gently place the bit in the horse's mouth

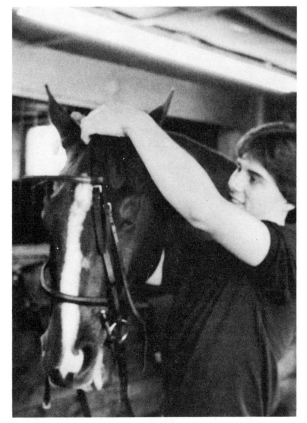

Pass the crownpiece over the ears

(PHOTOS BY SUE MAYNARD)

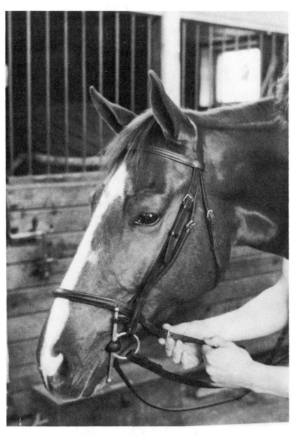

Fasten the throatlatch

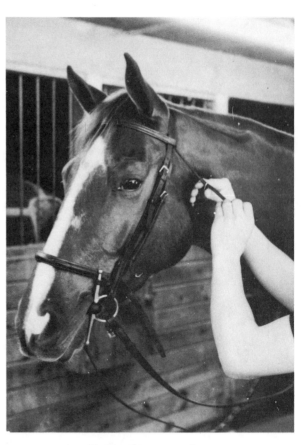

Fasten the crownpiece

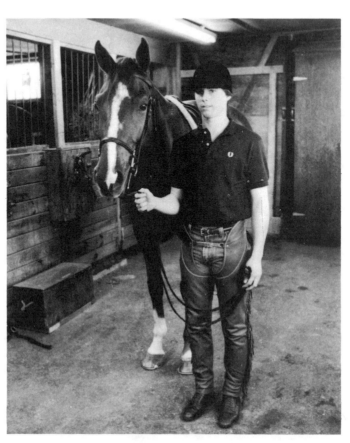

Prepared to ride

(PHOTOS BY SUE MAYNARD)

Chapter 8

HORSE DISEASES AND AILMENTS

As any animal owner knows, there comes a time when the healthiest get sick—and when that time comes the greatest comfort lies in the proximity of a reliable veterinarian. There is no substitute for the training and experience of such a man, and the average owner will make no mistake in calling him at the first sign of trouble. The veterinarian would far rather make a call which proves to be for a very minor ailment, or even a false alarm, than to be called in too late—which happens far too often and sometimes with tragic results. However, there are certain treatments for minor ills and injuries that the horse owners should know of—always with the proviso that if you are in any doubt at all as to the nature of the ailment you call your veterinarian immediately. Many animals are lost every year because some owner sought to do his own diagnosing—and guessed wrong. In general all treatments involving accidents and illness are to be regarded strictly as

first-aid, until the damage can be examined by a qualified veterinarian. In the event that a veterinarian is not immediately available, your family doctor may be able to help in an emergency—if only with advice.

WORMS

All animals have worms to some degree or other. Horses have some fifty different kinds, which if they are kept in check, may not necessarily prove harmful. However, if these parasites are allowed to multiply, they will debilitate an animal to the point where he may eventually die. The symptoms of a serious worm infection are a generally unhealthy, droopy look; upset digestion; loss of weight, although the appetite is good (''poor doers,'' stablemen call them); a dull coat; and lackluster eye.

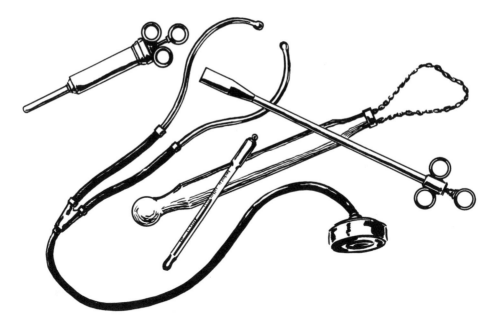

Worms are combated by doses of various sorts, some of which are necessarily very potent and should only be administered by a veterinarian or solely on his prescription. This cannot be stressed too much—strong doses of vermifuge can be dangerous and should not be given indiscriminately.

Almost all worms, or rather, their eggs, are taken in through the horse's mouth. From the mouth the eggs pass eventually into the digestive tract where they develop and live off their unsuspecting host. In turn their eggs, and there may be millions of them, are passed through the anal tract and so onto the ground. Here they are picked up by grazing and the cycle starts over again.

It should be pointed out here that care in feeding (hay not thrown on floor of stall, but fed from rack or manger) and pasture rotation will do much to keep worm infestations to a minimum. Most eggs can only survive thirty to forty days outside the host, strong sunlight being the best killer. If, therefore, a paddock or pasture can be left empty for a month or five weeks after the animals have been wormed, the eggs will die and the life cycle be broken.

The presence of worms may be suspected from any or all of the above symptoms. Sometimes the worms may be found in the droppings or around the anus and tail. Samples of the droppings should be examined microscopically by a veterinarian, who can determine the types present and if they are in dangerous quantity.

Some owners treat this condition with a drug called phenothiazene, but horses are exceedingly sensitive to this drug—for instance, the dose for a thousand-pound horse is the same as that for a hundred-pound sheep—so its use should be confined to administration under a veterinarian's direction and prescription. Most veterinarians prefer to use other drugs which are not only as effective, but more easily controlled.

The most dangerous of the intestinal parasites are of the strongyle group, the most important of which to the horse owner is *Strongylus vulgaris*—more commonly known as the bloodworm. In the case of this particular worm the immature state of the parasite is more dangerous than the mature state. In its immature state Vulgaris is present in the blood vessels which provide nourishment to the intestines. By forming clots these parasites can cause gangrene in parts of the intestines, or in some cases, rupture of the blood vessels and hemorrhage. Compared to this, the damage done in the intestines by the mature worm is of minor importance. An infected horse may pass up to 10,000,000 eggs in a single day. Strongyles can also lodge in the iliac arteries, cutting off the blood supply to the hind legs, thus causing lameness.

Ascaris—or the common roundworm—is the worm most frequently seen in droppings. The eggs are picked up by the grazing animal and pass into the intestines, where they hatch. The immature worms bore through the intestinal walls, enter the circulatory system and pass to the lungs. Here they bore into the air sacs, pass up the trachea, and are swallowed. In cases of massive infestations in young animals this can produce signs of pneumonia. The worms then mature in the intestines where they breed, and the eggs are then passed, to be picked up by the same animal or other horses, and the cycle repeats itself. An adult Ascaris may be eight inches to a foot in length. They irritate the intestines and, if they are present in sufficient numbers, may even cause an obstruction. Like all parasites, they thrive at the expense of the host, whose condition deteriorates as their numbers and size increases.

One remedy often recommended was carbon disulphide, given by pill or capsule. This is a powerful and dangerous vermifuge. Fortunately there has been great progress in the development of vermicides in recent years and the veterinarian who keeps abreast of the times (and unfortunately there are some who do not) has safer and more effective drugs at his command.

Pin worms (*Oxyuris equi*), while not in themselves particularly dangerous, cause horses considerable discomfort, which in turn can lead to poorer condition due to constant fretting. The eggs of the pin worm are ingested, as are other worms, and upon hatching, live in the rectum, where they are a constant source of irritation to their unhappy host. Symptoms are rubbing of the buttocks against posts, stalls, etc., and a consequent loss of hair. The old treatment was by enema, but new drugs have supplanted that method.

Another form of internal parasite is the larvae of the horse botfly (not to be confused with the common and vicious horsefly, which is a bloodsucker). The female fly, a fair-sized insect sometimes exceeding an inch in length, lays her eggs on any portion of the horse's anatomy which can be reached by the horse's mouth, most particularly on the lower legs. The eggs, about the size and shape of the egg of the common black ant, are attached to the hairs, and are usually found in clusters. They are licked up by the horse, and hatch (some species lay directly on the animal's lips) and eventually the larvae find their way to the digestive tract. Here they fasten and feed, until the following spring, when they pass out with the droppings. Pupation occurs in the soil and the flies emerge to continue the cycle. Like the other worms, the larvae, which reach two-thirds of an inch in length, are sometimes in sufficient numbers to interfere with digestion.

The fly season is short; and if spotted, the eggs can be removed by scraping, or washing with hot water or kerosene. If the larvae become established, the treatment is the same as for Ascarides. In massive infestations they can produce a form of colic.

COLIC

Generally speaking, colic means any internal pain. It can be due to gas (flatulent colic); an obstruction of the intestines caused by a ball of undigested feed; or what the veterinarians call acute abdominal catastrophe. This latter may be a twisted or telescoped intestine or a rupture of the intestine or stomach. These acute forms can be treated only by surgery, and, unfortunately, at the moment, with little chance of success. Such operations have only been attempted in recent years, and the horse is a bad subject for abdominal surgery, being prone to peritonitis, and going easily into shock.

Flatulent colic can be caused by improperly cured or moldy feed, or by watering directly after a heavy feeding of grain. Even a change of feed will disturb the horse's easily upset digestive system. Change of feed should be done gradually, mixing increasing proportions of the new feed in with the old. Sudden release after long stabling onto lush pasture will also produce colic, much as a surfeit of rich fare will produce severe stomach ache in humans. A great deal of gas is generated and this, besides being exceedingly uncomfortable, can lead to more serious stomach disorders. Animals with colic show every sign of extreme discomfort. They paw the ground, roll, kick and bite at their sides, which swell and become stiff. At the first sign of colic, call the veterinarian. While waiting for his arrival, get the horse into an open space where he cannot hurt himself if he kicks and rolls around. Walking the horse for short periods may help. A colic remedy, if you have one in your medicine cabinet, should be administered according to directions. Colic can be fatal, so you have to work fast. In severe cases, like the occurrence of gas in the cecum, the veterinarian may have to cut a slit in the flank (trocharization) to relieve the pressure.

Fodder poisoning is an ever-present danger in the stable, and often proves fatal. Horses have great difficulty in vomiting—they cannot do so at will like the dog or cat—and so anything they eat must be got rid of through elimination. Hence the horse is particularly susceptible to any form of food poisoning. Sometimes such poisoning can be traced to poisonous weeds, although animals will not normally eat these unless grazing is exceedingly scant. Most localities have at least one weed which is poisonous to horses, and it is a good idea to familiarize oneself with the appearance and growth habit of these through your county agricultural agent. In most cases, unless the horse is to run wild over a large area, the weeds can be controlled or eradicated.

By far the most danger comes from use of spoiled feed and moldy hay. Unlike, say, a goat, which is exceedingly fussy about the freshness of its feed, a horse will eat moldy feed with apparent relish. The results are always serious and often fatal. The recent fate of two fine work horses in my own neighborhood will serve to point the moral to this tale. A handyman (?) cleaned out several days' accumulation of leftover feed from the cow's trough and fed it to the horses. One died painfully the next night and the other the following day, and this despite the attendance of a highly competent veterinarian. A horse suffering from a mild case of food poisoning will not eat and will show signs of extreme restlessness and discomfort. In severe cases, the poison in the system produces gangrenous encephalitis. The mouth will hang open, and the horse will be unable to swallow due to paralysis of the muscles that control this function. A weakness of the hindquarters will become noticeable and is followed by complete paralysis and death.

Feed nothing but good clean hay and clean up and dispose of any grain which may have spoiled. Feed only the best you can procure. Remember, many fine animals have been lost because the owner tried to economize on the quality of his feed.

RESPIRATORY DISEASES

Broken wind or the "heaves" is a disease affecting the respiratory system. It is somewhat similar to an attack of asthma in humans. Difficulty in breathing and a bad cough, coupled with heaving of the flanks, mark this illness. A young healthy horse is seldom affected, but an older horse, especially if overworked and underfed, may suffer from it. Dusty hay is one cause—overstrain and poor feed, another. Cough medicines should be given and the hay and grain wetted down slightly before feeding. The disease corresponds roughly to the "nasty 'ackin corf" of the broken-down industrial worker of pre-union days. Rest and care are about the only relief. There is no real cure and damage is permanent. Special feeds are now available, beet pulp being one of them.

Strangles is an acute infectious disease, caused by *Streptococcus equi*. Its characteristics are high temperature (104 degrees to 106 degrees), inflammation of the nasal mucosa and abscesses in the regional lymph nodes. This infection will run its course in two to four weeks and is seldom fatal, unless followed by complications. Treatment is usually by ad-

ministration of antibiotics. Infected animals should be isolated, the premises disinfected and their bedding burned.

Horses, like their owners, are subject to coughs and colds, with somewhat similar symptoms. Like the human variety they are contagious and may pass from horse to horse, from one end of the stable to the other. Coughing, discharge at the nostrils and elevated temperatures are the signs, and a veterinarian should be called. Colds are often caused by drafts and the victim should be kept warm and well blanketed. Hot bran mash is recommended, but many animals with colds refuse to eat. The contagious shipping fever (so called because animals introduced into new surroundings, to new food, change of water, etc., are prone to it) also produces the same symptoms (stockyard pneumonia or equine influenza are other names for it). Apparently the resistance of some animals is so much lowered by the changes, however slight, listed above, that they fall prey to the slightest infection acquired en route or from animals at their destination. Here again the veterinarian should be called in. Sulfa drugs and antibiotics may help, and the newcomers to the stable should be isolated for a few days. Inoculation before shipping will help protect both the travelers and the animals at the point of arrival.

Coughs, colds and shipping fever may result in the glands under the jaw becoming swollen. Rubbing with camphorated oil a couple of times a day may reduce the swelling. If not, the glands will probably have to be lanced by the veterinarian. Animals suffering from contagious diseases such as the above should be isolated as soon as possible.

GLANDERS

Glanders or farcy is an infectious disease caused by a bacterium. It is characterized by the formation of ulcers and nodules in the lungs, in the nasal mucosa and the skin. Its ravages were known to the ancients, and were described by the Greeks before 400 B.C. It is, or was, very prevalent where large numbers of horses were herded together, especially in wartime in camps and remount centers. Horses dispersed from these centers spread the disease throughout the country. Effective methods of control under wartime conditions were not found until the time of the First World War. Much of the disease in Europe spread from Russia, a source of supply of many animals but where hygiene, both animal and human, was primitive.

The disease, which can be transmitted to man and carnivorous animals, is usually passed from diseased to healthy animals through discharges from nose, lungs or skin. These discharges contaminate mangers, water troughs and pails, utensils, harness, food and bedding.

Tests can be made on suspected animals and those which react positively are destroyed. Glanders is now very rare in the United States. There are several forms of this disease. The symptoms of acute glanders are chills and a high fever—106 degrees to 108 degrees—followed by rapidly spreading ulcers and suppuration of the nasal mucosa. These are followed by swelling of the lymph glands under the jaw, formation of nodules and abscesses on the skin and swelling of the limbs. Death usually occurs within a week. In the chronic type the animal often lives for years without showing marked symptoms, meanwhile spreading the infection.

EQUINE ENCEPHALOMYELITIS

Equine encephalomyelitis is also known as sleeping sickness, blind staggers, brain fever, or horse plague. This is an infectious disease transmitted primarily by mosquitoes; consequently, the peak season for contracting the disease is from July to frost. There are various strains throughout the world. Three of them have appeared in the United States: Eastern, Western and Venezuelan, which moved north several years ago and was prevented from reaching epidemic proportions only by stringent government measures.

Symptoms include high temperature; prostration, often with running movements when down; walking in circles; paralysis of various exterior parts and loss of sensation. A return to normal or subnormal temperatures is often followed by death.

Treatment includes good nursing, forced feeding and watering, and injection of serum. Recovery results in lasting immunity. Horses can be vaccinated against it, giving immunity for one year.

INFLAMMATION OF THE BACK MUSCLES

Many ailments of the horse used to be attributed to kidney trouble. Horses which flinched when the small of the back was groomed, or who appeared to suffer discomfort when mounted, were often suspected of suffering such trouble. Actually, although it is true that a horse's kidneys are close to the surface, horses almost never have kidney trouble. There is a great deal of folklore involved in horse medicine, and some of the old beliefs—of which the horse's proneness to kidney ailments is one—die hard. Inflammation of the long back muscles due to bruising—very possibly brought on by the thumping of a particularly heavy and inept rider, or to overwork—will produce the symptoms once attributed to injury of the kidneys, which are protected by the transverse processes of the lumbar vertebrae.

WOUNDS

For the treatment of minor cuts and scratches apply an antiseptic. There are many on the market and several come in pressurized spray cans. Antiseptic dusting powders can also be used. If wounds show signs of infection (become swollen and heated) it is a good idea to consult a veterinarian. All severe wounds or lacerations should be attended to by a veterinarian as soon as possible. Don't try to play surgeon—and risk losing your horse.

Puncture wounds, which seldom clean themselves by bleeding, should be soaked in a hot lysol solution and then treated with tincture of iodine or any good wound lotion. All grass-eating animals (particularly horses) carry the germs of tetanus in their intestines, such germs also being present in the soil in some localities. Therefore there is always the chance of an infection from this germ. If tetanus, or lockjaw, is contracted it is usually fatal. It is advisable to have the veterinarian administer tetanus antitoxin as a preventative measure.

A yearly antitetanus injection will guard against all such infections. Tetanus toxoid is one of the few 100 per cent effective vaccines. As all stable areas and pasture and tools used in and around stables are almost certainly contaminated by the tetanus germ, a yearly preventative shot is also a highly recommended safety measure for all people working around such areas.

LEG AND FOOT AILMENTS

In comparison with the weight—his own and his rider's—which a horse carries, his legs are built on the delicate side, and it is not surprising that a good deal of the troubles which afflict the horse would have to do with ailments or injuries to the feet and legs.

Lameness can come from many causes, from an ill-fitting shoe, a stone bruise or a strained tendon. The signs are usually easily seen, and when a horse begins to favor a leg or a shoulder, it should receive immediate attention. By a process of elimination, first testing the foot, then the leg, and finally the shoulder for heat, swelling or tenderness, it is generally possible to pinpoint the source of the trouble. When signs of lameness first develop, examine the animal's feet carefully. This examination is one which should accompany the daily grooming, and will often lead to the discovery and treatment of the trouble before it has time to develop into a serious condition. Care of the feet is of the utmost importance. There is an old saying, "no foot, no horse," and true it is. First clean out the foot. This cleaning process will usually reveal any wounds, caused by stepping on glass, nails, sharp stones, etc., as well as bruises or corns.

The foot is enclosed in a horny case, the hoof. This hoof consists of the wall, which supports the horse's weight on its lower part, the bars and sole, and the frog, which is the horny triangular pad between the bars and sole. This pad serves as a sort of cushion to absorb the shock of footfall, and also to some extent prevents slipping. The horn of the hoof, which acts somewhat like a human toenail, grows at the rate of roughly one-half inch per month. As the new horn grows down, the old horn of the frog and sole wears and flakes off.

Thrush, or Foot Rot, is probably the most common ailment of the foot. In this disease the sole, and particularly the frog, becomes rotten and soft, and gives off a telltale odor of decay, often coupled with a discharge of pus.

It is usually due to lack of grooming, which involves, or should involve, care of the feet. It is obviously impossible to guarantee that a horse will at all times step only on an immaculately clean floor. What the owner can guarantee is that the packed dirt and manure is regularly picked out of the animal's hoofs and around the shoes, as illustrated in the chapter on grooming.

To treat this, the hoof should be thoroughly cleaned out and washed with some disinfectant. Then some patent thrush remedy or powdered bluestone (copper sulphate) or calomel should be applied to the frog and packed in with cotton. This condition can be persistent and prolonged treatment may be necessary.

Founder, or Laminitis, is an inflammation of the sensitive part of the interior of the hoof, caused by injury to the blood vessels of the feet. The reasons for the damage to these vessels is not clear, but contributing factors may be overfeeding, improper cooling-out after violent exercise, as a follow-up to an acute infection, and in mares, following a difficult foaling.

The disease is accompanied by intense pain. Usually the two front feet are affected, more rarely one foot or all four feet. The fleshy leaves about the toe are affected and this sometimes results in the separation of the horn from the sensitive part of the hoof. The foot bone is displaced, in extreme cases sometimes actually penetrating the sole. A simultaneous sinking of the coronet of the toe changes the form of the hoof and often produces a characteristic wrinkling of the front wall of the foot. This causes severe lameness and results in permanent damage to the foot. As with many ailments of the feet and legs, considerable warmth will be felt in the whole foot. There will also be noticeable pounding of the pulse in the lower leg.

A goodly number of cases of founder are caused by horses and ponies getting into the feedbins. All grain storage bins should be made with sturdy, well-fitting tops which can be securely fastened. If metal drums are used (and they make excellent containers), the kind with the latch-on tops should be used. Otherwise even a heavy drum may be knocked over, and the top become dislodged.

Horses afflicted with founder may be partially cured but will seldom be fit for anything but the lightest work. Sometimes the results of founder may be mitigated by corrective shoeing.

Scratches. This condition is shown by raw wounds, sometimes with a discharge, above the heel at the back of the pastern. It is akin to chapping in humans. It is caused in severe weather by cold wet mud adhering to the back of the pasterns, aggravated by dirty stable conditions. If the pasterns are well cleaned and dried when the animal comes back into the stables, this will not occur. Shire horses, with their hairy fetlocks, are particularly susceptible to this condition. Riding horses with unclipped legs are likewise more prone to scratches than their clipped brethren. To treat scratches, soak the feet in warm water and Epsom salts or boric acid. This softens the scabs, which are then removed; then the parts should be dried and dusted with an antiseptic powder.

Occasionally a fragment of hard foreign matter will get in behind the wall of the hoof and work its

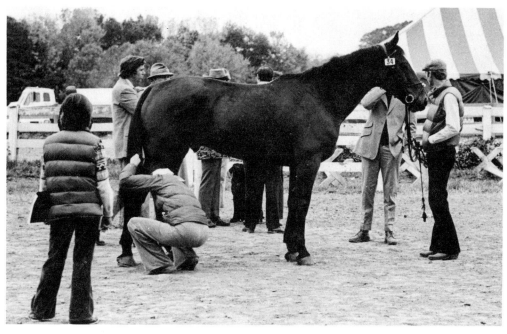

A vet check during a Three-Day Event (SUE MAYNARD)

way upward to, and eventually out of, the coronet. This will cause more or less lameness, and can often be detected by heat in the wall. Later a small pimple will form at the point of exit, and will eventually break and the foreign matter may be removed. Treatment with hot compresses of Epsom salts and water will hasten the opening of the pimple, reduce inflammation and help prevent infection. As when a splinter or brier works out of the human body, the process is usually more painful than dangerous.

Tendons are the elastic fibers by which the muscles are attached to the bones. These fibers are often subject to great tension, and, when strained or pulled, become hot and swollen.

Curb is a swelling of the tendon below the hock, at the back. This may not be readily visible, but can be detected by the fingers, and by the heat. There are many liniments on sale for the relief of curb and other ailments of the muscles and tendons.

Bowed Tendon is partial rupture of a tendon behind the cannon bone, giving a thick bowed look to the leg. This is serious and a veterinarian should be called in.

Capped Hock is a swelling of the upper part of the hock bone. It can usually be relieved by use of a penetrating medicine. Capped hock is usually the re-

sult of recurrent bruising, lying on a hard surface or rubbing. Treatment must be accompanied by removal of the cause of the injury.

Blistering is sometimes resorted to in treating the above ailments. This is done by applying an ointment, often containing a mercury salt, to the affected parts. This blistering ointment (and blistering is best left to the veterinarian) is strong enough to burn and blister the skin. Its effect is to stimulate the circulation, which in turn promotes healing. While the ointment is on (perhaps twenty-four hours), the horse's head should be secured in such a way that he cannot rub his nose in the ointment, which would result in burning that part of his anatomy too. At the end of the time the ointment is washed off. The affected part will swell and grow hot, and the hair will gradually come off. Meantime the horse should be rested. In severe cases it may be necessary to repeat the treatment.

Bog spavin is another hock ailment. It is swelling of the hock caused by the oversupply of the natural lubrication of the joint. It is usually brought on by a strain or an injury due to a fall. It is not usually serious and may be treated with some of the commercial remedies on the market.

Wind puff is similar to bog spavin, except that the

swelling occurs around the ankles. The treatment is the same.

Splint is an injury to the splint bones, which lie between the knee and the fetlock joint. While not likely to cause permanent damage, it will cause temporary lameness. Medicines can be applied, or, failing this, a veterinarian can treat by blistering. In severe cases, especially in cases of fracture, surgery may be indicated.

Thoroughpin is a swelling of the tissue surrounding the hocks. It does not usually cause lameness, and can be treated by the application of a commercial remedy. Cold water and cold compresses are recommended for sprains.

Corns are usually caused by bad shoeing or injudicious dressing of the hoof. There is almost always a staining of the horn due to rupturing of some of the small blood vessels. The blood penetrates the horn tubes, and causes the stains, which are carried downward as the horn grows until they become visible under the foot when the hoof is pared.

Contracted heels are also caused by poor smithing or badly fitting shoes or both. Weakening of the back half of the hoof, leaving too long a toe; or improper trimming of the spurs of horn which grow from the buttresses and press on the frog, are the usual causes. Use of shoes with branches too wide apart, or inclined inward so that the weight of the body tends to squeeze the heels together, is another cause.

Proper trimming and paring and corrective shoeing will usually cure both corns and contracted heels. In extreme cases of contracted hoof, V-shaped springs are sometimes used in connection with special shoes. The springs press the buttresses outward, and in time, with successive shoeings, the hoof may be forced back into its proper shape.

Navicular disease is a degeneration of the interior of the hoof affecting the navicular bone. It is often caused by stone bruising and contracted quarters. In very rocky country, pads are sometimes worn as a protection.

Cracked hoof: Horses sometimes develop cracks in the wall of the hoof. There are numerous dressings for hoofs on the market and use of one of them will probably prevent or cure these cracks. If they appear very large and deep, a veterinarian should be consulted. Many cracks of the hoof are also attributable to poor shoeing, putting unequal strain on the walls of the hoofs. Surface cracks are usually treated with neatsfoot oil or a commercial hoof dressing, which prevents the drying out of the horn. For more serious cracks, some of which extend all the way through the wall to the sensitive tissues underneath, small iron plates are often used to hold the wall from further cracking, held in place with small wood screws, much as one might treat a split in a piece of wood. Other methods are drilling and riveting with nails or by spiked clamps.

Most hoof ailments can be prevented by proper dressing before shoeing, frequent oiling of the hoof to stop drying out and exercise. Allowing the animal to go unshod whenever possible is also beneficial.

STRESS

Stress is a major preoccupation of riders and trainers involved in strenuous activities such as Endurance Rides and Combined Training. While it is, strictly speaking, neither a disease nor an ailment, it can cause temporary or permanent unsoundness—or worse. This is why officiating veterinarians in the above events, as well as solicitous owners, try to detect symptoms of stress in a horse during and after exceptional exertion by checking his temperature, pulse and respiration (TPR).

The horse's temperature is taken rectally with an oversized greased thermometer with a string attached to it. Normal temperature varies, but it is usually about 99.5°F. or 100°F. when the horse is at rest.

The horse's pulse can be felt along the jawbone where the external maxillary artery crosses the bone, inside the left elbow, and at the temple artery near the eye. Count the beats for fifteen seconds and multiply by four. This, too, varies, with the average around forty.

Respiration is visible in the flanks. Again, count for fifteen seconds and multiply by four. It generally varies between eight and sixteen breaths per minute at rest.

The point is to be perfectly familiar with a horse's behavior, physical appearance, and TPR in normal circumstances in order to be able to detect signs of stress during training or competition, because what is important is the recovery rate. Obviously, the TPR rises considerably during exertion but should soon return to normal, ideally within ten minutes. If the recovery rate is very much slower than this, it either means that the horse is not in condition for the work

An equine dental session: "floating" the horse's teeth (LOUISE L. SERPA)

demanded of him or that he is suffering from stress. First aid measures should be taken; veterinary attention may be necessary if there are other stress symptoms, such as dehydration or lathery rather than watery sweat.

THE MEDICINE CHEST

Medicines and equipment for home care need not be numerous. A medicine chest cluttered up with an accumulation of old remedies, salves and liniments is often more of a nuisance than a help.

There are a few things, however, which should be kept on hand for general treatment and emergencies:

1. A blunt-ended veterinary rectal thermometer is a necessity, the kind with an eye in the top. Several feet of string is looped through the eye before insertion, so that there is no danger of losing the thermometer in a deep insertion (coating tip with vaseline will facilitate entry). Two minutes should be allowed to obtain an accurate reading. 100.5° F. is normal, 104° F. shows a moderately high fever and anything over 106° F. is dangerous and denotes a serious condition. In an emergency an ordinary clinical thermometer will serve.

2. Sterile cotton and gauze bandages.
3. A bottle of liniment for soreness.
4. A medicine for relief of colic.
5. A wound lotion—some of these now come in pressurized spray cans.
6. A can of antiseptic dusting powder.
7. Neatsfoot oil or some commercial preparation for treatment of hoofs.
8. Epsom salts, for use as a laxative and externally as a wet dressing for sprains.
9. Bluestone (copper sulphate) for thrush.
10. Vaseline.

Lotions, medicines, foot preparations, etc., are all made commercially and many reliable varieties are on the market.

I have not included a cough remedy for the reason that many times a cough is the first symptom of a respiratory infection which should have professional attention.

With proper care and frequent examination, many conditions may be found and checked, which, if neglected, might prove serious, if not fatal. As with humans, an ounce of prevention is worth a pound of cure. And remember, when in doubt—call your veterinarian.

Chapter 9

BREEDING

Horse breeding need not necessarily be a large-scale operation. For every large stable, with its herd of mares and its stallions, there are dozens of small owners with one or two mares who rely on the nearest suitable stallion for stud services. There is great satisfaction in arranging a breeding program and raising a foal, especially if the owner has children of an age to take an active interest in the raising process. There is no surer way for a youngster to acquire a lifelong interest in horses than to have a part in the raising and taking care of a colt.

The breeding program is all-important. The bloodlines and characteristics of both sire and dam should be carefully scrutinized, and evaluated with the qualities desired in the offspring. At the least, breeding should seek to maintain a high standard of quality in an already proved strain. If possible, the breeder should strive to improve. This is the whole principle of controlled breeding, and it is by rigid adherence to these principles that the general level of excellence of today's horses is due.

The brood mare should be completely sound. As most of the weakness of horses lies in the feet and legs, particular attention should be paid to these features. If the stallion is noted for prepotency, pay considerable attention to his faults (all horses have some) as well as his virtues. Disposition means a great deal in any horse, especially one intended to be used as a pleasure horse. High-strung Thoroughbreds bred for the track may be forgiven some idiosyncrasies, like the famous English racer, Diamond Jubilee, who savaged his jockey when dismounting, and, years later, upon hearing his voice again, tried to break out of his stall to finish the job. But any such tendencies on the part of a saddle horse are to be avoided.

Mares usually come into season every fourteen to twenty-four days (twenty-one is average), starting in

A newborn foal a few days old (COURTESY OF HELEN STEINKRAUS)

February (some do so earlier) and continuing through the summer and sometimes late into the fall. On the average a mare remains in heat two or three days. Relaxed genital muscles and frequent emissions of discolored and odorous urine are the usual signs, coupled with excitement when in the presence of a stallion. There is also often a mucous discharge which soils the hind legs and tail.

The average time of gestation is 337 days and this should be taken into consideration when timing the breeding. Spring foals are usually preferred. They have the advantage of good weather and grass, while winter foals need good housing and much additional care.

Service fees will vary with the reputation of the stud, and may be a factor in deciding on a sire. In some cases it is possible to obtain an agreement where part of the fee is withheld until the mare is definitely with foal or even produces a living foal. Boarding fees should also be agreed upon as the mare is usually left with the stud. This is often the case if the mare has to be shipped any considerable distance, in which case she is shipped to the stud farm before coming into season. The breeder will also supply a breeder's certificate from the stallion's owner, so that, if eligible, the foal may later be reg-

istered. This should be done—for personal satisfaction if the animal is to be kept, and, because for ultimate sale, registration is usually a necessity. A foal is usually recorded as being one year old on the first day of January following the foaling date.

After being bred, a mare may be exercised and ridden in a normal manner up to two months before foaling. During the last two months all strenuous exercise should be dispensed with.

Breeding should take place when the mare is obviously ready and will stand for the stallion, although in many cases hobbles are used on the hind legs to prevent her kicking. It is customary to try the mare with the stallion and breed her when she will submit. Forced breeding should not be attempted except on advice of a veterinarian. In most cases, if she is ready, the mare will submit to mating quietly, but hobbles are a good precaution, and it may be necessary to use a twitch (a loop of cord or leather on the end of a short pole). This loop is placed around the mare's upper lip and twisted tight—a rather drastic but efficient means of control.

Before breeding the mare's tail should be bandaged for some eighteen inches, to keep her or the stallion from being injured by stray hairs. It is usual for the breeder to wash the external genitals of the animals to prevent danger of infection. Stallions are not permitted to rush the mare, but should mount quietly from one side.

Thirty days before foaling time the mare should not be worked or ridden, and if possible should be turned out to pasture in the daytime. The mare should be watched carefully for a few days before foaling.

Use warm water to clean her parts if a discharge appears. Some prefer to have the mares foal outside, maintaining that in a good clean pasture there is less danger of infection. However, recommended practice these days is to have the mare foal in a clean, disinfected box stall, with fresh bedding. She should only be turned into this stall when she begins to show the first signs of labor.

The mare will indicate that labor is approaching by becoming very restless, frequently getting up and lying down, circling her stall and pawing the ground. A noticeable depression appears on either side of the tail head, due to the sinking of the sacrosciatic ligaments. Normally the labor period is short; if labor lasts more than an hour the veterinarian should be called. The mare will begin to sweat and then lie down. The actual birth is only a matter of a few minutes. The foal is normally expelled front feet and head first. If the colt is not expelled naturally in this manner, the services of a veterinarian will probably be necessary. Nonprofessional handling in such cases can cause serious damage. Good advice to amateurs is to have a veterinarian alerted and if possible standing by when the mare goes into labor. Experienced owners may be able to do much in assisting at a difficult birth, but a foal represents a considerable investment, and it is foolish to risk it, and possibly the mare, too, for the price of a veterinarian's fee.

Mares are not prone to trouble—foals are usually expelled in the proper position—but if there is difficulty it is usually serious.

In general, mares do not seem to appreciate an audience and will often appear to retain the foal until the attendants have left the stall. Birth-watching should be done as discreetly as possible.

If the cord does not break (it usually does), it should be broken some six inches from the body of the foal. In any case it should be treated with a strong tincture of iodine. The foal should be wiped dry with towels and the soiled bedding removed. The mare usually gets on her feet immediately after birth. She may then be given a bran mash and a drink of water with the chill taken off. It would be

Mare and foal a few weeks old (E. T. WHEELER)

well to note here that many mares undergo a violent change of personality after foaling. They develop an extremely protective attitude toward the foal, and even the gentlest mare may show viciousness during the first few days. Mare and foal should be left alone as much as possible during this period, and visitors should be politely barred from the stable. This may be difficult when youngsters are involved but firmness may avert unpleasant or dangerous incidents.

The foal will try to struggle to its feet shortly after birth—ten or fifteen minutes later, usually. It will wobble around and fall down a few times, but in a few minutes more will be able to support itself and be ready to nurse. There is a surprisingly short period between birth and movement. In the wild state there is no protection for mare and foal, save in speed and the ability to keep up with the herd. This the foal can do in a matter of hours. This need for speed and the ability to travel a few hours after birth is also the reason for the great length of the foal's legs in comparison with the rest of the body. The legs of a foal are very nearly as long as those of a full grown horse, and the cannon bone does not increase in length from birth to maturity.

Within an hour, or at most two, of foaling, the mare should begin to pass the afterbirth. This should be allowed to pass naturally. If the afterbirth does not appear within two hours the veterinarian should be called, for if she retains the afterbirth a uterine infection may ensue.

If the foal does not nurse within fifteen to twenty minutes the muzzle may be directed to the teats. Fasten the mare and hold the foal, or push him gently from behind, and with a hand under his jaw push his muzzle in the right direction. If necessary milk a few drops into his mouth—he will soon get the idea. Occasionally a mare with her first foal will not co-operate. It may be necessary to secure her and even hold a leg while the foal is being taught to nurse. Usually the relief of being milked out induces the mare to accept the foal thereafter. In rare cases foals have difficulty moving their bowels for the first time. If the foal has not had a movement in fifteen or sixteen hours the veterinarian should be called.

The sooner the foal becomes accustomed to handling the better. In some stables halters are put on for a few minutes within hours after birth, and many trainers do this within two or three days. Shortly af-

Yearlings (LOUISE L. SERPA)

ter this, the foal may begin to be led, very gently and for short distances. The whole idea at this stage is to get the little animal accustomed to people and to a halter, and every effort should be made to avoid startling it.

Colts are usually weaned at six months. Long before that they will be nibbling at pasture, in imitation of their mothers. When weaning, colt and mare should be stabled out of sight, and preferably out of sound, of each other. There will be considerable whinnying for about a week. The pair should remain separated for about a month. During this time the colt will gradually lose interest in his mother (he will, of course, be fed on grain) and the mare's milk will dry up, usually with no help. But if the bag becomes very tight she may have to be milked out a little to relieve her and her teats rubbed with camphorated oil.

The colt should be fed often, four times a day if possible, and should be given as much grain as he can clean up. A forkful of hay twice a day should be supplemented with good pasture.

During this time the colt should become accustomed to being handled and being led with a halter. It is an excellent thing at this age to occasionally cross-tie him and get him used to having his feet examined. At all times he should be treated with the greatest gentleness, and at the same time, very firmly. A spoiled colt, which has been allowed to "get away with murder," will be harder to train.

Chapter 10

SHOEING

It is a great pity that the vast increase in numbers of horse owners in recent years has not been matched with any like increase in the number of horseshoers. In fact, horseshoeing is rapidly becoming a lost art, and the services of the few who remain (and these are likely to be elderly, and set in their ways) are much in demand. One unfortunate result is that the owner has little or no choice of horseshoers, and must be content with any man he can get—when he is lucky enough to get him. Yet the craft of the horseshoer is a vital one and one not to be picked up in any correspondence course or from a month or two as some shoesmith's assistant. Besides being a metalworker the horseshoer must have considerable knowledge of the anatomy of the horse in general, and that of the foot in particular.

That even in the great days of the horse in this country horseshoers were not all as good as they might have been is evidenced by the following as-

sertion by a famous veterinarian, William Dickson, quoted in a book published in 1899.

"Far too many blacksmiths are ignorant alike of the anatomy, physiology, and economic relation of the parts. They mutilate, and they cut and carve as whim, prejudice, or time-honored custom dictates. Disaster, it may be slowly, but surely, follows, and all too often the dumb creature's suffering foots the bill."

Note the use of the word, "blacksmith." It is a clue in part to the troubles that Mr. Dickson was complaining about. The blacksmith was, as his name implies, one who worked in iron, or black metal— as opposed to a "whitesmith," who worked in tin. The village blacksmith (and the breed has all but vanished) was concerned with many things besides the shoeing of horses. He it was who made the massive hinges for the church doors, and hammered out the iron for the cemetery gate. He made and repaired

"Turning" the hoof (SUE MAYNARD)

the axles and other ironwork which went into the local wagons and carriages, and had a hand in much of the machinery of the neighboring mill, press and mine. Horseshoeing was but part of his trade, and perhaps it was too much to expect that such a man would have the necessary knowledge of the delicate mechanism of the horse's foot, and its relation to the rest of the animal. Much of what knowledge he did have would be, as Dickson wrote, compounded of "prejudice, or time-honored custom," more of which seems to linger around the horse industry than any other.

There were, however, many farriers, or shoe-smiths, who dealt in nothing but the trade of horse-shoeing, and these would, or should, have had more specialized skill and knowledge than the jack-of-all-trades blacksmith. Today's shoesmith, being heir, so to speak, to the accumulated knowledge of the ages, *should* be a highly competent performer. Unfortunately this is not always the case and some present-day smiths are prone to hastily tack on a set of

ready-made shoes, and call it a day. Beyond locating, and reserving (well ahead of time) the services of a shoesmith with a reputation for competency, the best that the owner of the average small stable can do is to become as knowledgeable as possible about the art of shoeing, and keep a sharp eye on the smith. If corrective shoeing is necessary, it is an excellent idea to have your veterinarian diagnose the trouble and advise the smith.

The horse's hoof is a complicated structure and its shape and general condition affect the whole equine machine. This foot bears a far greater load per square inch than does the human foot; also, in many cases a horse is carrying a rider, which perhaps might be comparable to a man carrying a forty-pound pack. Because of this comparative overloading, and because the domestic horse is often called on to use his feet and legs longer than he would in his natural state, in different and unnatural ways—harness racing and jumping, for instance—and at times on ground not well suited to horses (asphalt, cobblestones, etc.), the constant inspection and care of the feet is of the greatest importance. For this reason the average horse owner should have at least a general idea of the structure of the horse's hoof, and of the problems that the horseshoer has to meet.

The horse's foot is equipped by nature with a hard horny box or hoof. It is possible that in the wild state a process of natural selection weeded out those animals with weak feet. It is also true that wild horses could in most cases pick the ground on which they grazed or traveled. Whatever the reason, for domestic use it has been found necessary in the majority of cases to further protect this hoof with iron shoes. This is unfortunate, as even the best-designed and best-fitted shoes damage the structure of the foot to some extent. Each nail driven into the hoof wall destroys the tubular horn fibers and weakens the very part which has to bear the greatest weight.

Most horses need shoes, and are duly shod, but when animals are to be ridden mostly on woodland trails and fields, or in a ring, shoes may not be necessary—and the animal, in that case, is better off without them. Also, animals which are to be turned out to pasture for any length of time can have their shoes removed. In all such cases, however, the feet should be watched carefully for any signs of soreness or injury. On the other hand, shoes protect the hoof from extensive wear, especially on hard roads or stony ground, and in winter prevent slipping and falling on icy ground. It is also possible, by corrective shoeing, to cure, or at least improve, defective or diseased feet. Horses should be reshod every four breed of the horse. In the front feet it is the thickest at the front or toe, about three-eighths to five-eighths of an inch, and thins out at the back, the quarters, to perhaps a quarter to three-eighths of an inch. There is little difference in the hind hoofs between the thickness at the toe, the sides and the quarters.

The horny sole, which is about the same thickness as the wall, covers the soft undersurface of the foot, its upper surface exactly fitting the structure above. This lower surface of the sole is more or less concave, is rough and uneven, and is often covered by loose flakes or scales of dead horn.

The frog is a triangular section of soft and elastic horn, growing from the back of the hoof toward the front like a wedge, between the bars and between the edges of the sole just in front of the bars. It is joined to both these structures. The frog acts as a sort of shock absorber, and should touch the ground even when the horse is shod. If it does not, all the shock of the impact of the horse's weight falls upon the walls alone.

In cases where conditions allow horses to remain unshod, trimming will be necessary every two or three weeks. Only a few tools are necessary for this operation; a farrier's knife and pincers, a pair of nippers and a rasp. As in any grooming operation, pick out the feet, removing any manure and foul bedding which may have become packed into the foot during the night. This should be done daily. First the sole should be cleaned up with the farrier's knife (needless to say, this should be kept sharp to be effective). The bits of dead horn should be trimmed away from the frog, cutting away the pieces which tend to grow over the groove on either side of the frog, between the frog and the bars. Do not remove any more than is necessary. This frog and the horny sole act as a cushion and protection for the soft parts of the foot.

Preparing the shoe (SUE MAYNARD)

or five weeks because the hoof may grow as much as half an inch during that time (the average is about one-third of an inch per month); although it may not be necessary to renew the shoe, in which case the shoes can be reset.

The hoof or horn capsule is a very thick skin, which fits over and protects the horse's foot in the same way that a boot protects our feet. In its normal healthy state it is firmly fixed to the underskin or pododerm. The hoof is divided into three main parts: the wall, the sole and the frog. The part we see when the horse has his foot on the ground, is the wall. This protects the foot on the front and sides. It extends from the edge of the hair just above the coronary band to the ground. As it goes to the back of the hoof it decreases in height, and passes around the bulb of the heel and turns forward and inward and forms the bars, which finally merge into the edge of the sole at the frog. The angle thus formed is called the buttress.

The thickness of this wall varies with the size and

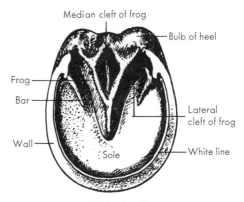

Right forefoot

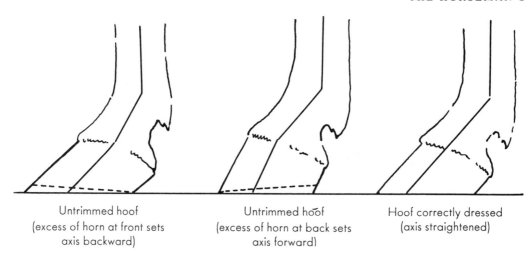

| Untrimmed hoof (excess of horn at front sets axis backward) | Untrimmed hoof (excess of horn at back sets axis forward) | Hoof correctly dressed (axis straightened) |

The hoof

Any unnecessary trimming or thinning should be avoided at all costs. Only remove those portions which natural wear does not seem to be removing, and which appear to be about to grow into or interfere with another part of the hoof.

Next, the rim of the hoof may need attention. If it has grown out ragged, or worn unevenly, it will need trimming to make it level. This is done with the nippers, and smoothed off with the rasp. Any sharp edges should be slightly rounded to prevent chipping and breaking.

To check the work, the horse should be made to stand on a hard level surface. In this way it is possible to see if the hoof is level, both from the side and from the front; and if the line of the front wall of the hoof is parallel to that of the pastern. This checking is important. If the heel is too high it will result in a stilted, mincing gait, which will throw too much weight on the toes. On the other hand, if the toe is too long it will force the foot back at an unnatural angle, thus straining the tendons.

The operation preliminary to shoeing is the examination of the animal at rest and in motion. The horse should be walked, on as level a surface as available, in a straight line both away from and toward the observer. The horse should be made to trot for a few steps. The animal is then allowed to stand, and the examination continued both front, back, and in profile. The sketches show the main faults. Sometimes these are defects in the animal itself, sometimes they are due to faulty shoeing, or to a combination of both. In many cases intelligent shoeing can correct the trouble, or at least mitigate it.

Basically the process of shoeing is divided into three steps. First the feet are trimmed and leveled.

Next the shoe is forged to fit the foot; and lastly the finished shoe is attached to the hoof. Step one follows the examination above, and should entail a minimum of cutting and hacking. Dickson stated that he would like to see the farrier's knife or drawknife omitted from the shoesmith's kit, in the belief that "if blacksmiths would use their knives less and their heads more . . . both horses and their owners would be better off." It is still the complaint that the more incompetent modern shoesmiths find it less trouble to trim the hoof to fit the shoe, than vice versa. Obviously the less done to the normal foot the better. Dickson comments on the "insane habit of trimming the frog and thinning out the sole til it visibly yields to the pressure of the operator's thumbs." He continues: "The frog is nature's cushion and hoof-expander; by its elasticity it wards off concussion from the less elastic portions of the structure, and by its resilience assists in maintaining the natural state, but the drawing-knife's touch is fatal to it. Once cut and carved and deprived of pressure, those very acts cause it to shrink, dry, and harden, and at once lose those very attributes which constitute its usefulness to the foot. Robbed of its elasticity and resilience, it is incapable of discharging its allotted function. . . ."

The only part of the foot which should ever need to be interfered with in preparation for fitting a shoe is the bottom of the wall and the portion of the sole which comes in contact with it. All the trimming necessary ought to be able to be done with the rasp. Great care should be given to trimming the hoof so that its angle will conform to the inclination of the limb. This step, and the leveling of the ground surface of the foot, are of the greatest importance. The fanciest shoeing job is worthless, and even harmful, if the preliminary leveling is not done correctly, because unevenly-borne weight causes distortion in the growth of new horn. Examination of the old shoes will usually indicate an abnormality in wear, which in turn will show the need for corrective trimming of the hoof, or even corrective shoes.

The foregoing dissertation on the need for careful examination and checking may be helpful, in the sense that the average horseman will at least know what should be done. The actual shaping and attaching of the shoes to the feet are in the province of the horseshoer and not the owner.

For anyone with the desire to learn about the horseshoer's trade, there are books to be had on the subject, among which *A Text Book of Horseshoeing* by Professor A. Lungwitz, translated by Professor John Adams of the University of Pennsylvania Veterinary School and published in this country by J. B. Lippincott Company, is still (it was first published in Germany in the eighties) a standard work. Once the job is done the following check list, originally from *The Horseshoer's Technical Manual* (U.S. War Department Publication 2-220), will help the amateur to go over the work with an intelligent and understanding eye.

Starting the inspection from a position in front of the horse, answer the following:

1. Are the corresponding feet the same size (toes same length, heels the same height)?
2. Is the foot in balance in relation to the leg?
3. Is the foot directly under the leg, the axis of the foot in prolongation to the axis of the upper leg bones, the weight of the body equally distributed over the foot structures?

Now move to a position at the side of the horse:

1. Does the axis of the foot coincide with the axis of the pastern (the slope of the wall from the coronet to the lower border should be parallel to the slope of the pastern)?
2. Has the lower outer border of the wall been rasped?
3. Do the conformation of the foot and type of shoe warrant the amount of rasping done?

Note the height and strength of nailing:

1. Do the nails come out of the wall at the proper height and in sound horn?
2. Are the nails driven to a greater height in the wall than necessary?

3. Is the size of the nail used best suited for the size and condition of the foot and weight of shoe?
4. Are the clinches smooth and not projecting above the surface of the walls?

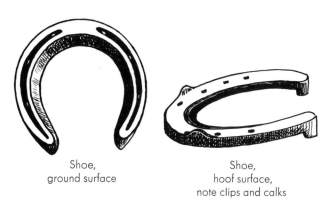

Shoe,   Shoe,
ground surface   hoof surface,
                          note clips and calks

The shoe

Note the outline and size of the shoe:

1. Is the toe of the shoe fitted with sufficient fullness (rounded) to give lateral support to the foot at the moment of breaking over and leaving the ground?
2. Are the branches of the shoe from the bent of the quarter to the heel fitted fuller than the outline of the wall to provide for expansion of the foot and normal growth of horn between shoeing periods?
3. Are the heels of the shoe of sufficient length and width to cover the buttresses?
4. Are the heels finished without sharp edges?
5. Does the shoe rest evenly on the bearing surface of the hoof covering the lower border of the wall, white line and buttress?
6. Is the shoe concaved so it does not rest upon the horny sole?
7. Are the nailheads properly seated?
8. Is the shoe the correct size for the foot?
9. Will the weight of the shoe provide reasonable wear and protection to the foot?
10. Have ragged particles of the horny frog been removed?

The shoes themselves should be chosen for the type and weight of horse, the work and the surface upon which most of the work is to be done. They range all the way from the comparatively clumsy shoes for draft horses, made especially thick to stand the wear of city streets, to thin racing shoes, discarded after a day's work at the track. The shoes should be as light as their use allows. "An ounce at the toe means a pound at the withers,'' goes the old saying. In winter special ''ground gripper''-type shoes are often used. These have projections called calkins underneath which give firmer footing on icy ground. These should be short, sharp and small. Shoes with high calkins serve no useful purpose, merely putting unnecessary leverage on the animal's legs.

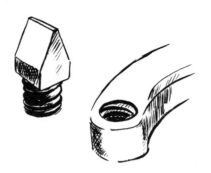

Screw calk; can be put in when needed

Chapter 11

RIDING

Age is no bar to learning to ride. Granted that the best time to learn is while a youngster, many middle-aged people have taken up riding and, with proper instruction, have acquired both confidence and skill.

In this chapter, it is taken for granted that the reader is a complete novice. Training itself should be done under the supervision of some competent instructor and in an enclosed ring or paddock. The trail or bridle path is no place to teach a beginner. I have emphasized the gaining of confidence as the most important part of your early training. Given the confidence of a firm seat in the saddle, the finer points of riding will follow in natural sequence.

The majority of riders use a double bridle, and so shall we in the following instructions. Actually you might be better off with a snaffle only. A novice is scarcely to be expected to have very gentle hands, and a curb bit may prove too much for the horse's

mouth. In any case you should understand the mechanism of the bits (see Chapter 7) and realize that they, especially the curb bit, are capable of hurting the horse's mouth. Western horses are customarily ridden with the curb bit only. Here again you might well use a snaffle, at least for the first few lessons.

If you are going to use a flat saddle, you will learn to hold the reins in both hands. This gives better control and balance. The exceptions are those riders whose functions call for one hand to be free. These include cavalrymen (and these are few and far between nowadays), mounted police and polo players. Because the cowboy has to have one hand free for roping, in Western-style riding the reins are carried in the left hand, the right hand resting on the rider's thigh.

It would be ideal to begin your riding instructions on a quiet well-trained horse with a soft mouth, sensitive to every command and schooled so as to make up with his own knowledge some of the deficiencies you will have as a beginner. Unfortunately not all riders learn on such a horse. Actually the possessor of such a paragon would be unlikely to submit it to the clumsy handling of a beginner. The average ''learner's'' horse may be quiet, often to the point of seeming to be asleep on his feet, but there the resemblance to the dream ends. Numbers of heavy-handed beginners have coarsened his mouth by sawing at it in attempts to guide him, or by using the reins as a means of staying upright in the saddle. Countless contradictory, or meaningless, commands have given him a resigned, stubborn or even rebellious attitude toward authority, coupled with a shrewd knowledge that, if he doesn't do what his rider wishes, there is little that the rider can do about it. However, this may not be quite as bad as it sounds. There is, of course, a vast amount of practice necessary to become a good rider. Much of this is in learning balance, use of hands, seat posture, suppling-up exercises and, above all, confidence, and for this any riding stable nag will do, only providing he is steady. The fine points in the use of the hands will require a horse with a more sensitive mouth, but this will come later. The better the riding school, the better the class of horse the pupil will be given.

Under no circumstances should the novice be put up on a partly broken animal or one that has shown signs of skittishness or bad temper. The beginner is in no condition to cope with any shennanigans on the part of his mount and attempting to do so will result in loss of confidence, and, in case of a bad spill, may result in serious injury.

MOUNTING

One of the first things for the beginner to learn is not to make any sudden movements while working around a horse. The horse is a domestic animal, and has been for many centuries. But like most animals who in the wild state depended on speed rather than tooth and claw for their survival, the horse is naturally apprehensive and some highly-strung individuals are downright nervous. So bear this in mind and move accordingly. Above all, relax. Horses are quick to sense your feelings. Nervousness or excitement on your part is instantly communicated to your mount. If you are serene and calm, your horse will be reassured and steady. When about to clamber aboard for the first time, this may necessitate a show of bravado on your part, but do your best.

Stand by the left stirrup. Before mounting you must hold the reins so that you have control of your horse. Let the reins hang evenly over the horse's neck, so that when you go to pick them up you will automatically hold them in the middle.

1. Take the snaffle rein in the fingers of the right hand.
2. Hook the curb rein with the forefingers of the same hand.
3. Take hold of the reins loosely with the left hand, and with the right pull the reins through the left until you can feel a light contact with the horse's mouth.
4. Move the left hand until it is close to the pommel.
5. Holding the reins with the left, slide the right hand, keeping the reins around the proper fingers as above, down to the left. Release the reins with the left hand, and put the right hand, now gripping the reins firmly, on the pommel of the saddle.

Keep it there while mounting. It will not only give you a firm grip on the saddle but will prevent you from accidentally jerking the reins while mounting, thus probably causing your horse to move.

To mount:

1. Stand close to the horse, facing diagonally forward across the horse's shoulders.
2. Hold the stirrup with the left hand, your right hand on the pommel of the saddle.
3. Place the left foot in the stirrup, keeping your knee tight up to the saddle.
4. Put the left hand low on the horse's neck, in front of the right hand.
5. Gather yourself, and still facing forward across the horse's shoulders, spring up from your right foot. The left knee should still be close up against the horse. Begin to straighten your left leg.
6. As you come up, your weight will be all on your left leg. As soon as you are standing upright, transfer your weight to your hands so that the left foot is taking very little weight, the right leg hanging clear.
7. Balancing your body over the horse's shoulders, carry the right leg, knee bent, up and over the horse's back, weight still on your hands (be sure to carry over well clear; a kick or scrape will start your mount moving).
8. As the right leg comes down into place, the knee and the inside of the thigh should touch the saddle first.

Mounting ''face to the rear'' (SUE MAYNARD)

9. Transfer weight from hands to left leg and settle gently into the saddle. When seated put the right foot into the stirrups. All these motions should be carried out smoothly and slowly.

Some believe this method of mounting to be an improvement over the older system of mounting facing the rear of the horse. They feel there is less tendency to use the saddle as something by which the rider hauls himself up, and also less likelihood of his coming smashing down on the horse's back. The horse, being the creature of habit that he is, too often learns to associate the act of mounting with a heavy thump. To avoid, or at least postpone, this occurrence, he automatically moves, leaving the novice rider hopping on one foot like a would-be ballet dancer.

In the ''face to the rear'' way of mounting, the rider stands facing the tail by the horse's near shoulder, holding the reins in the left hand, with which he also holds the horse's neck above the withers. The rider then takes the stirrup in the right hand and

twists it forward to receive the left foot. Then placing the right hand on the cantle of the saddle, he pushes up off the right foot, at the same time straightening the left leg. He then carries the right leg over and eases down into the saddle.

One advantage of mounting in this way is that if the horse moves he will most likely move forward toward you and as you spring up, you will automatically be carried round into the saddle.

If you should at some time be having trouble with a mount who persists in sidling away from you, shorten the right reins so that his head is pulled sharply round to the right. Then when he moves, he will bring his hindquarters round toward you.

Facing forward or backward, the main idea is to move slowly and smoothly, keeping the weight of the body as close to the center of gravity of the horse as possible and avoiding any ''wringing'' strain on saddle and girth as will result if the weight is too far out. Although when written out ''by the numbers'' the instructions for mounting sound as if they are a

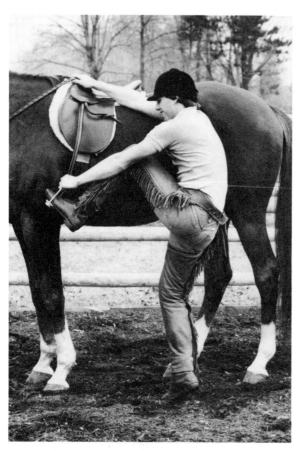

Mounting facing diagonally forward. . . .

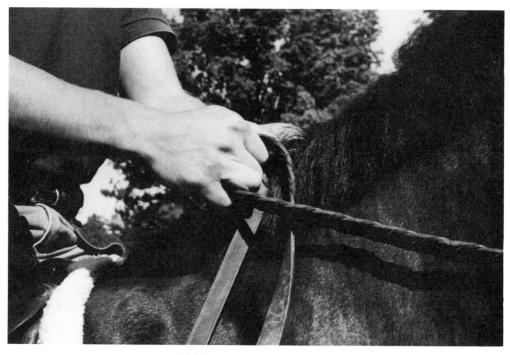

Holding the reins correctly

Final adjustment of the girth

Proper position of the body when mounted

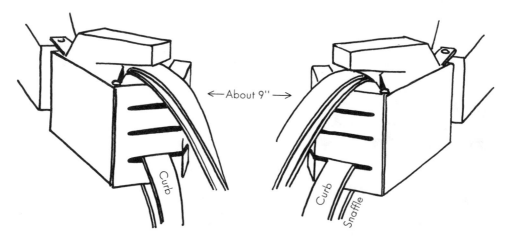

← About 9″ →

Curb

Curb

Snaffle

Pressure on mouth through flexibility of fingers and wrists

series of distinct motions, the whole action of mounting should be executed smoothly and gracefully and carried out as one continuous action.

The next step is the final adjustment of the stirrups. Take your feet out of the stirrups. When the feet are hanging, the bottom of the irons should be level with the ankle bone. (Riding Western-style calls for a longer stirrup leather. When standing in the stirrup there should be about three inches between saddletree and crotch.)

Replace feet in stirrups, lift the left flap, the reins in your right hand, and pull up or let out the leather the required number of holes. Shift the reins and repeat on the right stirrup.

Once in the saddle, take the reins in both hands. The hands should be positioned at the withers, knuckles out, thumbs up, about nine inches apart. The snaffle reins come into the hand beneath the little fingers, the curb reins between the little fingers and the next. They come up through the hands and forward, the thumbs closed down. The bight (the end of the reins) falls between the reins and to the right side of the horse.

Your hands do most of the controlling, and it is essential that their hold on the reins be both firm and gentle. Much of the pressure should be applied by mere movements of the fingers. The wrists should be supple and flexible and should be slightly bent, knuckles inward, giving more play to the hands and allowing them to follow and "feel" the horse's mouth.

THE SEAT

If your stirrup leathers are adjusted to the correct length you should now be sitting comfortably down in the saddle, with your thighs, knees and calves in close contact with the horse but not gripping violently. The ankle is bent, the heel down and the toes should be turned outward slightly. Notice that the stirrup straps are vertical. The stirrup iron should be under the ball of the foot, not jammed up against the heel of your boot.

Your shoulders should be back, the body erect but not stiff, the head high, elbows close to the side. Try to settle into the saddle and relax. At the moment your horse is stationary, but when he moves you must "give" with him. A stiff posture will destroy your balance.

Most of your success or failure as a rider will come from this sense of balance. Admittedly the ground can look mighty far away when you are perched on the top of a horse for the first time. If you have a poor sense of balance—and some people have—you are starting with a handicap, but much may be accomplished by exercises on a stationary mount. As you progress from exercises on a stationary mount to one in motion, confidence will increase and you will begin to feel that you are settling down and relaxing in the saddle instead of jouncing around on top of it.

That is why the seat is so important, both to your comfort and sense of security and to the horse's comfort and efficiency. The best way to acquire a good seat and at the same time improve your sense of balance and feeling of relaxation in the saddle is to carry out a series of limbering-up exercises with the horse standing still. These exercises should be done with the feet out of the stirrups. Here are some suggestions. First drop the reins so that they fall evenly spaced across the horse's neck. Then take your feet out of the stirrups. Try raising the knees as high as you can; first the right, then the left, then, thighs close to the saddle, bring the heels up behind you as far as you can. While retaining your seat, with thighs and legs in position close in to the horse, bend over and touch the toe of one boot with your fingers. Repeat on the other side. You should practice this one until you are secure enough in your seat so that when you bend over and down you have no feeling of slipping in the saddle and going over the horse's shoulder. These "off balance" exercises are important. Much of the insecurity which the novice may feel is due to the side-slipping motion of the horse, and the consequent feeling of being left behind, and that the body's weight is no longer over the center of gravity. The moment that happens there is an instinctive tensing of the muscles, which of course makes things worse.

These types of exercise teach you that by keeping the correct placing of the lower legs, knees and thighs, and by relaxing instead of stiffening, you can maintain a position far from the perpendicular without any danger of falling.

Another good limbering-up exercise is to extend the arms sideways, shoulder high, and swing the body to right and left, swiveling from the waist and keeping the seat firmly in the saddle and the lower limbs in position. Keeping the arms in the same position, lean back and touch the horse's croup, then lean forward and put your hand on his poll. Do this alternately, still keeping the knee and leg close to the horse. Spend as much time as you can on this type of exercise. It will pay big dividends when you come to the actual business of riding.

A word here about instruction. The primary duty of any instructor, as I see it, is to instill in the student, whether young or old, a complete feeling of relaxation and ease in the saddle. Without complete confidence and freedom from fear no amount of schooling as to posture, hands, seat or horse handling will mean anything. It has been said that horsemen are born, not made. In a sense this is true, and it is doubtful if any riders can equal the natural horsemanship of those people who are almost literally born in the saddle. That is why youngsters should be taught at least to sit on a pony as soon as they can walk. To these fortunate youngsters the horse becomes a familiar everyday thing, as comfortable and no more to be feared than a rocking chair. Those who take up horsemanship later in life, unless they happen to have the rare combination of perfect co-ordination and sense of balance on one hand, and complete lack of fear on the other, have to try to attain, by training and exercise, what a younger rider does almost by instinct.

So by all means do exercises, and plenty of them, before you as much as walk your horse. We cannot all ride like Mongols or Comanches, but a great deal of wonderful fun can be had on horseback, on the bridle path or even in the hunting field without the necessity of being able to pick up a handkerchief with your teeth at a full gallop.

DISMOUNTING

To dismount, take the reins in the right hand, the bight (the end of the reins) down through the bottom of the fist. Holding the reins firmly, grip the pommel with the right hand and place the left on the horse's neck, as you do when mounting. Keeping your weight completely on your hands, swing the right leg over the horse's back. As your right leg comes down level with your left, slip the left foot out of the stirrup. You will now be supported by your hands diagonally over the horse's withers, the weight straight down between his shoulders. Spring down to the ground beside your horse, letting the reins slide through the right hand as you do so. All this is done in one smooth co-ordinated movement. Like most people, horses appreciate a word of praise, so always make a point of making a fuss of your animal when you dismount.

THE HORSE IN MOTION

Once you have learned to mount and dismount, and presumably have gained some confidence and "feel" of the saddle, you are ready to put your horse in motion. There are various means of controlling your mount: by pressure and movement of your legs, and of your hands on the reins (the primary "aids"), by shifting your weight, by your voice and sometimes by riding crop and spur. Of these secondary aids we can rule out the last two for now, for the beginner has no business with either.

One thing to remember, don't fidget and make movements which your horse can interpret as an order to do something. Sit quiet and relaxed and when you do make a command movement be sure the horse carries it out. Some horses are stubborn and many are inclined to be lazy. Like many people, they don't believe in doing any more than they have to. Also, they are quick to sense whether the person on their back is an experienced rider in full control or only a passenger. Any person who deals with the training of animals (and this goes for the training of children, too, although many fond parents fail to see

(PHOTOS BY SUE MAYNARD)

it) knows that there are a few cardinal rules which, if they are not always applied, will lead to trouble. One of these is: don't confuse your subject with a multiplicity of commands, some of which are probably contradictory. Another is: if a command *is* given, see that it is carried out, even if it means endless repetition. Thirdly: don't give commands which are beyond the capacity of the recipient to carry out. Such commands only lead to frustration and bewilderment on the part of the subject, who often reacts by balking and refusing to co-operate further. Remember, in his quiet way your mount may be getting as exasperated as you are, and perhaps with more reason. A good rule to follow is to always blame whatever happens on yourself, never your horse. Good control and a sure touch, which you can acquire yourself in time, works wonders with any animal. If you don't believe it, just watch an experienced riding master take over a seemingly refractory mount from a novice. Instantly the horse obeys with all balking and jibbing stopping; the horse performs like an angel.

Before using your aids, "collect" your horse by tightening the reins enough so that he can feel a little pressure on his mouth, and apply some leg pressure. This alerts him and signals to him that you are about to give him a command.

WALKING

From the standing position, your horse may be made to walk by a slight pressure of the legs. This pressure is in the form of a strong squeeze (or squeezes, if the horse does not move out at once) with the lower part of both legs, applied behind the girth. This squeeze is so slight as to almost amount to a tap. However, don't get into the habit of kicking away at your horse's flanks. Beating a tattoo on his ribs will not get any better results and will certainly not make you a better horseman. A trained horse will move, because he knows that normally, with an experienced rider on his back, the next squeeze will bring a touch of the spur.

As the horse moves forward, his head will stretch forward a little. Your hands will naturally follow, to maintain the light touch on his mouth, and your body will incline slightly to the front. The hands should be as before, thumbs up, knuckles out, the fingers keeping the lightest possible pressure on the horse's mouth. The wrists should be allowed full play, and when motions need to be imparted to the reins, if slight pressures of the fingers are insufficient, a slight flexing inward of the wrists will be enough. As explained in the description of bits, the horse's mouth is very sensitive, and with the average

An outdoor exercise and training ring (LEROY SFIZZ)

horse very little pressure on the reins is necessary. Supple flexible wrists are most important.

To bring your mount to a halt, your fingers close gently on the reins, a slight pressure is given by the legs, and your weight, instead of being eased a trifle forward, is shifted to the rear.

When he has come completely to a halt, standing squarely on all four feet, make him back up. Your body weight is again exerted to the rear, your legs also press in, and light finger pressure is put upon the reins. This combination of small pressures will cause your horse to shift his balance to the rear and induce him to step backward. What you are really doing is giving your horse the signal to move (with your leg pressure) and at the same time checking him with the reins. He can't move forward so he moves backward. Relax the mouth pressure as soon as your mount starts to obey. Repeat this maneuver a few times, starting, walking, stopping and backing up.

After you have learned to make your mount start and stop, the next thing is to learn to turn him in the direction you want him to go. Say you want to move to the left. This is done by pulling gently on the left-hand reins. This pressure should be exerted as much sideward as the restricted position of your hands allow. The right-hand rein will at the same time press against the off side of the neck. Don't just pull straight back on the left-hand rein. At the same time the left leg gives a small amount of pressure to the rear. As he turns his head to the left you must slack off the reins on the right side a little to compensate. A small pressure on the reins is enough; you don't need to tug. You can "oversteer" a horse the same as you can a car or a boat. When you have turned sufficiently, relax the pressure. Reverse the procedure, turning to the right. Try turning the horse while he is standing still. Remember not to shift your weight forward as you do, otherwise your horse will start to move forward. Remember also that much of the "steering" depends on the action of your legs. When you exert pressure with a leg on one side, the horse's haunches are moved to the other side. Some horses have a tendency to sidestep; you can check this by proper use of the legs. Repeat these exercises until you can make your mount respond easily.

After you have had some time in the saddle and you are practicing walking, repeat the suppling-up exercises. At first, do these with feet in the stirrups. Then, when you begin to get the feel of it, without your feet in the stirrups. If you have had visions of vaulting into the saddle and thundering off across the fields, all this may seem pretty dull, but time spent at this stage will be well spent, and will give you greater confidence and "feel" of your seat, and the motions of your mount. Just proceed slowly and you will ultimately develop into a better rider than those who try to make quick progress at the expense of a good grounding in the fundamentals.

THE SLOW TROT

The slow trot is the gait which follows the walk. There is not much difference in speed, but it imparts an entirely different motion to the rider. In the walk the horse moves the legs on each side in close sequence. The two left legs moving, then the two right legs. This even motion keeps his back almost level and the rider experiences no jolting or jogging sensation. When a horse trots the legs move in diagonal pairs—the left foreleg and the right hind leg move forward together. The up-and-down motion of the slow trot is very slight. For that reason it is an excellent gait for the beginner as an exercise, although it is not a gait to be kept up for any length of time. The slight motion helps the rider learn to relax and to use the natural grip of the legs and the thighs to compensate for the rise and fall of the body.

To slow-trot your horse, lean your weight forward a little and open and close your legs in the same way as when you urged him from a standing position to a walk. However, at the same time you very slightly increase tension on the reins. By doing this you are at one time urging him to a change of gait but at the same time restraining him so that he will not go any faster. When he is slow-trotting you can then shift your weight back to the walking position and relax the pressure on his mouth. Try the slow trot without stirrups—it will help give you confidence.

THE FAST TROT OR POSTING TROT

To break into the fast trot, increase the pressure of your legs and bring your weight forward. The slight jogging sensation which was apparent in the slow trot is now accentuated. Just sitting in the saddle and letting the motion of the horse, transmitted through feet and legs, jounce you up and down, would prove uncomfortable after a short while. To change the tiring jogging motion to an easy up-and-down movement you "post." This means that you rise to the trot, rising in your stirrups on each alternate diagonal. The knees, lower legs and feet should

Position of body in walk (SUE MAYNARD)

Position of body in trot (SUE MAYNARD)

Position of body in canter (SUE MAYNARD)

not move. The upper part of the body moves up and forward, although no higher out of the saddle than necessary. Come down gently on the inside of the upper thighs and forward part of the buttocks. Don't crash down on the end of your spine; this will soon tire you and your horse. The rhythm is very pronounced and easy to catch on to. You either post on the right diagonal or the left. It makes no difference which, unless you are riding in a ring, in which case it is usual to post on the "outside" diagonal—that is, if you are going clockwise you post on the left diagonal. To post on the right diagonal you come down in the saddle as the right front foot strikes the ground. As he moves forward with his left foot you will be lifted up. When the left forefoot strikes, you hold your weight up out of the saddle for that beat, coming down as the right foreleg strikes, and so on. As your weight is always on the right foreleg and left hind leg it is important to even up the strain, occasionally shifting to the other diagonal by "skipping" a beat, just as you would if you found yourself marching out of step. While posting keep your hands in position. If you let them bounce around the chances are that you will put pressure on the horse's mouth. As he is responding to your command to go forward already, this go-but-stop business will only serve to confuse him. Save the rein pressure until you need it, in case, for instance, he starts to break from the fast trot to the gallop.

THE CANTER

The canter is really a slow, or collected, gallop. It is a three-beat gait. The sequence of footfall is as follows: right hind leg; left hind and right foreleg almost together and then the left foreleg. As the left foreleg is lifted there is a moment when all four feet are off the ground.

The left front foot describes a higher arc and reaches further out to the front than the right forefoot. A horse cantering with this sequence is "leading" on the left. When leading on the right, the sequence is left hind foot; left front and right hind; right front; suspension; left hind, etc.

In the West the canter, or lope as it is called, is a favorite gait. It is a most comfortable one and gives the rider a pleasant rocking-chair motion. Your body will incline more to the front; your head should be erect, keeping the back hollow by pressing the buttocks to the rear. Your seat should be firm but comfortable, with no tense gripping with the legs necessary.

In the canter the horse leads with either the right or the left shoulder. The hind leg on the same side also "leads" the other hind leg.

When a horse is cantering to the left, the left foreleg should lead and vice versa. A horse cantering to the left but leading with his right front leg is said to be cantering cross-legged. This is undesirable as, first, it makes for a rougher ride and, second, the horse is off balance, because when leading on the outside leg—i.e., the right foreleg when moving round the ring to the left—the horse has no "supporting" leg under him as he turns.

A child playing "horsey" across the floor will usually "canter," taking larger steps with one leg. If he is galumphing round to the left, chances are his left shoulder is to the front and the left leg is doing most of the prancing. If he makes a turn to the right, though, he will very likely change step and "galumph" with his right. He will do this because it will feel more natural and he will be in balance. Try it yourself (first pulling the shades, as this sort of thing makes the neighbors wonder). The horse changes step for the same reason as the child; he will be in balance. A stock horse or a polo pony which has to make very quick changes of direction is taught to change leads automatically, without command from the rider.

A trained horse is not put into a canter by merely urging him on from a fast trot. Such urging will only cause him to trot faster until he naturally breaks into a gallop. To canter you must first "collect" your horse. A horse is made up of two parts: the forehand, that is the head, neck, shoulders and front legs, and the hindquarters: the loins, hind legs, etc. When "collected," these two parts are brought together ready for action, just as a gymnast gathers himself ready for a move in any direction. The opposite of collected motion in a horse is the gallop, where the horse is stretched out. Much of a horse's drive and spring is in his hindquarters, so collection, as when preparing to canter, is mostly a matter of getting the horse's hindquarters under him, with his weight on his haunches.

When a horse is going collectedly much of his motion is in a vertical direction rather than forward. A horse so moving has been said to be able "to canter all day in the shade of a tree."

To put your horse into a canter with the left leg leading, turn the horse's head slightly to the right. At the same time shift your weight forward and a little to the left and urge him forward with the legs, exerting stronger pressure with the right leg. Turning the head "frees" or opens up the left shoulder, and the stronger leg pressure makes the horse move his hindquarters to the left. The effect of this is to make the horse travel forward in a slight diagonal, left shoulder and left haunch leading. Reversing the process brings the lead onto the right leg. In a well-trained horse this changeover is easily made at the command of the rider. If you are fortunate enough to be learning on a well-schooled animal your instructor may be able to give the command to the horse orally.

THE GALLOP

Everyone wants to gallop. There is exhilaration and excitement to the gait, with its pounding hoofs and flying mane. However, too often a beginner who is allowed to gallop without sufficient training, ends up sawing frantically at the reins or grabbing the pommel for dear life. Even the dullest animal likes to run at times, and a horse, once having got all that weight into motion, is sometimes reluctant to pull up to a trot again before he has barely got started. Be sure you have good control of your horse and feel reasonably secure at the other gaits before trying the gallop.

Galloping calls for a seat considerably more forward than you have used before. Practice standing in your stirrups, buttocks clear of the saddle and pushed out behind as a balance. The stirrup straps should be vertical—your weight entirely on the knees and heels. The knees should be slightly bent, not stiff, and close in to the saddle. Your shoulders should be back, your back hollow, and your head up. The arms should hang relaxed, wrists flexed, able to move forward with the horse when necessary. You can only do this when your body is in balance and secure. Don't overdo the lean forward or you will end up having to dig your knuckles into the horse's withers. A position too far back, on the other hand, will result in a "left behind" feeling and consequent use of the reins to retain balance. Always remember, the reins are not convenient handles to enable you to retain your equilibrium.

When at the gallop, most of your weight will be carried by the inner side of the thigh, and the rest by the foot, up through the knee. There should be no weight on the saddle from the buttocks at all. The

Gallop phase during which all four of the horse's feet are above the ground (SUE MAYNARD)

crotch should be about over the center of the saddle. The heels should be down and the knees should be relaxed enough to allow the inner part of the calves to lie constantly close to the horse.

The taking up of the gallop is called the "gallop depart." The gallop can be started from the halt, walk or trot. In the show ring the gallop is begun from the walk. In fancier riding, such as dressage, it is often begun from the halt. The cavalry usually began the gallop from the trot, and this is certainly recommended for the beginner. The horse is put into the trot, and, when moving out well, leg pressure is again applied and the horse will break into a gallop.

Be ready to apply pressure on the horse's mouth if you feel he is taking charge. A galloping horse should be under control at all times. When reining in from a gallop do so firmly but gently. There is no need to yank at the horse's mouth. Do your best to keep that balanced position when slowing up. If you don't you will find yourself with some of that picturesquely flying mane mixed in with your teeth.

WESTERN RIDING

The difference between riding in Eastern and Western style has diminished somewhat, as Western riding is being practiced more often for pleasure than for practical ranch work. The most striking contrast is in the tack and clothing used. But even where tack is concerned, the traditional Western saddle, with a deep seat, high pommel and cantle, has evolved in recent years so that modern recreational riding models are now built with a more level seat, and the stirrups, although worn longer than in Eastern riding, are hung farther forward than they used to be in order to accommodate a more upright, balanced, forward seat than in the old days. While the reins are held higher because of the saddle horn (which is lower in a Western riding saddle than in a roping saddle), there is a trend toward closer rein contact than used to be the rule. Only cutting horse riders now work with an extremely loose rein held very high, in order to demonstrate that the horse is doing

Western pleasure-style riding seat (LOUISE L. SERPA)

the job of separating a calf from the herd with no help from his rider.

The Western rider's control over his horse depends on weight aids and reining rather than on leg aids, which is why the stirrups are worn so long, leaving room for only about three fingers between the seat and the saddle when the rider is standing in the stirrups. Western horses are taught to neck-rein, changing direction in response to pressure applied to the side of the neck by one of the reins. They are also taught to stand ground-tied (with the ends of the split reins lying on the ground), to be hobbled (with the forelegs or hind legs tied together), or sidelined (with the foreleg and hind leg on the same side tied together).

Western gaits seem more relaxed and less collected than Eastern equivalents. There is a flat-footed walk, an easy jog-trot (to which the rider does not post), and the lope (a smooth, slow canter). These gaits are schooled, as in Eastern style, over circles and Figure Eights, the latter longer and leaner than the Eastern kind. Western horses have to learn to back faster and over a longer distance, and many are trained to perform a sliding stop. Among the more advanced Western movements are pivots, spins and rollbacks. The pivot is a 90° turn on the haunches, with the inside hindfoot almost stationary while the other feet push the horse around. The rollback consists of galloping straight along a certain distance, coming to a sliding stop and swinging around a half-circle in a single smooth movement, then galloping back to the starting spot on the opposite lead.

At its highest levels, Western riding is an art in which reining contests, for example, might be compared to Eastern dressage, and horse show stock events to combined training. However, for the average horse and rider involved in normal recreational riding, the Western style is based on the same foundations as the Eastern. The proof is that many horses and riders learn to practice both styles of riding with equal proficiency and enjoyment.

GOOD RIDING FORM AND MANNERS

At all gaits and at all times try to visualize yourself as you may look to someone watching you. Is your head erect? Is your back straight with shoulders back, or are you hunching over with shoulders rounded and chin on chest? Are your arms down and close to the body or are they flapping like a crow's? Are you riding like a centaur or a sack of grain? A mirror would be a splendid thing for every training

Leading a horse (SUE MAYNARD)

session and would do more to correct posture than anything else.

As in any sport, good form usually means good performance. If you intend to ride in a show ring, good form is a must. Watch others ride, and don't spare the criticism (to yourself, that is). Make a point of attending some top horse shows, where you will see really first-class riding. Above all, remember there are no perfect riders, and that even the most experienced horseman and horsewoman can benefit from practice and instruction.

You are now ready for your first ride down the trail. Start out from the stables at a walk—and if you have hard-surfaced roads to traverse before you reach the bridle path, you had best walk your horse until on soft ground. If there is much traffic, dismount and lead your horse. Many motorists have a bad habit of warning a rider with a blast of the horn—enough to send a skittish horse into a panic. Even if your riding grounds start at the stable, still walk your horse for at least ten minutes. This will give him a chance to limber up and get his blood circulating.

Good riding manners are an essential part of good riding, and following are a few "do's" and "don'ts." Some have been mentioned in the text—all are common-sense rules which, if observed, will make riding safer and more pleasant for the horseman, his companions and his neighbors.

1. Don't cluck or say "Giddap" to your horse while riding in company. Other horses may respond to your spoken command. Use leg pressure instead.

2. Don't gallop past someone proceeding in the same direction as yourself. Slow your mount down to their gait, and pass on the left.

3. If your companion stops for any reason, stop your horse also. If you ride on, their horse will be sure to try to follow.

4. If someone coming up from behind wishes to pass you, back your mount off to the side and turn him so that he faces the approaching rider (horses don't like to be "crept up on" from behind). This also applies when passed by a motor vehicle or tractor while in a narrow lane.

5. A fluttering piece of newspaper or a twig across the path sets some mounts to dancing and prancing. If your horse has any tendency toward skittishness, approach such hazards cautiously and make encouraging noises. If your horse balks at some particularly fearsome object—a noisy piece of farm machinery, for instance—it may be necessary to dismount and lead him past. Skittishness in some horses appears to be a sort of game. They will shy and rear at some object on the way out from the stable and on the return will pass it without a glance.

6. If your ride entails crossing a road or roads, bring your horse to a halt and check to see that the road is clear.

7. Don't let your mount graze while riding. This is a bad habit and should be broken. Stay alert for signs of this, and check your horse by a strong pull. Your horse should have his attention kept on his job, not on eating. Besides the danger of picking up sprayed grass, trailside eating may swell him so that the girth becomes too tight—a quick way to get girth sores.

8. Don't ride over people's land without permission.

9. Don't ride over land under cultivation.

10. Don't, when visiting, tie horses where they can get at shrubbery or trample flower beds.

11. Don't leave gates open, or bars down in a rail fence. If riding in company, the last rider through should close the gate or replace the bar. His companion or companions should wait for him until he has rejoined the group. A rider hurrying to catch up with a party of impatient riders may charge into the rear of the cavalcade, causing much confusion.

12. If thrown, don't let go of your reins unless in danger of being dragged into an obstacle. If you do let go, don't jump to your feet; you will only scare your horse, who may have stopped close by. Get up slowly. If you have a companion, stay on one knee or crouched down while they ride quietly up. If they stop, the chances are your horse will come over to be near your friend's mount.

Don't take off after a riderless horse. This usually only serves to make him move off a little faster. Try coaxing and if that doesn't work, have your companion turn his mount and head for home; the riderless horse will often follow.

13. If your horse bolts, don't panic. He won't go any faster than you would normally ride him at a fast gallop. Sit tight and pull hard on one or the other rein to make him turn his head. Usually you can feel a horse getting out of control, and that is the time to check him. An emergency is the true test of the good rider. There are many seemingly competent and even showy horsemen, people who have some experience even in the hunting field, who nevertheless "grab leather," as the Westerners say, with the zeal of a novice upon some unexpected antic of their mount. The confident rider, with a good seat, should be able to keep his saddle unperturbed during any crisis.

14. If another rider's horse bolts, don't gallop after it. The sound of your horse's hoofs will only make the runaway go faster. Follow slowly, or better still, stop for a moment. Horses like company and the act of stopping your mount may make the runaway slow down.

15. If you are ahead of the runaway, swing your mount across the trail or road. This will usually serve to check the bolting horse and give the rider a chance to regain control.

16. Don't ride full tilt down steep banks or rocky places. If your ride calls for negotiating a tricky spot, dismount and lead your horse. It may not look dashing, but it may save you and your mount from a nasty spill.

17. When climbing a long hill, walk your horse up it, or better yet, dismount and lead him.

18. Even a Thoroughbred is not a tireless machine. Rest your horse occasionally on a long ride. Dismount, loosen the girth, and walk him slowly till

he cools. Then let him stand for a few minutes before going on.

19. Water will have great appeal for horses in the hot weather. Keep good control of your horse, and keep him well away from the banks of ponds or streams. With a stubborn, thirsty riding-stable nag, this may take some firm handling.

20. Lastly, when returning from the ride, take the last ten or fifteen minutes at a walk. Don't come cantering in with your horse in a sweat.

A sliding stop in a reining pattern performed by Skid Frost, ridden by Earl Bimson (LOUISE L. SERPA)

Chapter 12

JUMPING

Some riders are content to learn enough to enable them to jog happily along trail or bridle path. Others, perhaps with the show ring or the hunting field in view, feel that their education is not complete until they have learned at least the rudiments of jumping.

Youngsters should certainly be taught to jump. It is not only exciting, but a great·builder of confidence, and demands both patience and skill. It follows logically after the mastery of the canter and the gallop (but no one should attempt to jump who is not quite at home on a horse in both those gaits).

Before learning to jump, the student should study how the horse moves when he clears an obstacle. When jumping, a horse uses his long neck and head as a counterbalance for his hindquarters. Because these movements of his head and neck are essential to his balance and to his recovery after the obstacle is cleared, the greatest care should be taken not to interfere with his head while he is actually jumping. After schooling (and horses are taught to jump) he will have a very good idea of where to take off in order to clear a given height. As he approaches the take-off point he will check and shorten stride as he places himself. In the actual jump, as he lifts his forehand (that part of the horse in front of the saddle), his head and neck go up, aiding this lift with their movement, as an athlete taking a standing broad jump uses his arms. The hind legs are in position well forward, under the weight, and as these immensely powerful limbs straighten, they launch the body forward and upward. As the forepart of the body passes the obstacle, the neck is brought down and straightened, thus by a shifting of balance helping to raise even further the hindquarters, as if the shoulders were for an instant the pivot between head and tail. As the body passes over the center of the jump the forelegs begin to extend, to take the shock of landing, while the hind legs are tucked up so that the hind feet will clear the obstacle. As the forelegs touch the ground the head comes up, again aiding as a balance and helping to recover and lift the forehand. The forelegs clear the ground *before* the hind legs touch. The whole leap is in the shape of a graceful arc or parabola.

Probably the most important thing to learn about jumping is that the horse needs the greatest freedom the rider can give him. This means maintaining a firm forward seat with the weight as much as possible over the horse's center of balance. Reams of questionable advice have been written about "helping" a horse over a jump or hauling up his forehand to pull him up and on when recovering. Actually, of course, no horse (or man either, for that matter) jumps better with a weight on his back. Beyond bringing the horse to the jump at the proper place and pace, the rider can do little but make his presence as unharmful as possible. Once the horse is committed to the jump, his rider cannot do much to help, but can do a great deal to hinder. A good horseman on a well-trained mount can lengthen or shorten his horse's stride as required so as to choose the point of take-off. On the other hand, horses must be painstakingly taught to jump, and a good jumping horse knows by experience the best place for him to take off to clear an obstacle of a particular height.

Many expert show jumpers insist that each horse has his own speed and pace at which he will jump best, and while he should be under perfect control all the time, the rider should attempt to interfere as little as possible. There is another school which prefers to regulate the horse's stride and pace so that he takes off at the exact spot which the rider chooses. To do this, the horse must be slowed down between jumps to a slow canter. The horse is then given his head two or three strides from the place where the rider has selected as the point of departure. This calls for real horsemanship on the part of the rider, but may cramp the horse's style somewhat, especially over a wide obstacle, where more speed before take-off is needed.

THE SEAT

The old-fashioned seat of our forefathers (you can see it in the old hunting prints) was about the worst possible for horse and rider. For one thing, the ri-

The Jones Boy, ridden by Katie Monahan (SUE MAYNARD)

der's weight was back somewhere on the horse's loins, a very bad place for it at a time when the horse most needed freedom in the hindquarters. For another, the legs straight out offered little to absorb the shock of landing, which must have been considerable. Judging by many contemporary photographs from the steeplechase or the hunting field, one can see that, at least as far as completing the jump goes, some modern riders are not much better. Not only do some of these pictures show the rider leaning well back in the saddle, toes pointing out past the horse's chest; but the rider, with outstretched arms, is pulling the horse's head up or to one side. A more unfortunate way to arrive on the other side of a hurdle is hard to imagine.

The forward, or Italian, seat, if it is properly maintained, is the best one, and is used by all of our modern riders in the ring and in the field. The saddle itself has something (some say a great deal) to do with the success of the forward style of jumping. A word of warning here. A type of saddle may be more efficient, or designed for more comfort, and its users may make extravagant claims for it, but *no* saddle, no matter how well designed, is going to make an expert out of a novice. A good horseman will look and ride well in a bad saddle, and the finest saddle will not be of much help to a poor rider.

The modern jumping saddle differs radically from the familiar English saddle. It is much deeper and the saddletree arms are inclined forward at an angle (which may be as much as forty-five degrees) allowing the rider to sit further forward, while the high cantle also tends to throw the body forward. A padded knee roll gives added support, and, coupled with the deep seat, helps prevent the rider's weight from shifting. According to Toptani, one of the foremost authorities on the art of jumping, it is the shifting weight which does most of the damage. An experiment he conducted seems to prove that he was right. A riderless horse was put in a jumping lane and made to go over an obstacle which it cleared easily. An average rider then took the horse over the same jump several times, dislodging the top pole. Refusing to believe that the added weight (175 pounds) of the rider caused the rapping, Toptani strapped a 250-pound weight to the saddle in place of the rider and sent the horse over the jump once more. This time it again cleared easily, and repeated the performance several times, as did other horses in the same experiment. The secret seems to be that the weight in the saddle is not the determining factor—*as long as it does not shift*. Toptani's objections to the English saddle were that it is too shallow in the seat and too

A bad landing

broad across the crotch, spreading the rider's thighs and preventing knee and calf grip. The bridge is too high, throwing the rider's weight too far back, and it does not offer any support to the jumper's knee. A further objection is that the English saddle raises the rider too far above the horse's back.

Other riders will take exception to this; in fact the divergent opinions on horsemanship in all its forms, from the position of the rider's feet to the proper way to trim a tail, are almost as fascinating as the art of riding itself. Surely in no other sport are so many seemingly simple procedures the source of such controversy. We can only recommend that the would-be jumper read some of the excellent books on jumping in its various forms which are available today and to make up his own mind.

One thing on which all experts agree is that no novice should start jumping until he has first learned how to ride. Without the confidence that comes with balance, a firm seat, and the knowledge that he can control his horse at all times, the beginner has no business attempting even the smallest jumps. In this speeded-up age, where everyone seems to be looking for a quick and easy way to do things, there is a tendency to try to rush the learning processes in many fields of endeavor, riding among them. However, a conscientious riding instructor will not allow his pupils to run before they can walk. For one thing, the confidence so carefully built up may be shaken by a tumble, while later on, a spill or two will be looked on as all part of the game. For another, the beginner who is nervous and not too sure of his seat will learn nothing by jumping. He will be far too concerned with sticking on to be able to give any attention to correct seat, hands, posture, and exact balance. The fine points will be wasted on him, and at the same time he may fall into bad habits which may take much time to eradicate later.

TRAINING THE RIDER

After the instructor is satisfied that you can handle your mount—and yourself—under all normal circumstances, and can walk, trot, canter and gallop without hands, stirrups and saddle, then you are ready for your first jumping lesson. It goes without saying that a well-schooled and steady mount should be provided. It is of the greatest importance that your seat be in no way dependent on your hands. It is absolutely necessary to avoid putting undue pressure on a horse's mouth at any time: it is doubly important while jumping. The untrained rider is handicap enough for any mount. But when in addition the rider is maintaining his own balance by pulling violently on the reins, the handicap is doubled and disaster may well lie ahead. Even the best-trained horse cannot perform under such circumstances, and much repetition of these tactics will ruin him for good. It is for this reason that for the first jumping lesson or two some instructors advocate a stirrup leather around the horse's neck just in front of the withers. The student holds onto this until he has learned balance, and to cushion the jolt of landing with his knees. Others suggest putting the hands on the horse's crest. Both are designed to give added confidence, but if the student has successfully completed his riding training these aids should not be necessary. It is excellent training to walk, trot and canter before each jumping lesson. These exercises warm up the horse and limber up the rider, and should be the preliminary to jumping instruction throughout the course. The exercises should repeat those of the earlier riding instruction—arm-swinging, body-bending, turning to face the tail, etc., done with feet out of the stirrups at the walk, trot and canter. After the preliminary setting-up exercises, which might take twenty to thirty minutes, you should begin (I am, of course, assuming that an instructor is present) by trotting your mount over a low jump—no more than thirty inches high and three feet wide, paying attention to seat and balance and leaving the reins slack.

When approaching the jump, keep a firm grip with the legs and knees, with the body inclined well forward from the hips, buttocks to the rear and clear of the saddle. The arms are extended to give the horse the maximum amount of play with his head. The toes are turned well out and the heels down, thus giving a strong grip with the calves. This balanced position should be maintained after the jump as well as before it. This is why it is so essential for the learner to acquire a really good seat before he attempts to jump.

The tendency at first is for the body to come heavily down into the saddle as the horse lands. This is not only uncomfortable for the rider, but also a poor reward for the horse for his effort. Worse still, the rider comes down just at the moment the horse is recovering his forehand. This violent shifting of weight at the crucial moment may cause the horse to stumble.

However, if the balance and leg position are correctly maintained there will be no tendency for the rider to end up digging into the horse's shoulders to prevent sliding up his neck. The body will be in balance and ready to resume the rhythm of the gait, and the horse will not have been hampered in his effort to regain his stride.

To obviate an involuntary tensing before take-off some instructors make the student refrain from looking at the obstacle at all. After negotiating the jump successfully several times, you should go over it without stirrups.

On successive days one or two more obstacles are added at widely spaced intervals, and these are taken in the same manner, with and without stirrups, then with only one stirrup (this is more difficult than jumping without any). The height of the jumps may then be raised four inches. Later on the same jumps should be taken bareback. This should continue for at least two months, the jumps being gradually raised to three and a half feet. The course is still taken at the trot with the reins loose, and you should at no time attempt to exert any pressure on the horse's mouth.

These jumping exercises are the finest kind of training irrespective of whether you later intend to do any jumping in the ring or field. The jumps are low and yet many of the sudden and unexpected movements with which a horse can disconcert and sometimes throw a rider are duplicated. For this reason many instructors prefer not to use wings on the jumps, so that the beginner is forced to cope with the sudden swerve of a horse who has decided to go around instead of over. The ability to successfully meet these emergencies is of the greatest importance, and mark the difference between a first- and second-rate rider.

With the addition of cavallettis (bars twelve inches

or eighteen inches high used for automatically regulating a horse's stride) the course may be taken at a canter. The cavalletti will ensure the horse taking one-, two- or three-gallop strides, according to the distance of the cavalletti to the obstacle, before taking off. As before, the jumps, which now can be raised to four feet, should be taken with and without stirrups, and bareback. They should next be negotiated in the same way but at first with one arm, then both, behind the back, and then outstretched. Next you should start to use the reins, shortening them until contact is made with the horse's mouth.

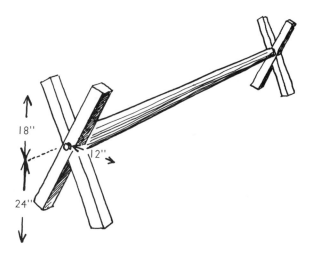

Cavalletti adjustable to three different heights

Jumping without reins has taught you to give your horse freedom. Now, with the lightest possible contact you will be taught to control your mount between jumps. From being a mere passenger you now become the driver, although you still allow the horse the greatest possible freedom of movement. Attention should be paid to jumping form, although if, as we are told, "form follows function," the foregoing months of instruction and exercise in the forward seat, using no reins and frequently no stirrups, will have developed good habits and a practical, and hence pleasing, style. I have mentioned the use of a large mirror in the riding school. A mirror is hardly practical in a jumping lane, but good use might be made of a Polaroid camera. A picture of a jumper's style may be developed almost before the rider has completed his canter round the ring, and might do much to help correct posture and style. Certainly a perusal of collections of photographs of the world's jumping "greats" taken in mid-air occasionally shows them in some peculiar positions, which they

may possibly have regretted when the pictures were reproduced. "Handsome is as handsome does," they say, and the graceful form displayed while clearing a four-foot fence may momentarily desert even the finest rider when striving to clear one seven feet high. But the novice should strive for perfection in style as well as clearing the obstacle.

The rider who successfully completes the schooling outlined above is on the road to becoming a better-than-average jumper. He has a long way to go before reaching competition standards, but the foundation will have been laid.

He will, of necessity, have acquired a firm seat, good balance and a sense of rhythm and timing which will stand him in good stead in the hunting field, and if he wishes to go on, in learning the finer points of show jumping in the ring. His further training will consist of higher and more difficult obstacles, placed at frequent intervals, and finally practice over courses laid out in the manner of the competition ring.

All experienced horsemen will agree that pace in the approach is important. Where the experts differ is on what the pace should be. Here again we have at least two schools of thought in opposition. One contends that the obstacle should be approached slowly and the horse allowed (or made) to "collect" himself—"jump off his hocks"—and so develop the full power of his loin and back muscles. Others claim that the horse is handicapped by being slowed too much—that there is no point in making a horse jump with two legs when he has four, and that with more speed the animal can clear the same obstacles with a great deal less effort. By this they do not mean that all obstacles must be taken at a mad rush. If such a rush occurs it means that the horse or rider or both are not sufficiently trained. The rider may have forced the horse into too great a pace, thus overriding the horse's own judgment as to its place of take-off; or an inexperienced horse may have misjudged his distance. In either case, the result is often a refusal, as the horse, approaching too close too quickly, senses his mistake and swerves at the last minute, sometimes with disastrous results to the horseman.

"All horses need to jump is: 1. Speed. 2. A free neck so that it can see the obstacle correctly. 3. A certain amount of encouragement from the rider (nervous riders make nervous horses). 4. Encouragement but *not* punishment. There is no sense in punishing a horse for the rider's mistakes. The worst thing a rider can possibly do is to slow down his horse. . . ." (Toptani, *Modern Show Jumping*)

Francie Steinwedell riding Dillinger in a jumping competition (SUE MAYNARD)

A rule of thumb given by some jumpers is that a horse should take off at a point not nearer than the height of the fence, and not further than eight feet. With a three-foot fence this gives five feet of leeway, but this leeway decreases as the height of the jump increases, so that the higher the obstacle the more care must be taken as to the exact take-off point.

Some horses seem to prefer a shorter take-off distance. I particularly remember one such at a local horse show. The horse was small and cobby (chunky), and carrying a very heavy rider. The animal invariably came close to the jump, appeared to stop momentarily, and then took off almost vertically. Surprisingly, although the style was peculiar, the little animal did very well.

Horse shows are an excellent place for you to pick up pointers on what or what not to do in the ring. Small shows, where perhaps the jumping will not be of uniformly high standards, may prove more instructive than exhibitions by the finest horsemen. By watching carefully you may recognize and study your own failings, and improve your own style by analyzing the faults of others.

TRAINING THE HORSE

The horse is not by nature a jumper. In his wild state, that is, on the open range, his instinct would be to run from danger and only jump in the event of being cornered against an obstacle of medium height. Jumping calls, therefore, not only for training in judging distance, pace, height, etc., but also for the use of muscles in a way in which the horse would not ordinarily have to use them. These muscles must be as carefully developed as those of any human hurdler, and this development plays as important a part in the training of a jumper as any of the other necessary skills. And here we come to another example of dissension in the ranks of the experts. For some say that even the greenest horse should begin his training with a rider on his back. Toptani is very firm about this, and sees no good coming from training begun without a rider. One of the arguments against riderless training is that the horse will never have to jump without a rider, so why not start him off with one and help condition him to the weight which he must eventually carry. Also, it is claimed that teaching a horse to jump riderless is to encourage it to jump paddock and pasture fences, with possible dire effects to himself and to his owner's neighbors.

However, the majority of trainers seem to agree that young horses should have their first jumping lessons without a rider. They should begin by being led over small obstacles: a low bank or pole laid on the ground, for instance. Anything will do as long as it is low. These obstacles may be raised gradually as the animal shows confidence. Another method is to use long reins or a lunge line as in the sketch. The pole acts as both wing and as a slide for the line. The height of the jump may be increased gradually as the young horse progresses. The wing should be reversed after a time, and the horse made to jump while circling in the other direction. Horses may also be schooled in a lane, either circular or elliptical.

The jumping lane should be fenced on both sides by railings at least seven feet high, so that the animal cannot see out and be distracted or frightened. It should be some fourteen feet in width and the obstacles should be the same. Here the horse is free, with no reins or lunge line, and made to circle the ring. At first the ring should be clear of obstacles, and the horse should be driven around at all paces and to either hand (clockwise and counterclockwise). After becoming accustomed to this a single low jump is put in and later other obstacles added at varying distances from the turns. In this way the animal gets practice at judging distances when suddenly coming to a jump. He also becomes accustomed to regulating his pace and judging his take-off positions when faced with obstacles placed fairly close together. If the horse tends to take off too close to obstacles, a rail (cavalletti) on, or just above, the ground some three feet out on the take-off side will help cure this. It must be remembered that young horses must be taught confidence in themselves, just as inexperienced riders must be taught. The animal should not be allowed to become excited—rushing around the ring will do him far more harm than good. The obstacles should be kept low, and the pace slow at all times. The main idea is to teach the animal to like to jump and to go over an obstacle as quietly and without more fuss than if he were trotting down the

road. Incidentally, such schooling is invaluable for any animal even if intended for no more than the trail or bridle path. An unschooled mount will sometimes make a great to-do about passing over even a small tree limb on a path, shying and balking as if the stick were a python or a five-foot fence. A brief training over only the lowest of obstacles will greatly improve his performance and add much to his rider's comfort and safety.

The schooling with a rider should repeat that of the free jumping: the obstacles should be low at first and heightened only when the horse has successfully cleared them. The jumps should be without wings, and the horse trained to jump the obstacle at the exact spot the rider selects. This is particularly important in a horse which is to be used for hunting. The horse's natural instinct is to jump where the obstacle is lowest, but other factors, such as a fallen horse and rider, may make this a dangerous matter. In such a case the horse which rushes for the nearest gap in the hedge is a positive menace, and here careful schooling over wingless jumps pays off.

A great aid to training is the trotting lane. This resembles a wide ladder lying on the ground, composed of some dozen poles raised up about eight inches. These poles should be eight feet wide and placed four feet apart. The horse is trotted into this lane, which teaches it to lift its legs very high and carefully.

This training of a young horse should not be hurried. At the famous Italian Cavalry School in pre-World War II days, the bars were never raised higher than one foot off the ground for the first six weeks. This seemingly slow progress resulted in horses that never refused or rushed their jumps.

Some horses, being by nature careless, lazy or both, soon find that the built-up obstacles of the show ring come down easily and that it takes less effort to knock down the top pole than to tuck the feet well up and clear properly. To break this habit, and to ensure clean jumping, a rapping pole is often used. This long, light pole, often of bamboo, is held by the trainer or assistant a few inches over the top rail of the jump. As the horse clears the jump the pole is raised and the horse receives a sharp rap on the shins or hoofs. A rap on the cannon bone of the forelegs will make him lift his forehand; if on the hind legs, it will make him raise his hindquarters; raps on the hoofs tend to make a horse pick up his feet.

Here again we have great differences of opinion. Some trainers swear by the rapping pole and use it constantly to keep their animals up to the mark. Oth-

Two famous jumping stars: Melanie Smith and Val de Loir (SUE MAYNARD)

ers see in it an unnecessary cruelty which often forces a horse to efforts beyond his strength and endurance, and which, by bringing in an element of punishment, makes the horse fear and dislike his work. These trainers, and there are many of them, prefer to make the lazy or careless horse punish himself by substituting an iron bar or piece of heavy-gauge iron water pipe for the top rail. A horse striking one of these—and they require a good hard knock to displace—will soon learn that it is less painful to go over the obstacle than into it. Even a light rap from a hoof will make a resounding ''bong'' which in itself is often sufficient to make a horse careful to tuck up his legs when jumping. It is a good idea when training a young horse to avoid hedge-type obstacles which can be brushed through too easily. If these are used, a piece of pipe concealed in the top of the obstacle will soon cure an animal of trying to take a short cut through the fence instead of over it.

Horseman and trainer must pick their own course through the conflicting opinions of the experts. What is clear and uncontroversial is that both novice rider

and green horse must be trained slowly and carefully. As with other athletes, overtraining is as bad as undertraining. Horses should be rested for several days at intervals. Too much schooling over the jumps may make a horse tired of his work, and therefore a poor and sloppy performer. Many people prefer not to jump more than ten or twenty minutes every other day. Certainly, jumping puts considerable strain on a horse, and an animal jumped in moderation will long outlast one that has been abused by being taken over the rails too often.

Punishing a horse because he does not jump well is useless. For one thing, nine times out of ten, a poor performance can be blamed on the rider. For another, punishment will only eventually disgust him with the whole idea of jumping. This is to be avoided at all costs, as the horse, as well as having a long memory, can be stubborn as a mule. Let him get it firmly fixed in his little equine brain that jumping is associated with pain, fear or discomfort, and he will be ruined for life. On the other hand, frequent rewards and praise will pay big dividends.

It will be seen that the schooling of a young horse

closely parallels that of the novice rider. However, it is a great mistake to attempt to combine the two. The novice should learn on an experienced animal, one that can be relied on—if possible, an old pro who will do the right thing whatever his rider does. In turn, the young horse should only be ridden by a trained horseman who is able to correct the animal's mistakes and give him the confidence he needs, at the same time keeping him perfectly under control at all times. This the novice is quite incapable of doing, and the net result of the combination of an inexperienced rider and an unschooled horse may well be faults that will be difficult if not impossible to alter later on.

Chapter 13

HUNTING

Hunting in all its forms was a passion with our ancestors, pursued with an enthusiasm which we moderns find hard to understand. Game of many varieties was hunted with hawk and hound. Most of the victims found their way to the table, and, indeed, hunting in olden times pleasurably combined the thrills of the chase with the laudable act of filling the castle larder. Notice I used the word "castle." The humble, and often underfed, peasant's meager larder was *not* stocked with game, not if he valued his life, that is; for the lords and squires were most jealous of their hunting rights, and woe betide the common serf if he dared poach on his lord's preserves. An occasional rabbit or small bird might find its way into the pot, but the killing of a deer meant the rope. Savage as the game laws were, even down to comparatively recent times, there were still daring souls who, for a thrill and a bit of extra food, would risk life or limb (for stealing small game in medieval times, the poacher might lose only a hand, ears or nose).

But as the lands grew more developed and the great forests and preserves shrank, the palmy days of hunting passed. The deer, the boar, the wolf and the bear vanished, or retreated to the more inaccessible of the wooded hill countries. All but the fox; in fact, he flourished. Plump chickens and goslings and baby lambs were to be had in ever-increasing abundance. Logically, this wily thief was hunted at first by enraged farmers, but later by the hunt-starved gentry, and great sport it turned out to be. In a comparatively short time the once despised fox was the favorite quarry.

It was a sport particularly suited to the boisterous squires and country gentry of England. The aristocracy of France, where the feudal system lingered on, after a fashion, much later than across the Channel, looked down with disdain at the helter-skelter cross-

The hounds of the Millbrook Hunt waiting for the huntsman to move off from the meet. With this pack of American hounds, he is carrying an American cow horn rather than the English copper horn which most huntsmen use (H. K. KIMBALL)

country dashes of their uncouth neighbors. It is impossible to accurately date the first packs used exclusively for foxhunting in England, but it was in the latter half of the seventeenth century. But before that, in 1650, Robert Brooke arrived in Maryland with a family and retinue totaling forty persons in all—and a pack of hounds. From this all-purpose pack sprang the Brooke hounds, famous in Maryland for more than two hundred years.

For it was inevitable that the hard-riding English gentry should introduce the sport into the American colonies, the Southern ones, that is—many of the Pilgrims and their descendants would have frowned on such frivolity. Here in Virginia, Maryland and the Carolinas it flourished from early times, although the earliest organized hunt club in America was the Gloucester Foxhunting Club, founded in 1766 by some sporting Philadelphians.

It is pleasing to know that the father of our country was a keen huntsman. Scarcely a page of Washington's diary dealing with his private life is without some mention of foxhunting, including more than two hundred references to particular hunts. On hunt days, the General and his guests breakfasted by candlelight, and were well away by dawn's first light.

"Went a-hunting and killed a bitch fox in an hour," reads one excerpt from his diary for September 22, 1769. "Returned home with an ague upon me." The ague, it may be added, did not prevent him from being in the hunting field the following day.

The hunting prior to the Revolution was of the hit-or-miss variety—and a pack might be expected to occasionally tangle with larger game than Reynard. Dr. Thomas Walker, first Englishman to build a cabin in Kentucky, writes in 1749 in the record of his journey, "Our dogs were very uneasied during the night." "Discovered," the next day's entry records, "the track of about twenty Indians." And later: "Our dogs caught a large he-bear." Further on we read that a bear broke one of his dog's legs and a companion's hound fell victim to a large elk. So game was mixed and the hounds of those days might expect to run into almost anything, from a fox to a Cherokee.

But later, as it had years before in Europe, civilization crept in and the elk and the red man departed to less populous places, leaving once more the wily fox as the chief target for horse and hounds. By the time of the Civil War, foxhunting had become the favorite sport of the landed gentry of Maryland, Pennsylvania and Virginia. After the war, foxhunting became more formalized. Many horses, hounds and hunt servants were brought from England and more attention was paid to style and system than before, although the English practice of stopping earths, or burrows, was not practical in this country. In 1907 the Master of Foxhounds Association of America (112 Water Street, Boston, MA 02109) was formed. This brought about better organization and regulation, and hunting territories were recorded and requirements set up for the recognition of packs.

Where in the very old days hunts were private affairs, with the "field" consisting of the owner of the pack and his family and guests, today they are mostly organized as clubs with the upkeep paid by subscription of the members. This upkeep includes kenneling of the pack, which may consist of as many as thirty couples (the term "couple" is used to denote two dogs, which, when proceeding to or from the field, are often coupled together with a short length of chain—also called a "couple"—to keep them from straying). It also includes in many hunts the services of a paid huntsman and also money for other expenses incurred, such as compensation for damage done to farm property.

THE MASTER OF FOXHOUNDS

The head of the hunt is the master of hounds or master of foxhounds, abbreviated MFH. His is the sole responsibility for the success of the hunt as an organization, the caliber of the hounds, the efficiency of the hunt servants, and most important of all, making the hunt popular with everyone in the community. This is not always as easy in this country as it is in England. Small farmers and landowners who have no interest in hunting themselves have to be talked into allowing passage of horses and dogs over their land. Stringing of barbed wire, the bane of fox hunters, has to be regulated as much as possible, a difficult task where great areas are involved. The indiscriminate killing of foxes in hunting country has also to be contended with. In England foxes are protected, but in America they are regarded, ex-

Going to draw the first covert (H. K. KIMBALL)

cept by the foxhunting community, as a nuisance to be exterminated by trap, poison or gun. On top of this there is the small, but exceedingly vocal, minority whose aim it is to see foxhunting banned as cruelty to animals. The fact that the fox they save from the hounds today may be poisoned or shot tomorrow—often to crawl away to die a lingering death—bothers them little. Because foxhunting was once reserved for the aristocracy—and still is hardly a poor man's sport—it comes in for some criticism from the social viewpoint. "The unspeakable in pursuit of the uneatable" was Oscar Wilde's scathing remark on the "horsey set." But with the easing of class antagonism and the increasing number of riders, these prejudices are vanishing and the hunt may someday achieve the same sort of popularity the once exclusive game of polo is now enjoying.

Some masters hunt their own hounds, but often the huntsman is a professional. As his name implies, he is in charge of the actual planning and working of the day's hunt. His is the strategy, his the praise for a successful season, his the blame for a poor one. The aim of every huntsman is to get his hounds away together on a fix, have them run together and kill together. This perfect pack work requires a great deal of effort, not only in the field, coordinating efforts of the hounds and whippers-in, but also in selection and training of the pack, without which no hunt can be successful. Besides this, the huntsman should have an intimate knowledge of his district, and know the likeliest place for foxes to kennel.

He must, of course, know his hounds and their voices and be able to tell by the cry whether they are gone away on a true scent, or are running rabbit or a deer. Like any hunter, his ability springs from long experience, amounting almost to instinct. This sixth sense tells him what his hounds are about and helps him (sometimes) to outguess the wily quarry. He knows the vagaries of scent, differing with temperature and humidity. He also knows that fields that have been treated with chemicals can profitably be avoided and cast around—even a heavily limed field will yield practically no line. In short, although the master of foxhounds is the commander-in-chief, the huntsman is general in command of the army in the field.

The huntsman is assisted by the whippers-in, whose duty it is to ride herd on the hounds, whipping them back into the pack if they start to stray. In broken wooded country, this is no easy task. A well-trained pack will hunt as an entity and not an uncoordinated mob, but even the best hounds will scatter on occasion. If the hunt is spread out, the whipper-in may find himself alone with the hounds, or some of them, and he must be able to sense whether to carry on with them, or to fall back to urge on tail hounds, as the laggards are called. If the hounds going away ("gone away" is the term used when the fox has been found and the hunt goes after him at full gallop) are only a few, he may have to decide whether to delay them long enough to allow the huntsman with the rest of the pack to catch up. Or a few hounds may follow one scent, while the rest of the pack have gone away, in which case the whipper-in does his best to get the hounds to leave their fox and join the pack. There is always the chance that the huntsman may be held up by wire, or a bad stretch of woods, in which case the whipper-in (there are usually two) nearest the lead must temporarily take over the place of the huntsman. For this reason whippers-in in this country often carry horns. Because of the legwork involved (the hunt staff are called upon to cover far more territory, much of it speedily, than any members of the field, and are usually out two or three hours longer), the whipper-in should, besides being a first-rate horseman, be as well if not better mounted than the huntsman. Besides this he should know the voice of every hound in the pack, and must be able to handle them, rating (disciplining by word or whip) them when necessary, firmly but not too severely. All in all, a whipper-in is almost as vital to a hunt as the huntsman. He, or they, if the system of hunting calls for a first whip and a second whip, on the right and left flank of the huntsman, must work closely with the huntsman. Teamwork is essential, and the longer huntsman and whips have worked together, the better.

Foxhunting in America is much different from, and far more difficult than, hunting in England. There are several reasons, chief among them being the nature of the terrain. Anyone who has traveled the English countryside has marked the almost park-like quality of the land: the neatness of the hedges, the numerous gates, the close-cropped rolling green of the fields and the small, neat, clearly defined coverts and woods. Much of the famous hunting shires—Leicestershire, Rutlandshire and Northamptonshire, home, among others, of noted hunts such as the Pytchley, the Belvoir and the Quorn—bear more resemblance to a vast golf course than to any terrain we know in this country. Wire fences, thanks to the efforts of the hunt committees, are few and far between, the fields being marked for the most part by ditches and hedgerows.

The foxes themselves are numerous, being pro-

A typical hunting scene, showing the whippers-in flanking the huntsman, followed by the field master and members of the field (FREUDY)

tected, and therefore also better fed (farmers' losses are also taken care of out of the hunt fund). There may be differences of opinion about the relative sagacity of the red fox of England and the foxes common to America, but there can be little doubt that the American fox, living, as he does, a harder existence, with every man's hand against him, is a tougher specimen physically than his more pampered English cousin. Then again, in England earths and drains are stopped the night before a hunt, while the inmates are out looking for their supper. Local gamekeepers and farmers know these earths (remember, it is a small country, and in England the woodchuck is unknown) and the stopping can be accomplished with little difficulty. Then again, the first covert to be drawn, and where a fox is almost sure to be found above ground, may be only five or ten acres in extent, seldom more than twenty.

In contrast, the American huntsman is faced with an entirely different problem. His hunting territory is far rougher, the fields less open, the fences frequently of wire. Pasture lands may lie adjacent to large tracts of thick scrub or swamp, and the coverts and woods are larger and lie closer together. In England a whip can usually station himself at a far cor-

ner of the little covert to be drawn and can usually get a view as the fox breaks cover. The American covert may well cover one hundred and fifty acres, far too large to afford a whip an opportunity for a view, and in scrub-covered country visibility may be limited to a hundred yards or less. A hunted fox is seldom viewed and the woods and hills muffle the sound of the hounds and obstruct vision. More important, in this country earths and dens are numerous and the territory is so large and rough that it is impossible in all but a very few localities to attempt to stop earths. This means that foxes may be well underground when the hounds are cast. Couple this with the fact that the foxes are not as numerous to begin with and you will see the disadvantage under which the American huntsman has to work.

However, a difficult task seems to bring out the best in man and beast, and many American packs regularly turn in brilliant performances finding and killing under unbelievably adverse conditions.

To the amateur the difficulty of finding and catching a fleet and elusive animal in an undefined area of rough, hilly wooded country, cut by roads, wire fences, streams and private property on which no hunting is allowed, may seem insuperable. The fox, unhindered by such obstacles, might well take off for parts unknown, leaving the field strung out across half a dozen counties. Fortunately the fox, like most wild animals, prefers to stay in his own locality. He will run, dodge, circle and perform various tricky maneuvers, but will remain in his own territory. Often foxes are killed within short distances of the spot where they were first viewed, in the meantime having led the hunt over a distance of many miles. Even so, the area in which a fox may be expected to operate may well take in some twenty square miles. In describing a hunt, the term "point" is used to denote the distance, in a straight line, between the two localities furthest apart covered in that particular hunt. The distance is the mileage actually covered by the hunt.

As we have noted, good hunting country in America is scarce. Farmers cannot be blamed for stringing wire. Labor costs have gone up and the once plentiful supply of suitable fencing woods, chiefly the now-vanished chestnut, has dwindled to the point where barbed wire is the only economical way to fence. Since the wars this has also been true to some extent in England, but in the hunting counties there the barbed wire is often removed (at considerable expense to the hunt committees) in the hunting season, and replaced afterward. In America, in areas where the conditions and interest warrant, wire is sometimes replaced for short stretches, or paneled. A few rail lengths of post and rail are substituted for the wire, or if the owner objects to having his wire cut, "chicken coop" paneling is used. Long boards are nailed to two-inch-by-four-inch joists to form inverted Vs, the apex of which is high enough to go over the usual four-foot fence.

Few farmers object to having gates put in their fences, but unless the gateposts are well set and supported these usually become difficult to open, even on foot, and can almost never be opened by a man on horseback. One of the worst hazards are areas where pigs are kept. Here stock fencing is used, often with barbed wire on top. This may completely stop hounds, as their only recourse is to attempt to clamber over, an operation which frequently results in injury, and sometimes death, as when a luckless hound gets hung up on such a fence in an unfrequented piece of woodland, and is not found until too late. In parts of the East, these fenced areas are large—thirty to fifty acres—and represent a real barrier.

Ideal hunting country should consist largely of pasture land—standing crops are naturally never ridden over, here or in England—but it is not generally realized that much farm land in the East has reverted to woods. Land once painstakingly cleared and fenced with chestnut or stone fences has been allowed to grow up, and only an occasional section of rotting snake fence or tumbled stone pile remains deep in the woods to tell the tale. In terrain where the combination of wire, impenetrable wood and swamp make regular hunting impossible, drag hunts are the only answer, the route "hunted" over being paneled or "cooped."

Besides a good terrain, there has also to be a supply of game. There are only two game animals in the East suitable for hunting on horseback, the fox and the coyote. Hare and the small cottontail rabbit are pursued on foot by beagles since their habits are such—the distance and points being so short—that they are not suitable for pursuit on horseback. In the West and Southwest, the game is coyote.

THE FOX

There are two kinds of foxes in North America, the gray fox *(Urocyon cinereoargenteus),* found from New England to South America; and the red fox *(Vulpes fulva).* This last is common to all Europe, North Africa, the temperate zone of Asia, and all North America as far south as Mexico. Red foxes are said to have been imported from England in 1730, but there is no foundation for the belief that the red foxes of the Eastern United States are descendants of these. Both are wily animals. The gray fox (which, by the way, can climb trees fairly well) usually keeps to the more hilly, wooded areas or swamps, while the red fox has adapted to changing conditions and, of the two, is perhaps more likely to be found closer to human habitations. Both den up in caves or burrows, the red fox excavating a sizable burrow for the litter of as many as ten cubs. In all but a few areas they are hunted as vermin. In Kentucky, where many farmers own hounds, and where there is much interest in anything pertaining to horses and hunting, they are protected by law; they are protected by custom in North Carolina and some local areas of other Eastern states where there is sufficient interest.

Deer are a frequent, and unwelcome, object of the pack's attentions. Hounds will often pursue their strong scent for miles straight across country. The great increase in the deer population in recent years has made them an increasing nuisance to the fox hunter. Taking everything into consideration it is not to be wondered at that in the average hunt, every day in the season does not result in a perfect day's sport. But while the few who "ride to hunt" may be disappointed, the true hunter takes these days in his stride, while the many who "hunt to ride" get their exercise anyway, and are usually well satisfied.

THE HUNT

Hunting techniques vary. Hunts with English hounds generally try to adhere to the English traditions and terms, while those with American hounds follow American customs. In both cases, the pack will be brought to a covert known to shelter, or suspected of harboring, a fox. The hounds will be sent in and the covert drawn, the huntsman and whips judging by ear the progress and direction of the hounds. If the covert is small enough, the whips will attempt to flank the covert, thus getting a view of the quarry when he breaks cover. The field meanwhile keeps well back and out of the way. The field also keeps quiet. The huntsman and whips are straining to catch the voice of the hounds, and conversation and unnecessary movement are a breach of hunt discipline.

If the covert is open enough for riding, a usual method is for the huntsman to advance through the center of the wood, flanked by his whips, at distances of two hundred to three hundred yards. Thus a line of some six hundred yards may be swept.

When the hounds "find" (first smell the quarry) they will "give tongue." The sound of the hounds differs not only with individual dogs, but varies at different phases of the chase, indicating to the trained ears of the huntsman the freshness of the "line" and the nearness of the quarry. Judging by the direction of the sounds, the huntsman will be able to judge the course the chase is taking and to anticipate to a degree the probable direction it will take. If the fox is viewed as it breaks cover (an unusual occurrence in this country), the cheer of "Tallyho" is raised, the traditional view halloo. The members of the field, while of course endeavoring to keep as close to the quarry as possible, should never ride so as to interfere with the huntsman and his staff, nor so close to hounds that there is any danger of riding into them. To ride into a pack and step on a hound is the worst possible offense.

Many hunts have been spoiled when overzealous riders, usually of the "hunt to ride" persuasion, have dashed madly through hounds at check, and swept them away with them. Most high-strung hounds will follow galloping horses, if not actively on a line.

If a rider cannot stop his horse when hounds check, he should turn away from the pack. Likewise, on finding oneself in front of the hounds, turn your horse's head the way they are running, get out of their way, and let them pass.

The scent of the quarry is often faint and elusive. Some ground may absorb it more than others, temperature and wind will affect it, while dry ground and dry air are usually a handicap. It may be crossed by other stronger scents—especially in this age of farm chemicals, gasoline and oil.

This scent may be likened to a fine silk thread, and when it snaps and the hounds check, it must be picked up again near where it broke. The location of the break can be told by the voices of the hounds, or rather by the lack of them (hounds do not cry when casting). The hounds themselves will cast around, trying to pick up the line. If the hounds are long at fault, and the huntsman thinks that the quarry may have taken advantage of a route giving poor scenting possibilities—a stone wall, or blacktopped road, for instance (a farmer once swore that he saw a fox jump on a sheep's back and ride its frightened steed across a pasture!)—he may make a cast with the pack, being careful to do so quietly, without getting the hounds' heads up.

Causing the hounds to raise their heads and their noses from the ground may lead to their interest lagging, thus delaying the search, and at worst may cause them to lose the scent altogether. For this reason, care should be exercised by the whippers-in in the use of horn or voice in bringing up the laggards, or hounds which have strayed or gone off on a false scent.

If the line is cold, and the hounds uninterested, the cheering on of another part of the pack may result in drawing the main body of hounds away from the line altogether. It is also the reason that any "whoopin' and hollerin' " by members of the field is strictly taboo. If the novice hunter feels impelled to yell, let him wait until he hears the "Tallyho" and the pack is off in full cry.

Casting consists of working the pack in ever-widening patterns until at last the line is struck again and the hounds give tongue and follow. It is obvious that a good hound, besides having a keen nose, must also have both physical staying power and mental perseverance.

Many a fox has met his end because a methodical hound has persisted when the others have given up. A hound must also have a good voice, especially in broken country with heavy cover, where the hunts-man must rely on ear alone, and must be able to count on receiving his hounds' signals loud and clear. If the hounds continue at a loss, and the hunts-man thinks he knows where the trail may be picked up, he may "lift" the pack with a whistle, a word, or a short toot on the horn and lead it off to where he feels the line may be picked up. "Lifting" is risky, but sometimes effective with a clever hunts-man.

Horn signals should be used sparingly for reasons given above, but in broken country are a necessity. Needless to say, huntsman and whippers-in should understand each other's signals perfectly. Thus a huntsman can signal change of direction to his whips, who are probably completely out of sight. Two notes of the horn indicate a turn to the right, three to the left. An occasional single note with some words in a cheerful, encouraging tone (hounds don't understand the words themselves, of course, but the tone in which they are uttered means every-thing) will serve to keep the pack at their work, and to let them, and the whippers-in, know where the huntsman is.

In the English style, if a reliable hound speaks, indicating it has picked up the line, a scream of "Hoicks" or "Yoicks" is raised, followed by a "Hark," to draw attention to the hound's cry, and a series of short notes on the horn. This will bring the rest of the pack in with a rush. As other hounds speak on the line, repeated shouts of "Yoicks, yoicks," with a succession of short blasts, spaced in threes and twos, will bring the pack together.

When hounds have truly settled on the line, and are giving tongue, the cry "Yoicks, yoicks, gone away, away, away, away" is raised, and a horn sig-nal of three short blasts and a long one, repeated over and over by both huntsman and whippers-in, serves notice to the waiting field that it is time to push on.

Should a covert be drawn blank, hounds are called off with long drawn-out cries of "Come aw-a-a-a-a-ay, come, come aw-a-a-a-a-y," and long undulating notes of the horn. This indicates to the whips and the field that the huntsman is moving on.

To stop hounds running riot (running game other than their fox), three long blasts are used, with the cry, "Ware riot." The whips should rate the offend-ing hounds with the same cry.

Occasionally a chase will be a short one and the fox will be "chopped" or "mobbed" (surrounded and killed without having a chance to run). More often it will be a chase involving many checks and finds. With luck, and if the country is clear and field well up, a final run with the fox in full view may end with a kill in the open with the whole hunt pres-ent. Then the "Whoo-hoop"—followed by short blasts interspersed with long tremolos—announces the death. But in most wild American hunting coun-try, kills are rare. Like as not the fox will be run to earth, in which case the clamoring hounds may be drawn off, and the fox later "bagged" for future re-lease. On other days the fox, if he be wily and fleet enough, will get clean away, nor will any true sportsman begrudge him his hard-earned victory.

Last call of the day is the "going home" call. Long and short blasts, lasting as long as the hunts-man's wind, tell that the day's sport is done.

In areas too built-up, broken by fields, and crossed by much-traveled roads to permit the safe hunting of a live fox, drag hunting is resorted to. A bag containing anise seed, or sometimes litter from a fox's den, is dragged over a carefully planned route. Later the hounds are put on the line and the hunt is on. Naturally, this form of hunting lacks the excitement and interest of a real hunt where the cun-ning of the fox is matched against the keen noses of the hounds and the cleverness of the huntsman.

However, as far as the majority of the field is con-cerned, a drag hunt will afford considerable fun and a chance to do some real cross-country riding. The drag line can be laid with a good deal of skill, pro-viding both hounds and field with a good workout. As well as ensuring a trouble-free route for both pack and hunters, it has the advantage of invariably affording a good run (which a fox hunt does not) and one which can be reasonably timed to give just so many hours of sport.

OBLIGATIONS OF THE HUNTER

A word about hunting manners, and the obligation that the members of any hunt owe to the landowners over whose land they ride. In England, where hunt-ing has been so long established, the responsibilities of the hunters are understood and honored. Lacking their tradition, some Americans are prone to disre-gard the rights and feelings of their temporary and sometimes rather reluctant hosts. Remember that for hunting to be maintained, it is necessary to have, besides considerable sums of money, the co-opera-tion of the local landowners. Crops ridden over, fences broken and gates left open do not endear the hunting fraternity to the farming community, and a hunting coat and a fine mount do not automatically make the rider monarch of all he or she surveys. Lack of consideration, and at times, downright rudeness, will undo much patient public relations work on the part of the master of foxhounds and the hunt committee.

Remember, too, that the words of the hunt officials—the master, the huntsman, and the whippers-in—are law. As we have noted, a well-organized hunt costs money, a lot of it. People who hunt regularly are expected to subscribe. A person might figure on supporting the hounds with which he hunts, to the tune, perhaps, of half of what it costs to feed his hunters. Certainly, costs differ in different localities and people wishing to hunt should obtain the details from the hunt secretary.

Participation in a hunt is for members of that hunt and their guests only. Guests should introduce themselves to the master of hounds when they arrive at the meet, and thank him at the end of the day. Besides the tips on behavior mentioned earlier, be sure that you ride in a manner which will not endanger other riders. There may be a certain glamour about breaking one's own neck while out hunting, but there can be very little in breaking someone else's. Don't crowd your neighbor, or follow dangerously close at his heels. Give the rider ahead of you plenty of time to clear a jump before you set your own horse at it, and be sure, if the jump is a "blind" one, that both horse and rider preceding you are well away before clearing the obstacle yourself. Many people and animals have been injured by a rider landing on them while they were rolling on the ground after a spill.

Again, remember to keep well clear of the hounds and the hunt servants. The latter have the right of way, and their orders are to be obeyed. Never try to pass them. Never speak to them during the hunt unless it is absolutely necessary. Do not disturb the master with conversation either, except for a polite "Thank you" at the end of the day.

Foxhunting immediately brings to mind pink-coated gentlemen in hard hats soaring over lofty fences. Actually, many followers of a hunt may be indifferent jumpers, or poorly mounted, or both, yet still enjoy a good day's sport. There are usually gates or openings for those who do not want to ride the fences, and skillful navigating through back lanes and bridle paths may enable the cautious, as well as the more venturesome, to be in at the kill.

DRESS

Last, the matter of dress. The guidebook of the Master of Foxhounds Association includes recommended hunting dress, but each master can make his own rules, and actual practice varies from one hunt to another. New members should ask the hunt secretary for information about the proper attire as well as local protocol.

The following formal hunting dress suggested by the MFA is that which has proved to be most practical, comfortable and comparatively safe over the years, and has therefore become traditional.

a) MASTER—Lady or Gentleman
Coat: Square-cornered, single-breasted frock coat, cut to suit the wishes of the owner. No flaps on waistline, and no pockets on the outside of the coat except an optional whistle pocket. A master who hunts hounds should have five "hunt buttons" in front; a master who does not hunt hounds should have four in front. For either, there should also be two buttons behind and two or three small "hunt buttons" on the cuff of each sleeve. The material should be of melton cloth or heavy twill. Scarlet is the most traditional color for hunting, but if the regular hunt livery is of another color, that color should be used. The collar and facing of hunt coats should be in conformity with the hunt's livery. No master, whipper-in, huntsman or member should wear his or her hunt livery (hunt colors and buttons) at another hunt unless invited to do so. It is correct that they wear a black or dark coat when participating in a joint meet without their own hounds.

Breeches: May be brown or white, of heavy cord, heavy synthetic stretch twill or other heavy material. Lightweight breeches of silk or synthetic knits are not correct.

Cap: Regulation black velvet hunting cap with ribbons down is preferred. A black safety helmet with the chin harness securely fastened is permissible.

Boots: Regulation hunting boots of black calf with brown tops sewn on, well polished, with tabs sewn on but not sewn down. White or brown boot garters (to match breeches) may be worn.

Spurs: Of heavy pattern with moderately short neck and no rowels (light racing spurs not permissible).

Gloves: Heavy wash leather or brown leather. String (rain) gloves may be carried under the girth.

Crop: Regulation hunting crop.

Horn: Regulation hunting horn carried either between buttons of coat or in a leather case fastened on either side of the front of the saddle. *No Horn Carried by Anyone Except Master or Huntsman.*

Wire cutters: May be carried in a leather case attached to the saddle.

Neckwear: Plain white hunting stock neatly tied and fastened with a plain horizontal safety pin.

Flask and sandwich case: Gentlemen may carry either a flask or a sandwich case (or both). Ladies may carry either a sandwich case or a combination flask and sandwich case.

b) HONORARY HUNTSMAN

"Turn out" the same as for MASTER. (Should have five buttons on front of coat.)

c) PROFESSIONAL HUNTSMAN

"Turn out" the same as for MASTER *except* that it should have five buttons on front of coat. *Flask and sandwich case* are not permissible.

d) HONORARY WHIPPER-IN

Same as HONORARY HUNTSMAN *except:*

Couplings: Should carry one set of couplings fastened to a D on off side of saddle.

Coat Buttons: Should have five in front.

e) PROFESSIONAL WHIPPER-IN

Same as HONORARY WHIPPER-IN *except:*

Flask and sandwich case are not permissible.

Coat should have a large "hare pocket" on inside of skirt. There should be five buttons on the front of the coat.

Stirrup leather should be worn outside of coat over right shoulder, under left arm, buckled in front with the point of the strap down.

f) GENTLEMAN MEMBER

Same as MASTER *except* scarlet coat should have rounded corners, *or:*

Coat: A black frock coat (same cut as scarlet coat) or black hunting coat is preferable to a "Shad-belly" coat. Buttons may be the regular buttons adopted by the hunt, but preferably a dark button with hunt initials or crest design in white. There should be three on the front of the coat. It is not customary to wear hunt colors on the collar of a black coat.

Hat: Top hat with scarlet coat, frock coat, or Shad-belly coat (hat guard optional). Bowler hat with formal black hunting coat. A safety helmet in black with chin harness fastened is also permissible.

Boots: Plain black calf without tops worn with black coat. White or brown boot garters (to match breeches) may be worn.

Hair: If long, to be confined neatly.

Neckware: Plain white hunting stock neatly tied and fastened with a plain horizontal safety pin.

Only masters of hounds, huntsmen, whippers-in, honorary secretaries and former masters are entitled to wear a hunting cap without permission.

g) LADY MEMBER (Astride)

Coat: Hunting coat of black, dark blue, gray or colored material, suitably cut, with buttons and collar trimming adopted by the hunt represented.

Breeches: Buff, brown or yellow (not white) cord or heavy synthetic stretch twill (not knitted) material.

Boots: Hunting boots of black calf, with black boot garters and patent leather tops optional.

Hat: Bowler or silk hunting hat (top hat). A safety helmet in black with a chin harness properly fastened is also permissible.

Sandwich Case (or combination *flask and sandwich case*): Optional.

Hair: Should be neatly confined. Hair nets are advisable and correct.

Gloves: Heavy wash leather or brown leather. String (rain) gloves may be carried under the girth.

Spurs: Regular hunting spurs.

Neckwear: Plain white hunting stock neatly tied and fastened with a plain horizontal safety pin. No other jewelry should be visible.

Crop: Light hunting crop with thong.

h) LADY MEMBER (Sidesaddle)

Same as LADY MEMBER (Astride) *except:*

Habits: Dark melton or other cloth, suitably cut.

Veil: Must be worn with a top hat but not with a bowler.

Hat: Top hat (silk hunting hat) to be worn with double-breasted dress hunting coat; bowler (derby) to be worn with plain jacket. Safety headgear in black with chin harness properly fastened is also permissible.

EXCEPTIONS TO THE ABOVE:

i) JUNIORS

It is not necessary for juniors to wear formal attire, as it is often both difficult and expensive to obtain properly fitting formal attire in small sizes. Whichever type of "turn out" is chosen, it should be immaculately clean.

A well-turned-out family group prepared for hunting (S. STROUP, COURTESY OF MRS. R. A. KIMBALL, JR.)

FORMAL ATTIRE: Same as for LADY MEMBER (Astride). Junior colors may be worn according to individual hunt customs.

Hat: A properly fitting safety helmet in black with a chin harness properly fastened at all times is preferable to a plain black velvet cap.

Crop: A lightweight hunting crop with thong, or a short crop.

Neckwear: A plain white stock neatly tied and fastened with a plain horizontal safety pin. Turtleneck shirts should not be worn except by very young children.

Hair: If long, should be neatly confined or braided.

INFORMAL KIT: A tweed coat in a muted color (no reds), tan or brown breeches or jodhpurs, shined brown jodhpur boots, string or brown leather gloves, a plain or colored stock neatly tied and fastened with a plain horizontal safety pin. "Ratcatcher" shirts are also correct with a neckband or neatly tied bow. Turtleneck shirts are for very young children only. Hat as above.

In hunting countries where extremes of temperature regularly occur, modifications to the foregoing suggested formal attire may be in order. Such modifications may be made by the master(s) of individual hunts as needed, particularly in cold weather, when parkas and heavy jackets are very warm when worn over regular coats.

Unfortunately, at some small hunts there is an increasing tendency toward informality in attire without the excuse of extreme weather conditions. Certainly, no one rides better for wearing an expensive scarlet coat, but it seems a great pity to see the traditional hunting costume giving way to an odd assortment of riding togs. There is much to be said for tradition, especially in a sport as old as hunting on horseback. As more young riders mature, perhaps they will find that riding can be as much fun in the attire that custom dictates, with the added fillip of knowing that they are correct. There is a little snob in most of us, and it is a much nicer feeling to find that you are the only one who dressed for the party than to know that you are the only one who didn't!

Chapter 14

PACKING

Camping out has always been a favorite American pastime, and with the advent of easier and quicker travel, and more leisure time, an ever-increasing number take to the hills each year.

Unfortunately, although the United States is very large and rich in forests (70 per cent of the land in New England is covered with woodlands, with 83 per cent in Maine and New Hampshire), the number of camping areas is comparatively small and the easy-to-reach locations are likely to be as crowded as Main Street. But there are still some fairly inaccessible spots, far from the beaten track, where the guest cabin and the restaurant are unknown. Some of these can only be reached on foot or by canoe, but many may be reached on horseback over some of the loveliest and wildest trails in the world.

Increased efforts have been made in recent years to develop and protect our wilderness areas. In 1968,

for example, the federal government created the National Trails System, which protects some 6,000 miles of scenic marked trails and is in the process of completing two major projects: the 2,500-mile Pacific Crest Trail from Mexico to Canada, and the 2,000-mile Appalachian Trail along the eastern mountain belt from Georgia to Maine.

A permit is required for riding through a national park, and sometimes a camping permit as well. Some parks provide horses that can be rented for an hour, a day, or up to several months, with or without the services of an experienced guide. You will be given a list of regulations to be observed when riding through a national park. Maps, guide books and timely information on weather and trail conditions are sometimes available as well. Information may be obtained from the National Park Office or Forest Service in the state where you plan to ride, or from

Saddling up early in the morning at a camp along the trail of the Weminuche Wilderness Area in Colorado (ALBERT MOLDVAY, COURTESY OF U.S.D.A.–FOREST SERVICE)

the Office of Public Affairs, National Park Service, U.S. Department of the Interior, 18th and C Street NW, Washington, DC 20240.

Most trail riders these days put themselves in the hands of professional packers—men whose business it is to outfit vacationers or hunters and see that they are mounted, guided, tented, fed and generally looked after and made as secure and comfortable as possible. On trips such as these, the amount of participation in the actual work of the expedition depends on the age, temperament and sometimes the wealth of the clients. Some revel in helping with camp chores; others won't lift a finger and expect the comforts of a hotel.

If you are interested in packsaddling a wilderness area with a private outfitter, you can obtain a list of these names by writing to the chamber of commerce in the various areas or cities bordering wilderness areas. There is also an affiliate of the American Forestry Association called Trail Riders of the Wilderness (P.O. Box 2417, Washington, DC 20013), which organizes pack trips in different parts of the country.

Some hardier souls prefer to do their own packing. I would advise no one to try this who has not had at least one trip into the wilds with a professionally-run pack train. A little practical experience is worth a good deal of theory. Fancy riding is not usually called for. Most pack-train work is done at the walk, with an occasional trot—and many who go on the professionally-run trail-camping trips have ridden little or not at all. However, for those who plan to go off on their own, familiarity with animals and their handling is a necessity.

A horse can pull a great deal more weight than he can carry on his back. But many times the places we want most to get to aren't exactly suited to wheeled traffic, which is usually why we want to go there in the first place. Few camps in the faraway places can subsist for very long on the supplies that can be carried in on the campers' own backs and so the need for the pack horse.

The ideal pack horse is short-backed, chunky and with sturdy legs. If he is experienced so much the better. A veteran of the trail will take care of himself and his load far better than will a novice, besides being easier to handle. A high-strung, excitable piece of horseflesh can be a nuisance anywhere—on a narrow mountain trail with a bulky load it can lead to a disaster.

While most animals are naturally sure-footed, they like to feel their way over rough going. Don't try to rush them; a horse probably knows better where it is safe for him to put his feet than you do. Also, pack animals develop a sixth sense about judging the width of their loads in relation to trees, boulders, etc. Of course, as the Bible implies, it is pretty difficult to lead a camel through the eye of a needle, and there will be places where things just won't fit and you will have to do a little clearing—but more on that later.

You ought not try to rush things in bad spots, but I don't mean that you should let your train get in the habit of dawdling either. A horse isn't the smartest animal in the world, but he has sense enough not to like to work. You must adjust the pace both as regards terrain and load weight, but after a bit you will find out exactly how much your animal or animals can tote over different kinds of country.

Don't expect your pack animals to carry too much. Most people make the mistake of thinking a horse is stronger than he actually is. While a horse can pull a good amount of weight on wheels, he cannot carry, pound for pound, as much as a man. Generally speaking, horses should never be asked to carry more than 20 or 25 per cent of their body weight. About 180 pounds is tops; if the load can be cut below that, so much the better. The use of light-

Trail Riders' pack train in Flathead National Forest, Montana (K. D. SWAN, COURTESY OF U.S.D.A.–FOREST SERVICE)

Riding through the forest at the start of an eleven-day trip into the Sawtooth Wilderness Area in Idaho (BLUFORD W. MUIR, COURTESY OF U.S.D.A.–FOREST SERVICE)

weight materials such as nylon, foam, aluminum and plastic, as well as modern food-preservation and packing methods such as dehydrated food in packets, can eliminate a lot of unnecessary weight.

The distance of a particular trek depends a great deal on the terrain, but in really rough country most packers figure that fifteen miles a day is about right—that is, if you plan on traveling every day. For one- or two-day hauls you can do a little better.

Since this is not a chapter on camping, it is assumed that all unnecessary items have been excluded from your packing list. If you and your partners are not experienced in camping out, a useful idea is to strip everything down to the bare essentials—and then halve it. Remember that people's ideas of "camping out" differ widely, and one person's "bare essentials" may be another's idea of accommodations at the Waldorf. Remember, too, that your animals can carry just so much, and that if possible it is better to have more horses with lighter loads.

OUTFITTING

Your pack animals and your mounts will need feed enough for a couple of good meals a day, perhaps in the form of hay and grain pellets and alfalfa cubes, fed in nosebags to avoid waste, and if possible supplemented by some grazing to provide more bulk. And don't forget salt blocks. You might take along a horseshoeing outfit—never mind the anvil and the spreading chestnut tree, but include spare shoes, nails, pliers, and maybe a hoof parer and a file. However, there is a fairly new invention, the lightweight urethane Easyboot, which can serve as a spare shoe and eliminates the farrier tools. You will also need plenty of rope, not only for hitches but for tieing, hobbling and more things than you can think of—and have rope for.

There are various kinds of pack saddles, and some packers prefer to devise and make their own. Some are made up of pads or blankets, often of heavy felt with extra padding on each end. Over these extra thick pads go wooden frames, curved to fit the back, and joined at the sides or bottom by wood cross-pieces or panels. Straps are fastened on either side, back and front, to take the breast collar and the breeching. Almost all pack saddles call for these two items: the breast strap to take the strain off the girths going uphill, and the breech strap to relieve the strain when going down. This last should have a strap across the back from side to side to keep the breeching from slipping down.

Some saddles use only one girth, relying on the breast straps and breech straps to keep the saddle in place; others use two, or even three. The well-known sawbuck rig, often seen on Western trails, has two. This saddle consists of two stout wooden X-frames joined by two panels fastened to the undersides of the bottom legs. These panels should be rounded on the ends and bent or shaved so that they curve slightly away from the animal's back. This is to avoid digging into the animal's back. They should also be sheepskin-lined. A thick saddle pad is put on before the saddle and should be long enough so there are three or four inches to spare on either end of the panels.

The two leather rigging straps crisscross around the bucks and down over the panels where they end in sizable rings. A cross strap connects these on either side.

The girths (cinches), which should be wide, are attached to and tightened by straps (latigos) which pass through the rings of the rigging straps. These can be knotted as on the old Western saddles, or buckled—either way as long as they can be readily adjusted and won't slip.

Personally, I am all for buckles—and also for straps, as opposed to short rope slings and hitches. You can't throw a diamond hitch with a strap and there are other places where rope is indispensable; but where possible, I will take a good stout canvas or leather strap with buckles, snaps, hooks or what have you, over a lot of fancy ropework, any day.

The best way to pack is in panniers. These containers (boxes, baskets, drums or whatever) are slung on either side of the pack saddle, usually with one of the more bulky but lighter items—a bedroll or tent—on top, and the whole secured with some kind of a hitch.

Panniers can be made of plywood, canvas, leather or a number of other materials, the lighter and

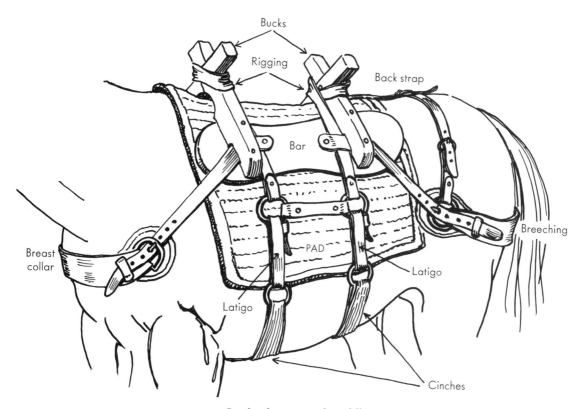

Sawbuck-type pack saddle

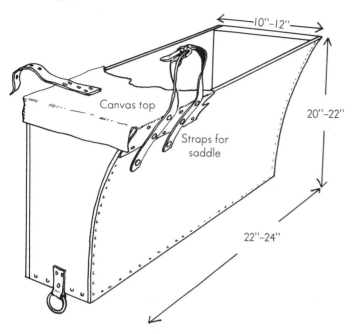

Pannier, plywood front and back

stronger the better. One piece of sheet aluminum for back, bottom and front, with sides put on with bolts or rivets, will make a strong light job that will take a lot of abuse and last a lifetime. While speaking of aluminum, there are sometimes containers of various shapes and sizes to be had in army surplus stores. These can be purchased at a fraction of their original cost, and while poking around you will find a wealth of straps, bags, knapsacks, webbing, buckles, snaps, rings and whatnot, some of which may prove exceedingly useful.

Panniers are usually a little longer than they are deep, about twenty-four inches long, eight or ten inches wide at the bottom and twenty to twenty-two inches high. Sometimes they are made with curves to fit the curve of the saddle. Even though a tarp is thrown over the whole load before the hitch is made, the panniers should have tops, if only of canvas.

The most important thing about making up a load is to keep it balanced. An unbalanced load is not only hard on the animal, but nothing, even if you cinch up tight enough to break his ribs, is going to stop that load from twisting sooner or later.

Joe Back in his fine little book *Horses, Hitches and Rocky Trails* recommends the purchase of a spring scale, the kind that will take weights up to 100–150 pounds. Then, when you pack your panniers, weigh them, and if they don't match up, switch things around a bit until they do.

The amount of supplies to be carried, and how

many horses you will need, will, of course, depend on the number in the party, length of trip and degree of luxury you demand. Two pack animals, carrying some 350 pounds, should do two campers for ten days.

If 350 pounds sounds like a lot, perhaps you have forgotten about oats. When you start out, one quarter of your available horsepower is carrying fuel only. Of course, you will be riding lighter each day by about twenty-five pounds unless you are on a hunting trip, in which case you will be coming back loaded too—you hope.

Don't count on your mount carrying too much. Besides yourself he will probably have saddlebags, rope, a rifle if you are hunting, and an ax. You will be live weight, which is easier to carry than the dead weight of the pack loads. Also you will be dismounting every so often, and will probably lead him over some of the rough spots. All the same, if you pack saddlebags, keep them light.

As mentioned before, you may have to do a little clearing—of deadfalls across the trail, or a couple of saplings a bit too close together. That is why the axes should be on the saddles and your saw should be strapped on the load of the lead horse, and where it is easy to get at.

A rough breakdown on supplies for two people for ten days works out about as follows:

Oats: five pounds per day per horse (two mounts plus two pack horses) (This is presupposing that there is some grazing where you camp.)	200 pounds
Hobbles, spare rope, stock salt, etc.	10 pounds
Small tent, bedrolls, mattresses (inflatable)	50 pounds
Tools, including a couple of spare horseshoes	10 pounds
Flashlights, bug bomb, first aid kit (including snake-bite kit), lantern, kerosene	10 pounds
Cooking and mess gear	5 pounds
Food: two and a half pounds per person per day	50 pounds
Extra clothing, toilet gear, etc., ten pounds per person	20 pounds
Miscellaneous	5 pounds

The oats are bulkier than feed pellets—a bushel (of oats, thirty-two pounds) takes up one and a quarter cubic feet of space—and you will need over six bushels. Use four sacks, feed out of each alternating, and be sure your sacks are in good shape. A little trickle of oats may be handy if you get lost and have to backtrack but it's an expensive way of trail blazing.

If you plan to do much camping, it might pay to make or have made four cylindrical canvas or nylon bags, each with loops or snaps or both for the pack saddle and a zipper opening in one end. Well made of good canvas, they would stand up to a lot of abuse, be easy to stow both as to the load and in camp, and be easy to feed from. A twenty-four-inch bag fifteen inches in diameter will hold about two and a quarter cubic feet or just over one and three-quarter bushels. Number them, so you will know which one you fed from last. A collapsible vinyl bucket is handy for watering horses as well as carrying water for camp use.

What between bags, containers, and panniers you should be able to keep a pretty neat camp. The older I get, the stronger my feelings about such things. Some people can turn a campsite or a boat cabin into a cross between a secondhand shop and a slum. Personally I like to be able to find what's wanted without sorting through a pile of junk, or falling over it in the dark.

LOADING

If panniers are used, and equal-sized feed bags, blanket rolls, and so forth, then the final lashing-up is made a lot simpler. Objects of diverse shapes and sizes pose more of a problem, but by using enough rope, a diamond hitch and a little care even the most awkward loads may be made secure. Nets are sometimes used. The advantage of the diamond hitch (there are several kinds) over a net, which it strongly resembles, is that the net is more or less rigid, while the "meshes" of the diamond hitch are adjusted to varied shapes of the load.

I prefer manila for all such lashings and slings, picket ropes and the like, and it is easier to work with than cotton, which is hard to untie after being pulled tight, especially when wet. Also, manila is easier to splice than cotton (and if you don't know how to splice you had better learn, because it is next to impossible to lash up a load with knotted rope). The Forest Service, however, recommends polypropylene rope for hitches since it is lighter and more durable than hemp; but hemp or cotton is recommended for picket and lead ropes.

In any case, you will need a lot of rope. A diamond hitch calls for some forty or forty-five feet. For slings, which are used in case panniers are not available or are impractical, ⅜-inch-diameter rope should be used. For the lashings use ⅝- or ¾-inch-diameter rope.

HANDLING THE TRAIN

How the pack train is to be handled when on the move depends on the traveling conditions. When the going is tough—mostly up and down, trails narrow and winding, and streams rocky and deep; or on mountain slopes where loose scree makes the footing tricky—the pack animals should be loose and allowed to pick their own way over and around the obstructions. The conditions which necessitate their being driven rather than led, plus the fact that horses are generally gregarious animals and prefer to go along with the crowd, will tend to keep them from straying. Usually a string can be driven across a bad bit of country without the necessity for much herding.

On good trails the usual practice is to tie the animals together, with the halter rope from one fastened to the saddle of the one ahead or tied to its tail. The halter rope is not fastened directly but is attached to a short piece of light rope which will break in case a horse slips, shies or bolts. The break line is in turn attached to a ring on the saddle. The halter rope on the lead horse is held by the rider. If not actually held in the hand this rope should never be attached firmly to the rider's saddle but held by a single turn around the saddle horn, so that it can be instantly let slip in an emergency.

Packers who handle large numbers of animals usually prefer to limit the number of animals in a single group to three or four, with a rider to each string. As most campers will probably not have more than two pack animals each, and often only one, the long pack train will not be a problem.

Tie the animals just far enough apart so that there is no danger of the lead horse kicking the animal behind. On the other hand, if too much rope is allowed the horses will be continually getting the rope around their feet.

When loading and unloading packs tie each animal's head high to a stout tree with a short halter. Never leave loaded animals standing around in camp longer than you can help. They should be unpacked and unsaddled as promptly as possible. They are then secured by picketing or hobbling.

Hobbles are leather or canvas straps made to

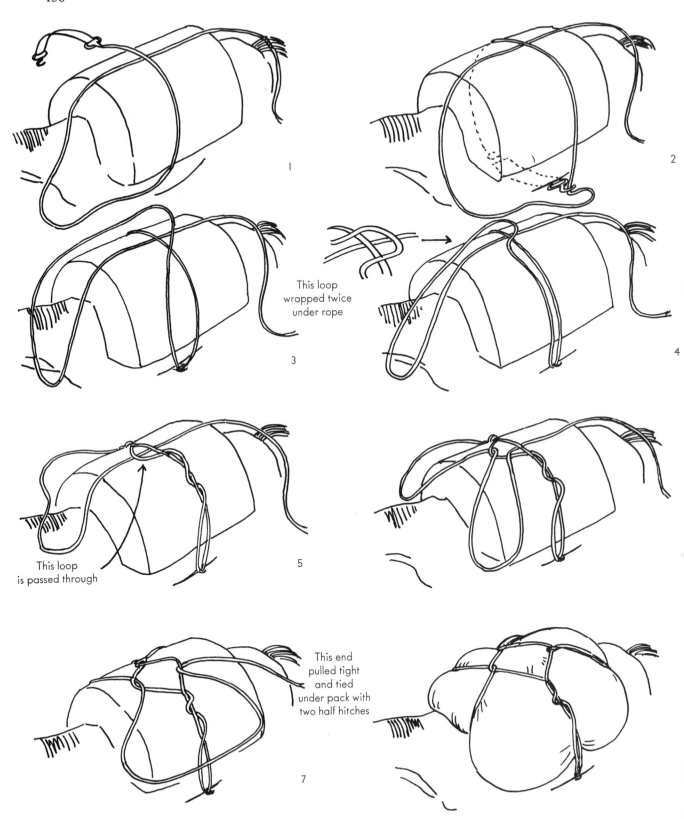

1

2

This loop
wrapped twice
under rope

3

4

This loop
is passed through

5

This end
pulled tight
and tied
under pack with
two half hitches

7

The diamond hitch

buckle around the feet and joined by a short strap or chain, much like a pair of handcuffs. They may be made to fit the two front legs, or a longer chain may be used and the forefoot and hind foot on one side may be hobbled. The use of the hobble is, of course, not to keep the animals stationary, but to restrict their movements, while still permitting them to find grazing, so that they cannot stray too far from the camp.

Some animals get very clever at moving in hobbles, and can stray quite a distance during the night. It is usual to hang cowbells to the necks of hobbled horses, so that they can be located easily.

A picket rope should be about thirty-five feet long, five-eighths or three-quarter inches in diameter. One end is secured to a strap around one of the horse's front feet, or around his neck. The other end is fastened to a picket pin—a stake driven well down into the ground. Because you may have to ride after strays you should always picket at least one riding horse, even if you hobble the rest. If the grazing is good and if you are lucky enough to camp in a box canyon or some kind of natural corral, you may be able to picket one and bell the rest and let them loose. When you stake out an animal, be sure that there is nothing within the area of the circle that he can wind the picket rope around. If there is, he will manage to do so. The picketed animals will have to be watered, and all should have a grain feeding before being turned loose.

If a permanent camp is to be made where there is good pasture, and the pack animals are not worked, the grain ration can be eliminated.

All this sounds like a lot of work—and it is—but it can be very rewarding, too. With pack horse and camping gear you can strike off the beaten path and, within an hour or two, begin to recapture some of the feelings of the mountain men, who first saw the grandeur of our Western mountains almost a century and a half ago.

Chapter 15

ENDURANCE AND COMPETITIVE TRAIL RIDING

Although the sport of long-distance riding is relatively new, the activity is ancient, even if the original goal was to transport armies, passengers or mail pouches rather than to win silver buckles and championship points. The riders of the Pony Express, for example, set some amazing long-distance speed records. But this was, of course, a commercial—and, sad to say, unprofitable—enterprise.

Closer to the modern sport were the long-distance rides of the U.S. Cavalry before World War II. The army used to condition its horses to cover up to 300 miles per week, carrying 200 to 245 pounds, and competitive rides were held as a selection test for equine cavalry candidates. One of them, starting in northern Vermont and ending at the Washington Monument in Washington, D.C., may have been the inspiration for the Vermont 100-Mile Three-Day Trail Ride, which was inaugurated by the Green

Mountain Horse Association in 1936 and is still a major trail-riding event.

But the individual who is generally considered to be the father of competitive long-distance riding is Wendell Robie, a California breeder of Arabian horses, who in 1955 founded the Western States Trail Ride, a 100-mile one-day ride from Lake Tahoe, across the old Sierra Nevada Pony Express route, to Auburn, California. The original idea was simply to complete the ride, which is a considerable achievement since it covers a wide range of elevation and terrain, including the extremes of snow at Squaw Pass to 100° heat in El Dorado Canyon. It is still considered the toughest ride in the country. In 1959, the Tevis Cup was first awarded to the rider with the fastest time, and since 1964 the Haggin Cup has rewarded the rider finishing among the top ten with the horse in best condition. Similar awards are offered by the increasing number of endurance rides that have been patterned after Wendell Robie's invention.

Today, numerous regional clubs and two major organizations, the American Endurance Ride Conference (6222 Thornton Avenue, Newark, CA 94560) and the North American Trail Riding Conference (1995 Day Road, Gilroy, CA 95020), sponsor and supervise long-distance rides in many parts of the country. Another good source of information is Trail Blazer Magazine (P.O. Box 1855, Paso Robles, CA 93446).

There are two distinct types of competitive long-distance rides: endurance rides and competitive trail rides. Both of them require well-conditioned horses and riders, both are controlled and judged by veterinarians at checkpoints along the way, where the horses' pulse and respiration—and sometimes temperature as well—are checked for signs of stress, unfit horses being forbidden to continue. Both are, of course, long-distance competitive rides, but their rules and goals are different.

The endurance horse must travel farther and faster, since an endurance ride is usually twenty-five, fifty, or a hundred miles long and is more like a race (especially the twenty-five-miler). The winner is the horse (the rider, actually) that covers the route in the fastest time while remaining sound throughout the ride as well as the morning after. The twenty-five-mile contest is often won in a total elapsed riding time of about one and a half hours; the fifty-miler in about four and a half hours; and the one hundred-miler in some eleven hours of actual riding time. There are usually two one-hour check stops and two spot checks during the fifty-miler, and three one-hour stops and several spot checks during the one hundred-mile ride. These may vary according to the weather and ground conditions of each individual event. Endurance riders may be assisted by a pit crew at the stops, and they are permitted to dismount and lead their horses (or be led by them uphill) if they wish. There are few formal rules—only eight of them for the Tevis Cup—but it is a more complicated, more competitive, more strategic and tougher contest than a trail ride.

A competitive trail ride is generally slower (four

Rhobamine, owned and ridden by Karen Petty, during a Western competitive trail ride (LOUISE L. SERPA)

to nine miles per hour), shorter (from twenty to a hundred miles), and may be spread over two or three days. It is definitely not a race. There are maximum and minimum time limits, generally with a thirty-minute difference, and a competitor can be penalized for going too fast or too slow. Unlike endurance rides, the riders may not be assisted and can advance only when mounted. The winners are determined by judges (some of them hidden at points along the trail) on the basis of condition, soundness, trail manners, carriage, and so forth, the idea being to select the ideal trail horse. Each ride has its own rules and prize list, which includes awards according to sex, weight and age of horse and rider, breed, sometimes even for such distinctions as having come from the greatest distance.

Needless to say, both of these types of competition require a fit rider and a well-conditioned horse, but not necessarily an expensive one. Beauty doesn't count at all, and conformation is important only in the sense that a well-built horse moves better and tires less quickly than does a poorly built animal. Full and part-Arabians dominate the lists of endurance winners. Part-Thoroughbreds, Morgans, Appaloosas and Quarter Horses possess suitable aptitudes too. But any horse over five years of age that is sound, has stamina, is well built, willing, properly conditioned, with good lungs, heart, legs, feet, and is possessed of an efficient ground-covering trot and a long, free-striding walk can compete honorably in a competitive trail ride.

You do not need expensive equipment or attire either, and entry fees are modest. Many competitors ride in blue jeans (with pantyhose underneath to avoid chafing), a long-sleeved shirt and a sweater or windbreaker. Endurance riders prefer reinforced running shoes or lightweight hiking boots to riding boots and breeches. Hard plastic helmets are popular because they can also be used as a bucket for cooling off the horse more quickly than with a sponge. Comfort and adaptability to varied weather conditions are more important than stylishness.

Despite the advantages of lightweight stock saddles and McClellans, the trend is toward flatter types, with stirrups adjusted fairly long. A number of manufacturers make a special endurance saddle, a modified McClellan type, which is the choice of many regular competitors. Whatever the model, it should be well broken in, comfortable for both horse and rider; care should be taken to detect and correct pressure points during training, because saddle sores spotted at the check stops are sure to lead to disqualification.

Some riders tailing their horses on the rocky trail up the Massanutten Mountains in Virginia (WINANTS)

Folded woolen blankets are often used instead of fleece or synthetic saddle pads, since they are cooler. Woolen or fleece covers on tack wherever possible help reduce chafing. String girths are most popular for the same reason and should be adjusted fairly loosely. A breast collar and crupper strap are indispensable, since there are bound to be steep uphill and downhill portions on the trail. As for bitting, some riders, particularly in the West, prefer hackamores or Bosals for longer distances; many use a snaffle, and a few experienced horses are even ridden in a halter.

Equipment varies according to the event and whether or not assistance is permitted. It may include tack replacements, water buckets, extra horseshoes or Easyboots, feed for the horse and snacks for the rider, bandages and liniments, electrolytes (mineral supplements), a stopwatch, grooming tools, sponges and a knife and flashlight (since you may

Midway of a hundred-mile ride, a mandatory one-hour stop for rest and a veterinary inspection—and for some a cooling swim (WINANTS)

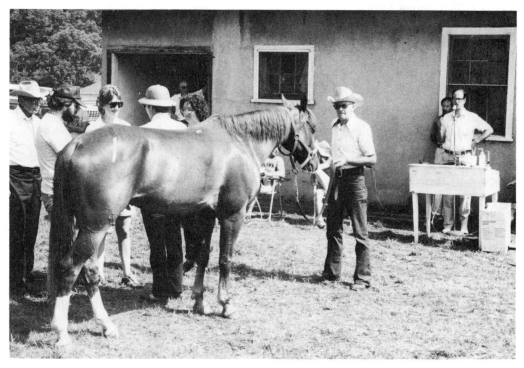

On the morning following a hundred-mile race, Buckshot is given a final check by veterinarians. At right of center is Dr. Matthew Mackay-Smith (WINANTS)

have to ride in the dark). The Western State Trail Ride, for example, starts at 5 A.M.; the contestants leave in heats of ten at two-minute intervals, and the first rider to cross the finish line usually arrives at nightfall.

Good horsemanship is just as important in long-distance riding as in other equestrian sports, if only because a good rider tires a horse less than a bad one. Careful planning and a certain amount of strategy during the ride are also necessary.

The conditioning program starts at least three months before a horse's first event, which should be a one-day trail ride, selected more as a part of training than with the intention of trying to win. When a controlled feeding program and gradually increased amounts of walking and trotting have developed the horse's stamina to the point where he can comfortably cover twenty miles in four or five hours, he should be ready for his first competition. Preparation also includes practice in riding with other horses and over varied terrain (including hard roads, steep hills, fording streams, crossing bridges), rating speeds, and developing a perfect understanding of the horse mentally and physically in order to recognize the first signs of fatigue or stress. He should be free from worms (but not wormed less than two weeks before a competition); vaccinated against tetanus, equine flu and sleeping sickness, and whatever other procedures are recommended for the region in which the event takes place. These are the basic essentials.

Experienced competitors develop quite sophisticated methods of training and conditioning.

There are also techniques and strategies involved in the ride itself: becoming familiar with the trail beforehand as far as possible; constantly adjusting the pace to the terrain, the weather, and the horse's condition; gaining time by knowing how to negotiate tight turns on woodland trails, for example; limiting fatigue by knowing how to handle steep hills, when to rest, when to water the horse inside and outside (dehydration being a constant risk during the warm weather months, when most of these events are scheduled); alternating the posting diagonal at the trot and limiting periods of gallop, a far more tiring gait; providing electrolytes to replace minerals lost in sweat; and giving the horse appropriate care at the timed checkpoints.

The friendly atmosphere of these events and of the awards ceremony and dinner afterwards is very different from the formal traditions and increasing professionalism of the horse-show world, which may be one of the reasons for the popularity of the sport and the enthusiasm of its supporters. Among these are many veterinarians who first became involved in endurance and trail riding in a professional capacity and then as active competitors. Certainly the sport provides a unique opportunity to observe the horse's reaction to stress and has already contributed much to the development of improved methods of equine nutrition and conditioning.

Chapter 16

COMBINED TRAINING

Combined training is an equestrian sport that originated in Europe as a military competition for officers' chargers, with the purpose of testing a horse's precision and obedience in performing on the parade grounds (by means of a dressage test); its speed, boldness and endurance on the battlefield (in a cross-country event); and its ability to recuperate quickly after strenuous activities (a veterinary inspection followed by a stadium jumping course). Since 1912, it has been one of the three Olympic equestrian disciplines, along with dressage and jumping. At that time, it was called the "complete test," or sometimes simply "the military."

After most of the world's cavalries were motorized during World War II, the sport became more widespread as a civilian activity. In the United States it is governed by the U.S. Combined Training Association (USCTA, 292 Bridge Street, South Hamilton, MA 01982) as well as the AHSA. Many local and regional organizations sponsor events of various degrees of difficulty which are listed in the USCTA and AHSA calendars and are advertised in horse magazines as well as locally. It has become increasingly popular among athletic riders whose horses may lack the scope to succeed in Open Jumping, or the beauty to win conformation classes, and who seek an energetic sport that is not devoid of thrills. A number of young women riders have proven that "the fair sex" is not necessarily the weaker one by excelling in eventing—even at the international level.

Horses over five years of age, of any breed or conformation, can compete in combined training events as long as they are sound, brave, well conditioned and well trained. You'll see Arabians, Appaloosas, and all kinds of mixed breeds, although whole or part-Thoroughbreds dominate advanced competitions, perhaps because their conformation

Michael Plumb and Better and Better during the dressage phase of a Three-Day Event (SUE MAYNARD)

Two-time World Champion Bruce Davidson riding Might Tango on a Three-Day cross-country course (SUE MAYNARD)

permits them to produce a good dressage performance, in addition to their inherited speed and courage.

Different levels of difficulty provide events for a wide range of capabilities: pre-training, training, young riders (ages 15 to 20), preliminary, intermediate and, finally, advanced, which is the standard for international and Olympic competitions. All of these categories may be broken down even further, according to the age of the rider or the experience of the horse.

There are four types of official events: (1) the combined test, a one-day event consisting of a dressage test and a jumping competition; (2) the horse trial, generally a one-day event but sometimes two, consisting of a dressage test, cross-country, and jumping (the order of the last two sometimes being reversed); (3) the Two-Day Event, consisting of a dressage test, jumping, and an endurance competition composed of four phases: two portions of roads and tracks separated by a steeplechase and, finally, a cross-country course; (4) the Three-Day Event, consisting of dressage, four-phase endurance, and stadium jumping, in that order.

Three-Day Events are the most difficult and hardest on the horse. The advanced cross-country course of the endurance test, for example, following up to 10 miles of roads and tracks and a steeplechase, is up to 8,106.54 yards long and includes twenty to twenty-five obstacles or more, with a required average speed of 623 yards per minute. But the demands of many One-Day Events remain well within the means of most good riding horses.

Whatever the event, the scoring is the same: Penalties incurred during each phase are totaled, and the horse with the lowest number of penalty points is the winner. In case of a tie, the best score in the cross-country event determines the winner.

While it doesn't necessarily take a lot of money to compete in combined training events, and though you don't need an expensive horse, you must be prepared to make a big outlay of time and energy. A lot more of both is spent during preparation than in actual competition. Due to the effort involved, it is customary to compete in a One-Day Event no more than once every three weeks; advanced Three-Day Events are so taxing that one or two per season should be considered the maximum.

When a horse has been well conditioned and well trained (which we'll come to later), he can be entered in a local combined test or horse trial at the pre-training level. This relatively modest beginning is far less formidable than the international events you may have seen in person or on television, but it is still an all-round test of a horse's capabilities. For example, at the pre-training level the dressage test consists of performing one of the AHSA training-level tests, which generally consist of walk, trot and canter in both directions of a rectangular area, circles 21.88 yards in diameter, and changes of lead across the diagonal. The horse should be relaxed, obedient and proficient in the different movements, but not overtrained in the test as a whole, because anticipation of any movement will be scored against him. On the other hand, the rider must know the test thoroughly.

The pre-training cross-country course is seldom longer than one mile, including some fifteen numbered obstacles not exceeding two feet nine inches, which are more varied and natural than the show ring kind. The required speed is usually 383 yards per minute, overtime incurring penalties. The terrain is apt to include fields, woods, ditches and water; the course is marked with red flags on the right, white flags on the left. Knockdowns are not penalized and are infrequent anyway, because the obstacles are, in principle, solid. The only penalties are for falls of horse and/or rider within a penalty zone (an area surrounding each obstacle), refusals (three at the same obstacle causing disqualification), going off course (unless rectified), moving backwards in a penalty zone, and failing to complete the course within the time limit (which is generous at this level).

Pre-training stadium jumping should also be within the scope of any good riding horse. The fences of the normal show ring type do not exceed two feet nine inches, and the test is scored as in a normal horse show jumper class. This score weighs less heavily in the final tabulation than do the other two, the cross-country score always being the most important.

How do you start once you have decided that you'd like to compete in combined training events?

First of all, you must get your horse in excellent condition, which means no fat, no worms, and a progressive, well-planned program of feed and flat work to build up muscles, wind and stamina. He must be taught the movements of the dressage test. He must be able to jump three feet with ease. He must be accustomed to riding over varied terrain, jumping any obstacles he may encounter willingly and boldly. He should be able to gallop twice the distance of the cross-country course of his level without showing fatigue or stress.

The actual training program has to be made to order for each individual horse, taking into account his

Torrance Watkins and Red Door clearing a water obstacle on a cross-country course (SUE MAYNARD)

age, ability, experience and temperament. In all cases, consistency leading to slow but steady progress is the best policy. This is not a sport for weekend riders! It generally takes several months to prepare a horse for his first combined training event, at least six months for a green horse. Some excellent programs are outlined in specialized books. One of the best is the chapter written by Jack Le Goff, coach of the U.S.E.T. Three-Day team, in *The U.S. Equestrian Team Book of Riding,* ed. William Steinkraus (New York: Simon & Schuster, 1976). He introduced to America the technique of "interval training," which was developed in Scandinavia as a training method for human runners and was subsequently adopted by horsemen. Without going into the complicated biochemical explanation for its effectiveness, the traditional program of increasingly long gallops is replaced by brief timed periods of fast work, interrupted by progressively shortened periods of recovery, the purpose being to condition the horse while avoiding stress or injury resulting from fatigue.

The rider may need conditioning too, as well as practice in developing a sense of pace, since the tests all have to be ridden at a specific average speed, and it is important to be able to "rate" the horse over the cross-country course. A sense of pace comes more naturally to some riders than to others. The best way to develop it is to ride a measured track with a stopwatch in order to acquire the "feel" of different speeds.

The competition itself requires mental as well as physical effort. For example, the official walk of the cross-country course is usually scheduled the day before the event. Experienced riders walk it at least three times, not only in order to become familiar with the course but also to plan the best way to negotiate each obstacle, since there is often an option between a short route requiring a bold jump and an easier jumping situation over a longer route, which therefore takes more time. They try to plan alternative strategies in case something goes wrong—for instance, if the footing deteriorates, the horse tires, the approach is wrong or the weather changes. Speed being a vital factor in the score, they try to spot portions of the track where seconds can be gained with minimum risk and effort, and those places where speed should be sacrificed in favor of safety.

Assuming that the cross-country event has been completed successfully, the rider must turn his thoughts to the veterinary inspection and give his horse the utmost care to help him recuperate from his efforts before tackling the stadium jumping test. He must also walk the jumping course, measuring the strides between fences, and so forth, as in a normal jumping class, and then prepare his horse for this final phase. This generally involves warm-up movements designed to gather the horse in order to produce a more rounded, cleaner jump (knockdowns now being penalized) than during the cross-country trek, which always tends to make the horse more extended and jump flatter.

There is no reason to be intimidated by the demands of combined training. At the highest level it produces some of the finest horses and riders in the world, but competitions at the lower levels remain within the capacity of any serious rider and good horse. As Michael Page, one of the most successful Olympic Three-Day riders, has said, ''Successful Event riding depends not so much on the extraordinary athletic capabilities of the rider as on his knowledge and understanding of the capabilities of his horse and his ability to prepare and use them.'' Most horsemen agree that of all the equestrian sports, perhaps only competitive long-distance riding develops such a complete understanding between a rider and his horse.

Tad Coffin and Bally Cor during the stadium jumping phase of a Three-Day Event (SUE MAYNARD)

Chapter 17

POLO

Polo is not only one of the fastest and most exciting games, it is also one of the oldest. It is supposed to have originated in Persia, and records reveal that it was played as early as 600 B.C., although there is reason to believe it was played long before this. From Persia it spread westward to Turkey and eastward to the high steppes of Central Asia and the hill country of the Himalayas. The name comes from the Tibetan word for ball, "pulu." It was known in China and was introduced into India during the reign of the Mogul emperors.

Old Persian drawings show that there were many similarities between the ancient game and the modern version. The mallets used, the goal posts, the bandaged legs of the ponies, all were much the same as we know them today. Although originally the game was pretty much of a free-for-all, it gradually became more organized. In the tenth century the first recorded "international" match was held, when the

Iranians played the Turanians. At this time the number on each team had been set at seven.

By the sixteenth century the field had been standardized at 300 yards by 170 yards and the number of players had dropped to four. However, rules seemed to have differed from country to country and from time to time. In India, at least in the early days of the game, there were numerous players on each side and no teamwork, each man attempting to score for himself.

The game naturally attracted the attention of the horse-loving English officers and officials stationed in India. Teams were organized and the First European Polo Club founded in 1859. In 1869 an article in a magazine aroused the interest of an officer of the Tenth Hussars, then stationed in England. His fellow officers took up the game enthusiastically and other cavalry regiments followed suit. In 1871 a regimental match was played between the Tenth Hussars and the Ninth Lancers, with few or no rules and eight players per side. It must have been a wild melee, and decidedly unscientific, but it evidently appealed to the hard-riding cavalrymen, for the popularity of the game spread from regiment to regiment and by 1873 the game was well enough thought of to be adopted by the fashionable Hurlingham Club. In 1874 the Hurlingham Polo Club was formed. Rules were drawn up and the number of players on a team reduced to five. In 1882 the rules were revised again, the number of players being reduced from five to four.

Polo got its start in America when James Gordon Bennett brought mallets and balls from England and introduced the game to his friends. The members of the Meadow Brook Club of Long Island took an interest in the game and soon there were several polo clubs in the East.

In 1879 a game between the Westchester Polo Club and the Queens County Club drew ten thousand spectators. In the eighties polo invaded the Ivy League, and during the same period began to be played in the United States Army.

Rules were still few and far between, and the length of time of the periods, or ''chukkars,'' was not limited. The game went to the team scoring two out of three goals. To keep up interest in the game, it was found necessary before many years had gone by to adopt some form of handicapping. Under the system adopted, a handicapping committee rates each player from zero to ten according to his worth in goals to his team. This handicap, which may be low at the start of his career, goes up as his ability increases. When a match is arranged, the handicaps of the four players are added up and compared with the total for the other team. The weaker team is allowed the number of goals between their aggregate handicaps and those of the opposing team.

This system enables even beginners to play with experienced players and weak teams to compete with crack outfits. Open tournaments and international polo are played without handicaps.

The modern outdoor polo field is 300 yards long and 200 yards wide, if unboarded; and 300 by 160 yards if boarded (boards are not over eleven inches high). As ponies frequently ride over the lines, there is a safety zone of some ten yards on each side and thirty yards on each end.

The goal posts are set eight yards apart, are at least ten feet high, and made to break off if crashed into by horse or rider. The four-and-one-half-ounce ball is made of willow or bamboo root, and does not exceed three and one-quarter inches in diameter. The

stick, or mallet, made of cane, is from 48 to 52 inches long, with a narrow wooden head set on at a slight angle.

The object of the game is, of course, to drive the ball between an opponent's goal posts. The officials in a match consist of two umpires and a referee. In the ordinary small game there is usually only a single referee.

The game is divided into periods, or chukkars. Match play calls for eight chukkars of seven minutes each with four-minute rest intervals after each, with ten minutes at half time. However, a less number of chukkars may be agreed on, as may an increase in time for intervals. Six chukkars is the usual game today, enabling a player to get by with a three-pony string.

Two players, Nos. 1 and 2, are forwards; Nos. 3 and 4 play the back position. These positions are flexible, and if a man playing No. 4 has possession of the ball and is in good position to dash forward to attack and possibly score, he does so, and one of his teammates automatically fills his position until he returns to it.

The game is commenced by the umpire bowling the ball underhand between the opposing teams, each team being on its own side of the center line. The ball is put into play in the same way after each goal is scored.

A ball knocked over the side lines is bowled back into the field by the umpire at the same point where it crossed the line.

Polo is a rough game. It is played at speed, and the combined weight of man and mount totals well over a half a ton. Collisions are frequent and many of the rules of the game deal with right-of-way and dangerous riding. Riding off, that is the forcing of a rider off his course and away from the ball, is permissible and forms a considerable part of team play. However, it must be done in such a way and from such an angle that there is a minimum of danger of bringing a pony down by collision or swerving in front of it. Using a mallet in such a way as to entangle the opposing pony's legs is also forbidden. Such safety-rules-of-the-road are rigidly enforced, and penalties involving free hits at the goal from specified distances are assessed against the team committing the foul.

Indoor polo is played with three-man teams; an arena 300 feet by 150 feet, with goal posts ten feet apart, is standard. If a smaller arena is used goal posts are closer together, but never less than eight feet apart. The ball is soft, not less than four and a quarter or more than four and a half inches in diam-

The "good old days" of polo on Long Island in the twenties and thirties (PHOTO TRENDS, INC.)

eter, and weighs a minimum of six ounces. Regulation games are of four seven-minute periods, with four-minute intervals, and a ten-minute interval at half time.

In the early days polo was played on whatever ponies were available locally. The enterprising Hussars who were first to play the game in England used cavalry horses at first, but it soon became evident that such large and relatively clumsy horses were not suitable to a sport demanding agility and quick changes of pace and direction. Irish ponies under fourteen hands were sent for, and were found to be an improvement.

Speed in ponies was not considered a great virtue in those days. The game was much slower than at present, teamwork was almost nonexistent, and maneuverability and endurance were the criteria. The Anglo-Indians played a faster game, and the native ponies were speedier, being likely to have a high

percentage of Arab blood. It was not long before it became obvious that the somewhat hit-or-miss method of obtaining suitable mounts would have to give way to something better.

The Polo Pony Society was formed in England, and issued Volume I of the Society's studbook in 1894. Thoroughbreds, Arabians, and some of the native British ponies were listed. Of these last, the Welsh was the favorite, both in view of conformation, hardiness and speed.

As time went on, a larger breed of pony was introduced into the game. At the beginning of the Anglo-Indian polo many of the Indians played on ponies no larger than twelve hands. This was too small for the heftier English, who preferred mounts thirteen or 13.2 hands. In 1888 the standard was raised to 13.3 and later to 14.2. That height had already been exceeded in England; and after the First World War, the height measurement was dropped alto-

Collisions between two horses and their riders, both going at high speed, and together weighing a ton and a quarter, can be a dangerous matter. Consequently most rules in polo have to do with right-of-way and safe riding. The decision as to what is safe riding and what is not is up to the judgment of the referee. For instance, in situation A, if White crosses a couple of pony lengths ahead of Black, who is proceeding slowly, there is no danger of collision, and no foul is called. However, if the pace is fast, White may not cross the line of the ball (and therefore presumably the line of Black's approach) at even the slightest angle. This applies both to crossing from in front or coming up from behind (see B and C)

A

If the pace of both horses is slow, or if Black is proceeding slowly, and White, fast, so as to clear, then there is no danger of collision, and no foul. This is true also of situations B and C. Calling a foul depends on both speed and distance. If the pace were fast, a foul would be called on White in all three instances

B

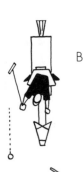

C

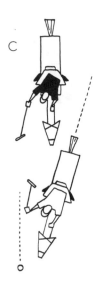

Even if angle is slight, if pace is fast a dangerous situation is created

D

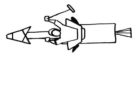

White may legitimately cut in from an angle and play the ball as long as he does not cross in front of Black

E

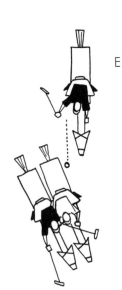

Here White is being forced into the path of oncoming Black. Foul is on Black for creating a dangerous situation

F

White may ride Black off the ball and take possession

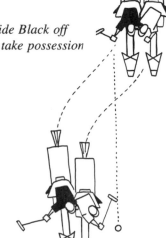

Polo fouls

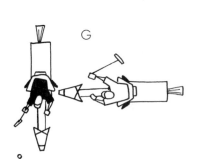
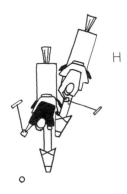

Bumping—White may bump Black at right angles, as in G, if pace is slow. If pace is fast, the angle must not exceed 45 degrees, as in H, where White may be at full gallop but angle is small, so there is little danger. However, if White were riding off Black, and at the moment of impact the shoulders of White's horse were in front of those of Black's mount, then a foul would be called on White

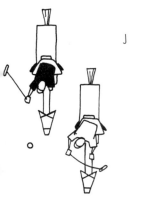

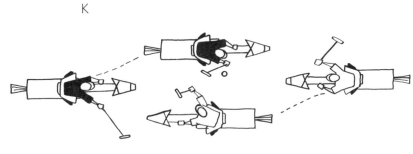

If White backhands his mallet into Black's pony's legs, it is a foul

Two players riding to meet head-on must give way to left and play the ball on the right side. (L) Fair; (M) Foul; (N) Foul; (O) Fair Hooking. A player must be behind or in front of opponent's mount, or on the side on which ball is being played. Hooking over (M) or under (N) opponent's pony is foul

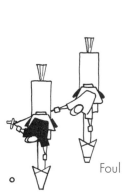

Fair Foul Foul Fair

Polo fouls

An intercollegiate polo match (COURTESY OF POLO MAGAZINE)

During a professional polo match, the 1980 Cup of the Americas. Left, the United States' Memo Gracida. Right, Argentina's Horatio Heguy (COURTESY OF POLO MAGAZINE/AMI SHINITZKY)

gether, as had already been done in Argentina and the United States. Today some mounts run 15.2 hands or over. This increase in heights to 14.1 and 14.2 hands brought about the importation of larger ponies into India, chiefly from Australia. In the United States many small Western horses were used, improved by breeding in Thoroughbred stallions. Today quarter horse and Morgan blood are featured in the bloodlines of many polo ponies, as is an admixture of Arab and Thoroughbred.

Argentina probably has more polo players than any other country, and the native Argentine ponies, the Petizo and the Criollo, have also made their mark on the type. The Petizo is a chunky short-legged animal, which found much favor in the days when the height standard was below fourteen hands. Bigger and more rugged than the Petizo, the Criollo is to the gaucho what the cow pony is to the ranch hand of the West. The original Spanish blood has been improved by Thoroughbred stallions imported from England. This Thoroughbred-Criollo cross has produced some fine ponies, many of which have found their way to this country.

Finding the right stock is only half the battle. The

top-grade polo pony must be clever. He must be able to dodge and swerve while going full speed, and to wheel and turn on the proverbial dime. Besides this, the successful mount must be able to follow the ball, and instinctively put his rider in a good position to hit it. He must be completely steady and unaffected by the waving mallets and yelling crowds. In addition, and no less important, he must have much courage, and not flinch from contact, sometimes violent, with another mount.

The training of the polo pony requires both time and skill. Speed, intelligence and agility by themselves are not enough; the pony must be schooled until he is as familiar with the game as his rider. Training, which used to begin with breaking-in of four-year-old stock which had been allowed to run wild on the range, has become more scientific. Many ponies now start their schooling when much younger, and training is continued for several years, five or six being considered none too long for a really good mount.

Many top players prefer a pony that plays with a slack rein. In any case a polo mount must be sensitive to the slightest signal from his rider, a light pressure of the reins on his neck or the smallest leg movements being sufficient to guide him. The rider must be able to give his full attention to the game, and the less "horse handling" he has to do, the better.

You will notice I said the "top-grade" pony. Such a pony costs a great deal of money. Even back in the twenties, nine or ten thousand dollars was not unusual for a fine animal.

In the "good old days" of the late twenties, when the estates of the North Shore of Long Island resounded to the drumming of hoofs, and when Hitchcock, Milburn, Webb and the other great ten-goalers were holding the stage, polo was truly a rich man's game. Strings of expensive ponies, grooms, fancy stables and all the paraphernalia which went with the game put it beyond the reach of all but the wealthiest.

Then came the great financial crash, and in a little while polo in America and England appeared to be on its way out, seemingly doomed forever by the depression and the ever-rising taxes. In the austere post-depression times, followed by the grim years of World War II, there was little room for a millionaire's sport. But then there came a change, brought about in part by the great interest in riding generally which has swept the country, bringing a corresponding increase in the number of breeders, riding schools and horse rental and boarding stables. Then,

too, financially there has been an increase in the number of young men with comfortable salaries and leisure time for recreation. Some of them took to sports cars, others discovered the joys of sailing, but some of those whose interest lay with horses found that polo, or at least a class of polo, was within their means.

The investment compares favorably with sailing, for example. While the upkeep of a twenty-two to thirty-foot yacht may not be as high, its initial expense is much greater. The average beginning polo player would need three mounts, which might very well be sound Western ponies that have had at least some training and played a game or two. In high-goal polo, of course, he would need more than three—and more highly trained ones, for at this level the ponies are pushed to their utmost and seldom play for more than one chukkar. But the novice, playing a much slower game, can use a mount that has rested for two chukkars. Then he would need the tack for these three ponies and his own outfit: helmets, mallets, knee guards, etc. Finally, there are the running expenses of board, veterinary fees, transportation expenses, and so forth.

If the owner is a "gentleman farmer," he may prefer to keep his string of ponies on his own land. While this is perhaps the ideal solution, it entails considerable work or expense or both, and requires means of transportation to and from the polo grounds. If owning and boarding-out mounts is not feasible, then ponies may sometimes be rented for so much per chukkar. Since there is no outlay for tack in this case, it is by far the cheapest way to enjoy the game. However, few players remain satisfied for long to rent their mounts. Even to the tyro, the difference between playing on ponies to which he is accustomed and on mounts which are strange to him is apparent. Frequently the renter eventually becomes the owner, and while his expenses increase somewhat, so does his enjoyment and his performance.

It should be made clear that the game, as played by the vast majority, is strictly low-goal polo. While there are some fine players in the game today, the quality as a whole has dropped, and top-flight polo is confined to a very few clubs. Out of more than eighteen hundred players eligible to play under the auspices of the U.S. Polo Association in 1982, only thirty were handicapped at over six goals, and of these only one, Gonzalo Tanoira, an Argentinian, was rated ten goals.

The average no-goal player, the man who likes to work off a bit of steam and perhaps a few surplus pounds on a weekend afternoon, has no chance of competing in first-class polo, and if he did he would be as out of place and as dangerous as a nervous student driver at Sebring or Le Mans. Anyone who can ride can learn to play polo. He does not even have to belong to a club, although most players do. Some hunt clubs sponsor polo teams, and some pony clubs have a polo program for training youngsters. Many small polo clubs suffer from a shortage of players and will welcome them on a pay-as-you-go basis. The United States Polo Association (1301 West 22nd Street, Suite 706, Oak Brook, IL 60521) can give you the location of the polo club nearest you.

Chapter 18

HORSE SHOWS

Horse shows, whether large ones sponsored by the American Horse Shows Association and its affiliates, or small, informal local shows, have increased in number and popularity in recent decades. Besides attracting those genuinely interested in horses, a well-planned show offers a sufficient variety of spectator events to draw the general public, especially when there is grand prix jumping featuring U.S. Equestrian Team members and other show-jumping heroes who have become full-fledged sports stars since major horse show events have been televised.

In all probability, the amateur owner and rider will at some point wish to compete in a horse show. He may want to display his prowess as an equestrian, or demonstrate his mount's ability; if a breeder, he may wish to bring his stock to the attention of the public. Nothing is more rewarding to a breeder than consistent wins at shows. The ribbons promote sales and stud fees, while the competition ensures continuing efforts to improve the breed.

The dates and locations of horse shows are usually listed in local newspapers and magazines devoted to horses and horsemanship. Once you have shown a few times, your name will be on a mailing list and you will receive prize lists for shows in your area. The prize list, which can also be obtained on request from the show secretary, specifies what classes will be scheduled, the conditions under which each class will be held, the amount of prize money and entry fees for each class, as well as the provisions for stabling, feed and water. It is, incidentally, customary to bring one's own feed to a one-day show. While water is always available, many owners prefer to bring their own because a change of water is upsetting to many horses.

The prize list will also specify the classification of

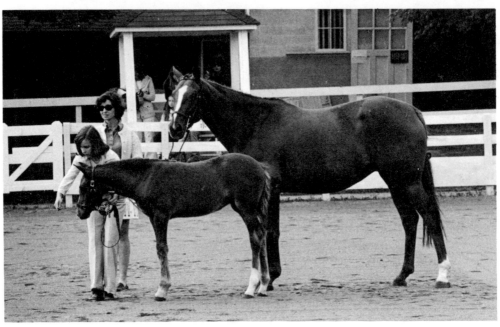

A breeding class (SUE MAYNARD)

the show, whether it is an informal, unrecognized event or whether it is recognized by, and therefore subject to, the rules of the AHSA (598 Madison Avenue, New York, NY 10022). All regular exhibitors join the AHSA, whose dues are modest, if only to receive the rule book and calendar and to be eligible for annual high-score awards. Nonmembers are required to pay a small registration fee when taking part in an AHSA show, in addition to the entry fees for each class. The latter vary widely, from a few dollars at a local show to several hundred for a stakes class in an important show such as Devon or Harrisburg.

AHSA-recognized horse shows are classified as "A," "B," or "C," depending on the amount of prize money and the number and variety of classes scheduled. There are various divisions, such as equitation, Saddlebreds, hunters, jumpers, etc., and a show may be rated "A" for one division and lower for others. "A" shows offer the highest standards and the keenest competition—and the most points towards annual high-score awards in each division, too. Although they also offer the most prize money, it is seldom sufficient to cover the cost of campaigning at this level, even without considering the value of the horse (and in this company you'll find the most valuable riding horses in the country). So most horse lovers who simply want the fun of competing from time to time limit their efforts to the numerous local, unrecognized shows that are organized by riding clubs, hunt clubs, boarding stables, breed associations, etc., which occur most often on weekends. There were about forty thousand of them in 1981

(compared to some eight thousand AHSA-sanctioned shows).

In recent years there has been an increase in the number of horse shows restricted to a single breed or group of breeds, such as Morgans, Palominos, American Quarter Horses, etc., usually featuring a wide variety of breeding (or "halter") classes, shown in hand, and of performance classes in the specialties of the particular breed. For example, Harness, Roadster, Trail Horse, Stock Horse and Cutting Horse, among others, for the Morgan; and for the Appaloosa a variety of English, Driving and Western classes, the latter including Trail, Reining, Stock Horse, Hackamore, Cutting, and Calf-Roping competitions.

After selecting a show that is within your horse's scope and your own, you must decide on the classes in which to enter him. The choice is generally so wide that the temptation is to enter too many events. Three to five would be a maximum for a one-day show, and the kind of shows you're apt to be interested in are almost always the one-day type. You have to study the prize list carefully in order to enter your horse in the classes for which he is qualified. Classes may be subdivided according to size, age and breed, as well as other criteria, such as being bred by the owner or owned by a local resident. Model, halter and breeding classes, in which the entries are shown "in hand" rather than ridden, are divided according to sex as well as age, height and breed.

At most local shows there are many children's classes, including equitation, jumping, and gymkh-

Shadwell, shown in a Conformation Hunter class conducted by Bill Ellis (SUE MAYNARD)

An attractive entry in a family class (SUE MAYNARD)

ana games such as egg-and-spoon races, musical chairs, etc.

Just to give an idea of the number and types of classes that may be scheduled, the following is a list of Green Working Hunter classes in the AHSA rule book—and there are the same ones for Regular Working Hunters, and just as many for Green and Regular Conformation Hunters!

Open, Stake, Under Saddle, Small, Lightweight, Middleweight, Heavyweight (or) Middle and Heavyweight, Thoroughbred, Non-Thoroughbred, Three-Year-Old, Four-Year-Old and Over, 1st Year Green, 2nd Year Green.

In this Working Hunter Division there are also "Miscellaneous Hunter Classes," including Maiden, Novice and Limit Hunters, Hunter Hacks, Bridle Path Hacks, Pairs of Hunters, Hunt Teams, Three-Year-Old Hunters, Amateur-Owners, and Hunter Classics (Regular, Amateur-Owner and Junior).

Specific requirements as to performance, tack and clothing are described in the rule book and often in the prize list, which, to repeat, should be studied with care. When dress is not prescribed, conservative attire is preferred. Boots and breeches or jodhpurs with a tweed coat, white shirt, plain tie, and a felt hat are suitable for many events. Attire for hunter classes is more rigorous, and a hard cap is obligatory for jumping events. Loud coats, shirts and ties are frowned upon—in the Eastern show ring, at least. Even in events where dress does not count, a well-turned-out rider always makes a more favorable impression.

Good ring manners also impress the judges as well as the public. When the classes are called to the ring, the entrants should be prepared. Announcements are made over a loudspeaker and notification is given when it is time for a class to get ready. Not only is it very bad form for an inattentive contestant to be hurriedly saddling up when the others are already in the ring, but if a rider in an AHSA show does not appear at the in-gate within three minutes after his class has been called (one minute in a jumping competition), he is automatically eliminated.

The ring procedure, which varies according to each class, is described in the rule book. Unrecognized horse shows can set their own rules, but they generally pattern them after the AHSA rules. In most classes, the riders circle the ring to the right (counter-clockwise) close to the rail. If one horse overtakes another, his rider should pass him on the left. If, as often happens, there is a bunch of horses on one side of the ring while the horses on the other side are strung out sparsely, it is permissible to ride across the ring to a less crowded spot along the rail. Sometimes the judge will instruct one or more riders to cross the ring in order to space the horses he is evaluating more evenly.

The riders must, of course, pay attention to the judge as well as to their mounts at all times. Requests to stop, to change gait or direction, etc., should be carried out promptly and smoothly. If a horse "acts up," he should be discreetly wheeled out of line until he has quieted down, and if this doesn't happen quickly, he may be asked to leave the ring. When the horses are lined up for inspection in the center of the ring, they should be spaced some ten or twelve feet apart.

Horse show procedures inside the ring as well as "behind the scenes" may seem a bit confusing at first. If you consider your first few horse shows as part of your horse's training and your own, without expecting to win a ribbon, you will not be disappointed. You might even be pleasantly surprised!

It goes without saying that good sportsmanship is expected of all horse show competitors. Unfortunately, while preserving all the forms in dealing with their fellow contestants, riders too often permit displays of bad temper when dealing with their mounts. The show ring is hardly the place for discipline and correction. A loss of temper or injudicious use of whip or spur create a very bad impression.

Most people know enough not to criticize another rider's performance, but often they will not hesitate to make disparaging remarks about his horse. Invariably, the owner, breeder, or a member of his family will be standing right behind, which causes embarrassment all around. People are touchy about their favorite breeds, too, and are annoyed to hear them

The show ring at the Sunnyfield Farm Horse Show in Bedford Village, N.Y., set up for jumping (SUE MAYNARD)

Rodney Jenkins on Idle Dice clearing the final fence of the jump-off course
. . . (SUE MAYNARD)

. . . and racing through the finish line to win the Ox Ridge Grand Prix (SUE
MAYNARD)

Mark Leone riding Tim in the Nation's Cup at Lucerne, 1982 (FINDLAY DAVIDSON, COURTESY OF U.S.E.T.)

criticized by fanciers of another type of horse or style of riding. The worst breach of horse show manners is to criticize the decisions of the judge. His name has been announced in advance, and by entering the show the exhibitors are implying that they will accept his decisions, whether or not they agree with them.

Still, the atmosphere around most horse show rings is usually friendly and festive. If it weren't, horse shows wouldn't be as successful as they are—so successful, in fact, that it is advisable to make your entries early. It is first come, first serve, and popular classes in attractive horse shows are quickly filled. Small shows often permit "post entries" on the day of the show, but it is safer for you and helpful to the show's management if you send in your entries early.

Dolly O'Lena ridden by Ross Churman in an open cutting competition (LOUISE L. SERPA)

Chapter 19

TRANSPORTATION

For the owner who plans to show, hunt, race, play polo or participate in rodeos, some form of transportation for the horse is necessary. There are many firms who specialize in shipping horses. This shipping is usually done in large vans, which hold from three up to nine horses. This may prove ideal for transporting a number of animals—a string of polo ponies, for instance—but for the person who owns only one or two, such means of transportation may prove excessively expensive. For one thing, while the horse vans may only be in actual use on the road for two or three hours, they will be standing by all day at a show, and the waiting time must be paid for. If the show, meet or what have you, lasts two days, two round trips must be paid for, or the van and driver held overnight, at a considerable addition to the price.

Another drawback is that occasionally such transportation is in short supply. When the show season is on, everyone wants shipping facilities and there is often a mad scramble for space.

Organizations such as riding schools and hunt clubs frequently charter a large van to take their members' horses to a show, and there may sometimes be an empty stall available for a nonmember. Perhaps a neighboring horse owner will be able to accommodate your horse in his van or trailer if you are going to the same show or meet. But, obviously, these solutions require a certain amount of luck as well as sharing of expenses.

All things considered, it often pays the small owner to do his own hauling. Today there are many fine two- and four-horse trailers which can be towed behind many types of car. Of course, you must make sure that the horsepower of your car is equal to the task of hauling the trailer you select, that the brakes are also adequate, and that the hitching system is installed and/or verified by an expert. The trailer

Horse transportation at a carriage meet (SUE MAYNARD)

should be checked for safety inside as well as outside (no sharp edges or projections, no glass windows, horse-proof door latches, etc.), and it should be of adequate size to accommodate your horse(s) comfortably. If the trailer is combined with a built-in caravan-type camper body on a small truck, or something on the order of a Volkswagen van, then house and stable are combined, with complete freedom of movement and a considerable saving in expense. Secondhand horse trailers are often advertised in horse magazines.

Whether new or used, both the trailer and vehicle to which it is hitched should be maintained in perfect condition, checked and double-checked before each trip, including verification of the supply of spares and tools, the soundness of the flooring and the hitch.

Even when you are vanning your horse a short distance to a show or meet, he should be protected from possible injuries. Some sort of padding should be provided in the front of the van. An old mattress covered with canvas will serve the purpose. A tail chain is used to prevent horses from getting too close to the tailgate and to prevent them from kicking. The chain should be fastened so that it stretches across about one foot below the underside of the tail. To avoid rubbing, it should be covered with canvas or a piece of rubber hose.

The horses are tied in their stalls by a chain with heavy snaps on both sides of the halter; it should be long enough so that they can reach the hay net or manger but not long enough to allow them to reach

over the divider of a two-horse trailer and bite the horse in the adjoining stall. If you are transporting two horses, you should load the heavier one on the left; roads are higher in the center, and you have more control of a load if the greater weight is on the higher side.

In spite of your best efforts to drive smoothly, especially when starting, stopping and turning, there is always the possibility of a horse's becoming frightened during transport. Halters and other gear should therefore be extra strong. To avoid chafing, it is advisable to use a sheepskin cover on the halter. To avoid head injuries, many owners fit their horses with a head bumper, a sort of padded crash helmet designed to protect the poll, which is held in place by passing the crownpiece of the halter through loops in the bumper. Felt shipping boots should be used to protect the horse's legs, or the legs should be well wrapped in shipping bandages. It is a good idea to use a commercial or homemade tail wrap, too, in order to prevent rubbing, especially in the case of show horses.

When a completely enclosed trailer is used, blanketing should not be necessary. Horses generate a considerable amount of heat in an enclosed space, even when it is well ventilated, as all trailers should be. However, if there is a danger of drafts, the horses should be blanketed; this is mandatory when an open-top trailer is used. During wet weather, waterproof blankets should be placed over the regular blankets.

For comfort during the trip—even a short one—

the nonskid flooring should be covered with a deep bed of straw. Most owners also provide a hay net and a bucket of water, the latter being only partially filled in order to avoid splashing.

LOADING

Loading a horse in a van or trailer can be difficult if the animal has not been trained to enter it as a youngster. His first objection is to the ramp, which feels and sounds strange and gives him a sense of insecurity. Then there is the horse's instinctive reluctance to enter a strange enclosure. To overcome this, you should place the trailer in such a way that daylight enters it so it does not appear to be a deep, dark cavern. The trailer and ramp should both be perfectly stabilized, and the ramp as well as the floor should be covered with a nonskid mat. A little straw strewn on the ramp may make it more inviting.

The first step when loading an inexperienced horse is to give him a chance to examine the trailer. Then try to lead him up the ramp, encouraging him with your voice and tempting him with oats or sugar. The idea is to make moving forward into the trailer sufficiently attractive to overcome his qualms. If he balks at stepping on the ramp, try moving his feet yourself, lifting one and moving it forward a little, then moving the others, always keeping the horse straight.

If this doesn't work, you can try a method which requires two helpers. Fasten two lunging lines, one on each side of the trailer entrance, and cross them behind the horse's rump, with a helper holding onto each end. As you lead the horse forward by the halter, the helpers move forward too, and the lines draw the horse's rump ahead. When extra help is not available, you can use one line, fastened to one side of the trailer and looped under the horse's tail. When loading singlehanded, it may help if the halter rope is run through a pulley fastened to the front of the stall. In this way the horse can be led in with one rope, leaving the other hand free for the line. Another method that often works is to have two people clasp their hands behind the horse's rump and heave him up the ramp. If you have a two-horse trailer, load an experienced horse first and the other will usually follow him without the slightest difficulty.

During all of these efforts, the important thing is to avoid undue noise and nervousness. The more calm and patient everybody is, the more tractable the horse will be. Remember that you are trying to teach him to load, not simply to get him into a van or trailer just this one time.

Once in the trailer, the horse should be rewarded. When you are training him to load rather than setting off for a show, for example, let him stand inside for a few minutes, then back him out and repeat the procedure several times. It is better not to move the trailer the very first time. Consider this first loading

Loading a horse in a van (SUE MAYNARD)

as a practice run. Horses soon become accustomed to traveling, and if their introduction to it has been gentle, they rarely give any trouble afterwards.

Young horses can be trained to enter a trailer by parking it in the paddock and feeding the animal oats or hay in it. With a very shy animal, you can start by putting the oats at the near end of the ramp and gradually move them into the interior of the trailer. Once the connection has been made between trailer and feed, the horse will usually walk up the ramp forever after in cheerful anticipation of a handout.

LONG-DISTANCE VANNING

Long-distance transportation of horses requires careful organization, attention to detail, and an expert driving technique, which is one reason why it has become a specialized profession. Nevertheless, many experienced owners transport their horses over the same routes just as successfully.

If you are planning interstate travel, you must check the various state regulations concerning vaccinations and health certificates and make sure that your horse's papers are in order. A negative Coggins test performed within twelve months of the transport is required by most states nowadays, as well as a veterinary certificate of good health. As of 1982, the state of Florida even requires a certificate showing that out-of-state vans and trailers were cleaned and disinfected under veterinary supervision prior to loading. You should also carry owner's papers or proof of registration.

Since horses are prone to constipation during long trips, you might try to avoid it by feeding a bran mash several evenings before the departure. Alfalfa hay during the trip will help to keep them loose. You'll need to plan stops for leg stretching (slow walking) and urination, because many horses refuse to urinate in a moving van. Since standing for many hours may reduce circulation, care should be taken at the end of the journey not to exercise the horse or allow it to run for at least an hour after unloading.

Overnight stops can pose a problem in some parts of the country, as riding stables which used to provide equine hotel accommodations in every hamlet have become a thing of the past. The most practical solution is to plan your route, then phone the local chamber of commerce in the areas where you intend to stop overnight, requesting information about stabling facilities. You can then adjust your itinerary accordingly.

Chapter 20

DRIVING

The practice of driving horses rather than riding them has existed for many centuries. The horse's ability and willingness to pull a vehicle was exploited on the farm, the battlefield, in industry, on highways, byways and city streets until the advent of the railroad around 1830, and particularly of the automobile in the early 1900s.

In the days when "horse power" still referred to the strength of a living animal, a fine turnout of horse and carriage was a status symbol, carriage making was an art, and skilled coachmen were greatly admired. Inhabitants of rural areas have never ceased to appreciate a horse that can be driven as well as ridden, but there was quite a long period during which the most conspicuous example of driving in America was in harness racing and Westerns. Then, during the 1960s, there was a revival of interest in driving as a sport and a leisure activity. The American Driving Society (79 Southgate Avenue, Hastings-on-Hudson, NY 10706) and the Carriage Association of America (P.O. Box 3788, Portland, ME 04104) have promoted the sport with such success that driving events are now included in the programs of the AHSA and the Fédération Équestre Internationale (FEI), the international equestrian organization (Schosshalden 32, 3006 Berne, Switzerland). There is even a chance that driving will become an Olympic equestrian discipline.

Nevertheless, many people who consider it quite normal to take lessons in order to become a good rider think that anybody can hitch a horse to a wagon, climb in and drive off. After all, there are wheels, brakes, horse power, and reins to steer with! But there is a lot more to driving than this. Special skills and techniques are involved, and the best way to master them, as in riding, is to take lessons from an experienced instructor.

Almost anyone can learn to drive a horse. There

Walter Warren breaking a horse to drive (LOUISE L. SERPA)

is virtually no age or weight limit, and the physical demands are mild compared to many other equestrian sports. An increasing number of horsemen turn to driving after abandoning some more strenuous riding activity. Prince Philip, an ex–polo player, and Philip Hofmann, an ex–fox hunter, are two prominent examples.

Likewise, almost any sound horse with the proper temperament can be taught to drive. The following breeds, however, are better suited than others due to their conformation, gaits and temperament: Morgans, Standardbreds, Saddlebreds, Hackney and Tennessee Walking Horses, Hackney, Shetland and Welsh ponies, for example, as well as crossbreeds bearing these strains. Many ranch horses, which are often part Quarter Horse or Appaloosa, are driven as well as ridden as a matter of course.

TRAINING

Being ground-driven in long lines, with the trainer walking behind, is part of the traditional early education of all riding horses, because a young horse can thus be introduced to bitting, saddling and rein signals long before he is strong enough to carry a rider on his back. In long lines he is taught to move straight and in balance, to make transitions from one gait to another, and to learn elementary rein and voice signals; he gets used to wearing tack, develops muscles and suppleness, gets exercise, and learns to collaborate with a human partner. This is the first step in training a driving horse, too, except that the latter is ground-driven in full harness as soon as possible. Only when he is perfectly at ease with the harness is he hitched to a vehicle.

Several assistants should be present the first time a horse is hitched to a cart, preferably in an enclosed area. Professional trainers often use a special breaking cart with extra long shafts at this stage. As in all training, the procedure is a gradual one: first, leading the horse with the unhitched cart simply held in place behind him; then leading him with the cart hitched but unoccupied; and, finally, getting into the cart with an assistant still leading the horse and maybe another one pushing gently from behind, until the horse has become accustomed to the weight. All early work is done at a walk, using voice commands which are gradually reinforced by rein signals. It is impossible to estimate the length of time it takes to train a horse to drive. It could be days, weeks, or months, depending on the horse and trainer.

VEHICLES AND HARNESS

A wide variety of vehicles is used in driving. A light two-wheel cart is the best choice for a beginner, because it is the easiest to maneuver. A four-wheel topless buggy is the vehicle required in the horse show's fine harness division. For driving competitions in which appearance is scored, as is almost always the case, owners take great pains to discover and restore fine antique vehicles. For ordinary pleasure driving, workmanlike modern equivalents are manufactured in a wide price range.

There are different kinds of harness, too, the basic

Mrs. John West driving a Quarter Horse to a Hempstead cart (FREUDY, COURTESY OF THE CARRIAGE ASSOCIATION)

components always being: the bridle; a breast collar; a crupper strap; a backpad held in place by a surcingle or girth with rings on the sides to which side straps for the shafts of the vehicle are attached, and rings on top through which the reins pass. Two side reins or an overhead check rein are used to keep the horse's head in position, and blinkers are usually added later.

Bitting is particularly important because the only communication with the horse (aside from voice and whip) is through the reins acting on the bit. The most widely used is a Liverpool curb bit with curb chain. A snaffle is required in fine harness show classes as well as in harness racing.

DRIVING TECHNIQUE

Driving reins are heavier than riding reins, measuring at least one inch wide. Experienced drivers ("whips") hold them in the left hand, with the buggy whip in the right. The off rein is passed over the first finger and down through the hand, while the near rein is brought around the outside of the little finger and up through the hand. Beginners should start by holding one rein in each hand, taking care to keep the forearms horizontal, the hands close together and steady.

Because a broken piece of harness can spell disaster, it should be maintained in perfect condition. The

Mrs. Kathleen Whaley driving a hunter to a gig (BUDD, COURTESY OF THE CARRIAGE ASSOCIATION)

proper fitting of each piece of harness also requires a lot of care—and often a certain amount of experimentation in order to find the perfect balance between comfort and control.

The latter is vital, too, if only because a poorly balanced vehicle greatly increases the horse's load. The driver's seat can contribute to this. He generally sits on the right side of the cart, in a straight, well-braced position.

The basic movements to practice at the outset are walking and halts; then trotting, backing, turning corners (wide and slow at the beginning), going uphill and downhill. The latter is apt to frighten the horse at first, and he may have to be led downhill with an empty vehicle until he is used to the feeling of its weight pressing against the breeching.

In actual practice, all of this is simpler than it may seem, at least on the pleasure-driving level. It becomes more complicated when dealing with more than one horse: a pair, for example; a tandem (with one horse in front of the other); a unicorn (a pair, with the third horse alone in front); and, even more difficult, a four-in-hand, which is the most spectacular as well as the most difficult and thrilling type to drive.

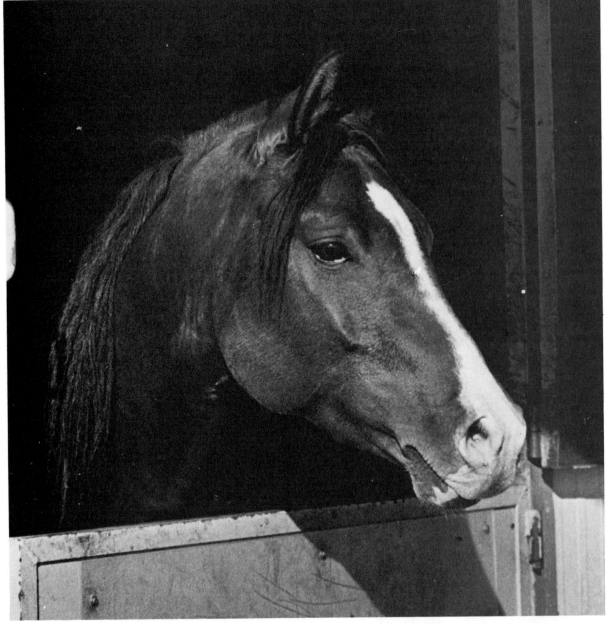

(LOUISE L. SERPA)